STO

A

P9-AFR-985

DISCARDED

FEB 27 '75

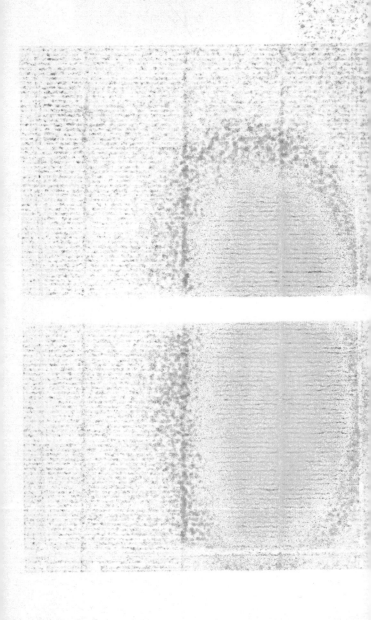

ENGLISH RECUSANT LITERATURE
1558–1640

Selected and Edited by
D. M. ROGERS

Volume 225

ALFONSO RODRIGUEZ
*A Short and Sure Way
to Heaven
1630*

ALFONSO RODRIGUEZ

*A Short and Sure Way
to Heaven
1630*

The Scolar Press
1975

ISBN 0 85967 209 3

Published and printed in Great Britain by
The Scolar Press Limited, 59-61 East Parade,
Ilkley, Yorkshire and
39 Great Russell Street,
London WC1

1835660

NOTE

Reproduced (original size) from a copy in the
library of Ampleforth Abbey, by permission of the
Abbot and Community.

References: Allison and Rogers 733; STC 21144.

A SHORT
AND SVRE WAY
TO
HEAVEN,

and present Happines.

TAVGHT IN A TREATISE OF
OVR CONFORMITY
WITH THE WILL OF GOD.

Written by the Reuerend Father
ALFONSVS RODRIGVEZ
of the *Society of Iesus*, in his worke in-
tituled, *The exercise of perfection and*
Christian vertue.

Tranflated out of Spanish.

Ira in indignatione eius: & vita in volun-
tate eius. Pfal. **29**. **6**.

Wrath in his indignation: andlife in
his will.

Permiffu Superiorum 1630.

TO
THE REVEREND
AND
RELIGIOVS MOTHER
ANNA OF THE
ASCENTION.

PRIORESSE OF THE ENGLISH
Teresians in Antwerpe.

Euerend & Religious Mother,

Many excellét Treatiſes haue ſeene light by the happy péne of F. Alfonſo Roderigues, that great Maſter of ſpirit. But this alone may worthily ſeeme to carry the nature of a Centure, wherein all the lines of perfe-ction drawne through his o-ther workes come iointly to meete . The higheſt ayme of vertue both in time and eter-

*2 nity

nity, is to set an exact conformity betweene our soule and
God : & the best wayes of spirit, such, as leade to this toppe.
What store of excellent precepts, solid helpes, and most ef-
fectuall meanes our Author
hath heere collected to so noble an end, diligent perusal wil
discouer. To which purpose as
I chanced vpon the worke apparelled in English, so my singular affection and respect to
your selfe & yours, would not
permit me to stád long irrde-
liberatió whether I should first
addresse it, after it had recei-
ued life from the print. For to
whom can a treatise of diuine
conformity be more due, euen
in rigour of claime & challége,
then

then to a family of that illustri-
ous Order, the Foūdreſſe wherof reflected vpō the world admirable light of exāple in this
kinde; hauing bene trained in
ſpirit as herſelfe teſtifieth, vnder the conduct of three moſt
eminent men of the Authors
Profeſſion; as of B. Father Borgia Duke of Gandia and third
Generall of the Society , *Bea-
tified by the holy Church* , Father Baltazar Aluarez, whō by
diuine reuelation she vnderſtood to haue bene the greateſt Saint then liuing in this
world, and Father Francis Ri-
bera, whoſe rare vertue was ac-
cōpanied with equal learning.
And who more worthy of the
firſt view, then a Superiour of
                              the

the same family, by whose dis-
creet and pious gouernment
the whole cōpany maintaines
in flower & vigour the primitiue spirit of their Foundresse,
especially in this high point of
true Conformity. Accept therfore Reuerend Mother of this
little presēt, rather as a pledge
of cōgratulation,then a spurre
of new incitemēt,with my best
wishes that your house may e-
uer prosper,grow vp,& florish,
as it doth , to the glory of our
Lord , the honour of your
Foūdresse, the Cōfort of your
soules , and the good of our
whole Nation.

Your R. euer humble seruant
in Christ Iesus.
                    I. C.

A TREATISE OF OVR
CONFORMITY VVITH THE
will of God.

Ian. 28.

THE I. CHAPTER.

*In which there are laid two princi-
cipall foundations.*

On *sicut ego volo , sed sicut tu,* not as I will, but as thou wilt, O Lord. The Holy Fathers af-signe two reasons , why the sonne of God would descend downe from heauen, and become perfect man by yesting himselfe with our humanity: the one was, to redeeme vs with his pretious blood ; the other, to shew vs by his example , and teach vs by his doctrine the right way to heauen. For as it would haue auailed vs nothing to haue knowne the way, if we had been still detained

Matt. 26. 39.

A   in

Ber. fer.
2. in Cir-
cumcif.
Dom.

in prifon; fo likewife (faith *S. Bernard*) it would haue little profited vs, to haue been deliuered out of prifon, if we had not knowne the way: and feeing God was inuifible, it was neceffary (vnto the end we might fee him, and by feeing imitate him) that he fhould become vifible and cloath himfelfe in our humanity, as fhepheards goe apparelled in the fkins of fheep, that their flocke may be allured to follow them, by feeing in them their owne refemblance. And fo that holy Pope. *S. Leo* fais; *Nifi enim effet verus Deus, nõ adferret remedium; & nifi effet verus homo, non præberet exemplum.* Vnles he had been true God, he could not haue brought vs remedy; and vnles he had been true man, he could not haue afforded vs an exãple. But he hath done both the one and the other moft aboundantly, out of that exceffe of loue which he bare to man, and therfore as our redemption hath been moft amply great, *& copiofa apud eum redemptio*, fo alfo hath his doctrine been, fince he hath not deliuered it vnto vs alone in words, but much more by the example of his works, *capit Iefus facere & docere*, faith the Euan-

Leo Papa 1. fer.
1. de Natiui. Do.

Pfal. 119
7.

Euangelift *S. Luke*, *Iefus* firft begun with the practife and execution (and that for the moft part of his Bleffed life) and afterwards began to preach in the laft three yeares, or two yeares and a halfe, before dyed. Act. 1.

Now among many other things which our Sauiour Chrift hath taught vs, one of the principall is, an entire conformity with the will of God, in all occurrences and occafions: the which he teacheth vs not only in words, when fetting downe vnto vs a forme of prayer, he tells vs, that one of thofe things which we are to befeech, and begge of our heauenly Father, is: *fiat voluntas tua ficut in cælo & in terra*, thy will be done in earth as it is in heauen: but he much more confirmes this doctrine by his bleffed exáple, feeing he profeffeth to haue defcended from heauen vnto no other end, *defcendi de cælo non vt faciam voluntatem meam, fed voluntatem eius qui mifit me*. I haue defcended from heauen not to do mine owne will, but the will of him who fent me. And on that facred day, when hauing inftituted his holy fupper, and almoft ended the worke of our redemption, Mat. 10.

A 2   tion,

tion, in that prayer of his in the Garden, although his flesh and blood, and sensitiue powers had a naturall horrour, and auersion from death, by which he witnessed

Mat. 26. 39. that he was perfect man, saying; *Pater mi, si possibile est transeat à me calix iste,* Father if it be possible let this chalice passe from me: notwithstanding his will was alwaies prompt & desirous, to drinke of that chalice, which his Father sent him; and therefore he presently adds, neuerthelesse, be it not as I will, but as thou wilt ô Lord.

But vnto the end that we may descend vnto the very depth, to ground our selues very well in this conformely, we must first lay two briefe, but substantiall foundations; vpon which as vpon two hinges our whole matter must be sustained. The first is, that all our profit in vertue and perfection consists in this conformity with the will of God, which according as this shall be more full and perfect, shall likewise be more excellent and great. This foundation is easy to comprehend, since it must be graunted, that perfection essentially consists in the charity and the loue of God, and that the more

perfect

perfect we shall be, the greater shall our loue be to Almighty God: the holy Euangell is full of this doctrine, as also the Epistles of S. *Paul*, and the liues of Saints. *Hoc est maximum & primum mādatum &c.* This is the greatest and the first comaundment, *Charity is the band of perfection and the greatest of all these is charity,* the loue of God is of all things the most high and perfect, and the most excellent and dearest part thereof, and (as it were the abstract and quintessence of this charity) is an intire conformity with the will of God, in desiring nothing but what may be most pleasing vnto his Diuine Maiestie. *Eadem velle, & eadem nolle ea demum firma amicitia est,* saith S. *Hierom* borrowing the sentence from another Philosopher: so that the more one is conformable and vnited with the will of God, the better and more perfect he shall be, it being moreouer most certaine, that the will of God, is the most excellent and perfect thing, which may be imagined, and so by consequence he is better and more perfect, who comes the neerest to the will of God. And it was the Argument of an other Philosopher; if God be

Mat. 22. 38. & Colos. 3. 14. 1. Corin. 13. 13.

Hier ep. ad Demetriad lib. de amicit.

A 3   the

the most exquisit and perfect thing of all, the nearer on comes for to resemble him, the more exquisit and perfect he shall be.

The second foundation is; that there can chaunce and happen nothing in the world, but by the will and ordinance of God, sinne ōly excepted, of which God is neither Author, nor cā possibly be. For as cold is naturally opposit to heat, warmth to water, and darkenesse to the sunne, so much and infinitly more, is it repugnant to the eternall goodnes of Almighty God, to haue any friendship or commerce with wickednes, as the Prophet *Abacue* testifies: *Mundi sunt oculi tui, ne videas malum, & respicere ad iniquitatem non poteris,* thy eyes are pure that thou maist not see sinne, & thou maist not looke vpō iniquity. Affirming that he cannot, nor may not looke vpon it in that sence as we vsually say a man who hath a horrour frō a thing cannot abid its sight, whereby he giues vs to vnderstand, the great auersion and detestation which God Almighty hath from wickednes that he cannot endure the sight of it. *Quoniam non Deus volens iniquitatem tu es.* Seeing thou art not a God (saith Dauid) who hast any will

Abacu.
2. 3.|

Psal. 55.

will that iniquity ſhould be: and againe, Pſal. 44. *dilexiſti iuſtitium & odiſti iniquitatem,* 8. thou haſt loued iuſtice & hated iniquity. In briefe the holy ſcripture doth euery where abound, with teſtimonies of Gods mighty hatred and deteſtation of ſinne; and therfore he can no waies be Author of it. But excepting ſinne I ſay, all other things, all miſeries and all calamities, inflicted on vs for our puniſhments, proceed from the ordination and the will of God: which foundation is moſt infallible; there being no ſuch thing as chaunce or fortunate in the world, as the Heathens erroniouſly did faine. neither are thoſe goods which the idle world abuſiuely cal goods of Fortune the donatiues of any ſuch thing, as Fortun, or of chaunce; ſince there is no ſuch thing as they are ſaid to be, bu they are gifts beſtowed by the hand of God ; As the Holy Ghoſt teacheth vs by the wiſeman, *bona & mala,* Eccl. 11. *vita & nors, paupertas. & honeſtas à* 14. *Deo ſun,* both good and euell, life and death, puerty and riches are all procceding from Almighty God.

A nd lthough theſe things are often by other ſecondary cauſes brought to

A 4 paſſe,

paſſe; notwithſtanding it is moſt certaine,
that there happens nothing in this great
Republique of the world, without order
from this ſoueraigne Emperour who
hath all dominion in it, there is nothing
by chaunce or accidence to God. but all
which happès to vs, firſt paſſeth through
his hands, and his diſpoſure of it. He hath
numbred all the bones of your body,
and keep a iuſt account of euery haire
of your head, of the which there doth
not moult or periſh one, without his particular prouidence. but what do I ſpeake
of men? ſeing our Sauiour himſelfe affirmes in the Euangell, that not a ſparrow
falls into the Fowlers nette, without his
ordinance and permiſſion. *Nonne duo*
paſſeres aſſe veneunt, & vnus ex iis non
cadet ſuper terram ſine patre veſtro?
Neither is there any leafe ſhaken with the
wind, but by his good pleaſure: and alſo
the wiſeman ſays ſpeaking of lots, *ſortes*
mittuntur in ſinu, ſed à Domini tempe-
rentur. Howſoeuer the lots are caſt into
the Lapp, yet according to the pleaſure
of God they are mingled there, & by his
appointment drawne out and diſtributed,
cecidit ſors ſuper Matthiam the lot fell
vpon

Mat. 10.
29.

Pro. 16.
35.

Act. 1.
26.

vpon Matthias but not by chaunce, it being the pleasure of God by that means, to elect him for his Apostle; This verity, the better and more morall Philosophers, haue by the only helpe of naturall light found out, and so they say, that diuers things, in respect of their secondary causes, are fortuit and casuall, wheras if you regard their primitiue cause, they are no waies casuall, but done with mature deliberation and designe : which they declare by the example of one sending a seruant vpon some occasion to a certaine place, and dispatching another vnto the same place, by another way ; now they meeting both together there, & one not knowing of the others sending do straight imagine that they are met by chaunce, whereas vnto him who sent them it is no casuall thing, but done with purpose & deliberation. In like manner although oftentimes som things for as much as men can perceaue fal out as it were by chauce, because they are vnexpected vnto them, neuertheles vnto God Almighty they are no waies so, he hauing so ordained them, for ends secret and hidden to the eyes of men, and only knowne vnto his pro-uidence.

uidence . That which we are to gather
from these two foundations , which we
haue laid , is the conclusion of what we
haue propoſed: which is , that ſeeing all
thinges which happen to vs, are proceeding from the hand of God; and that all
perfection conſiſts in the conforming of
our ſelues vnto his will ; we are therfore
to receaue all thinges as coming from
his hand , and conforme our ſelues in
them, vnto his diuine and holy will , we
are not to eſteeme any accident to come
by chaunce , or that any man hath had
his hand in it;for this only ſerues to vexe
and diſquiet vs: neither are we to thinke
that this or that is happened vnto vs , by
any one procurement , and that otherwiſe it would not haue chaunced,for ſuch
and ſuch reaſons as may occure vnto vs.
But letting paſſe all ſuch imaginations,we
are to receaue all things, as being ſent vs
from the hand of God , by what way
ſoeuer they arriue vnto vs. For it is he
who doth direct them ſo . One of thoſe
renowned Fathers of the deſert,was wont
to ſay , that a man ſhould neuer attaine
true quietnes and content, vntil he could
perſwade himſelfe , that there was no
body

body els in the world but God and he; **Doroth.**
And S. *Dorotheus* says, that those autient **doct. 7.**
Fathers were very conuersant in receauing all things as coming from the hand
of almighty God, how sleight so euer they
were in themselues, and in what manner
so euer they chaunced to them, and that
by this meanes, they attained vnto a great
quietnes and peace, leading euen in their
mortall bodies heauenly liues.

THE II. CHAPTER.

Wherein the second foundation is more
amply declared.

IT is a verity so confirmed by holy
scripture, that all afflictions, and euills
which happen vnto vs for punishment of
our sinnes, are proceeding from the omnipotent hand of God, that it were needles for vs to spend more time in proofe
therof, did not the diuell seeke to obscure
it with his malicious craft, seeing from
an other verity which we affirmed to be
infallibly true, to wit that God is neither
Author nor cause of sinne, he infers a false
and lying conclusion, in perswading some
that,

that , how euer thofe harmes which are
incident vnto vs by naturall caufes,and by
creatures deuoid of freafon , as fickneffe
famine, fterility and the like, are all proceeding from the hand of God.feing that
they commit no finne , in what they do;
neither is it poffible they fhould , in that
they are incapable of finning:neuertheles
thofe harmes and domages which arriue
vnto vs through the faults of others , as
when any one doth ftrike and wound,
or robbe and iniure me , are not proceeding from the hand of God,neither hap-
ning through his appointment and pro-
nidence,but through the malice and per-
uerfity of the others will; which errour,
and fuch who receaue not euery thing
as coming from the Almighty hand of
God, *S. Dorotheus* doth excellently re-
prehend where he fais.*We when we heare*
any word fpoken againft vs , or chaunce
" to be iniured of any one, do imitate dogs,
" who when any one throwes a ftone at
" them, not regarding him who threw it,
" do runne and bite the ftone ; fo we con-
" fider not God Almighty to be him, who
" procured vs this affliction, to clenfe vs
" from our finnes, but ftraight runne vnto
the

Doroth.
doct. 7.

the ftone, which is to wreake our anger „
on our neighbour. „

To free vs from this errour, as alfo to
ground vs furely in the Catholicke truth,
the Diuins confider in the finnes which
man comits two thinges which do con-
cure ; the one is the motion and exteriour acte ; the other the diforder of the
will, whereby we come to tranfgreffe the
comaund of God . Of the firft God is
the Author; and of the fecond man. Let
vs put the cafe ; on entring into quarell
with an other kille him: vnto the killing
of him.there is required,that he lay hand
to his fword, that he lift it vp, that he let
fall his arme, and giue the blow; with diuers other naturall motions, which may
be a part confidered by themfelues, without the diforder and commotion of that
mans will , by whofe interuention that
other man is kild : and of all thefe motions by themfelues and confidered apart,
God is the Author, and produceth them
as he doth all other effects in creatures
deuoid of reafon;feing that as nothing of
it feife , without the helpe of God can
put it felfe in acte , or motion ; fo alfo
(without him) this man could not haue
                                                        ftired

ftired his arme, nor handled his **fword**,
and moreouer thefe naturall actes **in the-**
felues are not bad, feeing that if a man
fhould make vfe of them in his defence,
in a lawfull warre, or as executioner of
Iuftice, and fo kill an other, he fhould
cōmit no finne; but of that fault, which
is in the diforder of the will, by which
this wicked wretch cōmits that outrage,
and of the difaray of reafon, God is not
the caufe, how euer he permit it, in that
he could haue hindered it, and yet out of
his iuft iudgments, doth not. They vfe
to declare this by a comparifon, a man
hath a wound in his foot, and by reafon
therof he haults, the caufe why he doth
go vpon his foot, is the vertue and motiue power of the foule, but the occafion
of his lamenes in his wound, and not the
vertue of his foule: fo likewife, in thofe
actiōs by which men come to finne, God
is the caufe of the action; but the defect
and finne, proceeds meerly from the
mans free will.

So that although God neither is nor
can be the Author of any finne, yet we are
affuredly to hold, that all the euill inflicted on vs for punifhment of our fins,
whe-

whether they arriue by intermiffion of caufes naturall, or els by vnreafonable creatures, by what way, or in what manner fo euer they are directed, are all proceeding from the hand of God, and fo ordained by his high prouidence, it is God alone, who lifts vp that hand which ftrikes you, & moues that tongue which reuiles and iniurs you. *fi erit malum in ciuitate quod Deus non fecerit* fays the Prophet *Amos*, is there any euill in the Citty that God hath not done? the holy fcripture is full of this verity, attributing all the euill which one man doth to another, vnto God, & faying that God alone is Author of it.

In the fecond booke of the Kings God tooke the inflicting of that punifhmēt vpō himfelfe, where with he punifhed *Dauid* by meanes of his fonne Abfalon, for that adultery and murther which he had committed, faying: *Behould I will raife vp against thee, a plague from thine owne houfe, and bereaue thee of thy wiues before thine eyes, & giue them to thy neighbour: thou haft committed this (thy wickednes) in primat, but I will bring to paffe that which I haue faid, in the fight of all Ifraell,*

Amos. 3 6.

2. Reg. 12. 11.

Israell, and in the face of the sunne.
whence also it is, that those impious
Kings, who with great pride & cruelty
did execute most cruell vengeance on the
people of God, were called by the holy
Scripture, instruments of the diuine Iustice, *wo vnto Assur the rod of my fury,*
and of Cyrus King of *Persia*, by whom
God purposed to punish the Chaldeans,
he sais, *cuius apprehendi dexteram* whose
right hand I haue laid hold of. *S. Au-*
gustin herupon discourseth excellent well:
their impiety (saith he) is become as the
,, axe of God, they are made the instrumēt
,, of the angry, but not the kingdome of the
,, well pleased. God vsually doth, as we see
,, men to do. a man sometimes when he is
,, angry, will snatch vp some rod which lies
,, next at hand, perhaps some twig or o-
,, ther, with which he beats his sonne, and
,, afterwards casting his rod into the fier,
,, he doth reserue the inheritance for his
,, sonne: in the like manner God sometimes
,, by the euill, teacheth & amends the good:
,, by vsing them as instruments and scour-
,, ges of his wrath.

We read in the Ecclesiasticall History,
that *Titus* Generall of the Romaine
army,

Isai 10.5

Isa.45.1.

Aug. su.
psal. 73.

Hist.ecc.
P. 1. lib.
3. c. 11.

army, fetching once a circuit about the walles of Hierusalem, which he then held besieged, and seeing the ditches all filled with the dead corses and carkaifes of men, and all the neighbouring country, infected with the horrible stench of thē, lifting vp his sorrowfull eyes to heauen, to direct thither his lamentable voice he cald God to witnesse for him, that he was no waies the cause of so great a slaughter and butchery of men. And also when *Alaricus* was in his expedition to sacke and ruine Rome, it is recorded that a venerable auncient Monke, went to meet him on his way, beseeching him that he would not be the cause of such great euills, as were imminent that day, ouer that wretched Citty: vnto whom he answered, that he went towards Rome out of no proper inclination of his owne; but there is, said he, a certaine person, which importuns me daily & euen seems to hollow in mine eares, go to Rome, and distroy that Citty; And thus we see all things are proceeding from the hand of God, and disposed according to his will & ordinance. And so the Royal Prophet *Dauid* whē *Semei,* reuiled and curst him,

p. 2. li. 9. c. 2. hist. left.

B   throwing

throwing downe sand and stones againſt him, ſaid vnto thoſe who counſailed him for to reuenge himſelfe; *The Lord hath commaunded him, to curſe and reuile Dauid*, and who ſhall dare *to ſay, why hath he done ſo?* as much as to ſay, the Lord doth vſe him as his inſtrument to puniſh and chaſtiſe me with all.

But what marueile iſt, to acknowledge men, the inſtruments of Gods Iuſtice and diuine prouidence, ſince euen the Diuels are ſo, how euer otherwiſe obſtinat and enhardned in their malice, and ſeeking nothing more then our perdition, *S. Gregory* notes it excellently well, vpon that place of the firſt booke of Kings, *Spiritus Domini malus arripiebat Saul the 'euill Spirit of the Lord did ceaze on Saul,* the ſame ſpirit being called the ſpirit of the Lord, and alſo an euill ſpirit; euill (to wit) becauſe of the deſire of its miſchieuous will; and of the Lord, for that he was ſent by God, to afflict Saul with that plague and torment, which God by its meanes did execute vpon him, and ſo it is declared in the ſame text ſaying, *exagitabat eum ſpiritus nequam à Domino* the wicked ſpirit from the Lord, did torment and

vexe

2. Reg.
16. 10.

Greg. li.
18. mo-
ral. c.3.
1. Reg.
16. 23.

1. Reg.
16. 14.

vexe him, and for this reason sais the saint, doth the holy scripture call those diuells which torment and persecute the iust, the Thieues of God, Thieues because of the malicious will they haue, to hurt and damage vs, and of the Lord, to giue vs to vnderstand, that all the power they haue for to do any mischiefe, is deriued vnto them from almighty God. And so *S. Augustin* obserues very well, that Iob did not say, *Dominus dedit, Diabolus abstulit*, the Lord hath giuen, and the Diuell hath taken away; bur he attributs it all to almighty God, saying *the Lord hath giuen me, the Lord hath take away*: knowing right well, that the Diuell could proceed no farther in hurting vs, then God permitted him. And this Saint prosecutes his discourse saying; acknowledge God the Authour of thy scourge and punishment, seeing the Diuel can do thee no harme vnles he first permit it, who hath all superiour power. Let no man say this mischiefe is happened to me by the Diuells meanes, but attribut all your punishment & affliction to Almighty God: since the Diuell can do nothing of himselfe, not so much as touch the least haire

Greg. li. 14. mor. c. 16., Iob. 19. 12.

Aug. in psal. 31. Iob.1.21

Aug. in psal 31.
,,
,,

　　　which

which lies vpon our garments, without
the permiſſion of God; neither could he
enter into the heard of ſwine as the E-
uangell teſtifies, without hauing firſt obteined leaue of our Sauiour *Chriſt*, to do
it. how then ſhall he be able to tempt or
indomage vs, without the permiſſion of
Almighty God? He who had no power
to touch the ſwine , how ſhall he come
to annoy the children?

*Math. 8.
31.*

THE III. CHAPTER.

*Of the great good and profit, which is in-
cluded in this Conformity with the
will of God.*

S *Aint Baſil* ſays that the height of all
the ſanctity and perfection of a Chri-
ſtian life, conſiſts in attributing the cauſes
of all things to God, how little or great ſo
euer in themſelues they be , and to conforme our ſelues in them vnto his holy
will. But to the end that we may the better comprehend the importance and perfection thereof, and be incited by our affection towards it, to ſeeke and procure it
with greater diligence; we will more par-
ticu-

ticularly declare the great good and profit , which is contained in this conformity with the will of God . The firſt is
that intire and perfect reſignation,which
the Saints and all Maſters of ſpirituall
life do extoll ſo much,pronouncing it the
root and offſpring of all our tranquility
and peace, as being that whereby a man
is wholly ſubmitted and reſigned into the
hands of God, as a peece of clay into the
Potters hands.to be faſhioned and moul-
ded as he pleaſes,without deſiring to haue
any intereſt longer in himſelfe,neither to
liue, to eate, to ſleepe, or labour for himſelfe,but wholly and intirely for Almighty God : and this is effected by this conformity,ſeeing that man thereby reſignes
himſelfe wholly vnto the will of God in
ſuch manner , as not to deſire any thing;
but only that the diuine will may be moſt
perfectly accompliſhed in him ; as well
in point of what he is to do, as in all accidents which may happen to him, aſwell
in proſperity and conſolation , as in anxiety ánd aduerſity. Which is a thing ſo
gratefull and pleaſing to Almighty God,
as for this only reaſon, he ſtiled *Dauid* a
man according to his owne harte.*Inueni*
virum

virum secundum cor meum, qui faciat omnes voluntates meas, he hauing prepared his hart so plyable and obedient to the hart of God, so readily wrought to a delicate aptnes to receaue each forme which he should please to impresse in him, either of ioy and contentment or of paine and griefe, as softned waxe was not more supple to receaue the figure which a man should imprint in it: and therefore he said, and repeated it againe, *Paratum cor meum Deus, paratum cor meum*, my hart is prepared, ô God, my hart is prepared. Secondly he who hath this intire and perfect conformity with the will of God, must with all haue attained to an intire and perfect mortification, of all his passions, and vitious inclinations; We are not ignorant how highly necessary this mortification is, how much it is commended and extolled in the sacred scripture and by the B. Saints. Now this mortification is a meanes which of necessity must precede the attaining of this conformity with the will of God, this being the end, and mortification the meanes to arriue vnto it; and we know the principall end of any thing is vsually more sublime

1. Reg. 13. 14.
Actuum 13, 22.

Psal. 56. 8. & Psa. 107. 1.

lime and perfect then the meanes . That mortification is a necessary meanes to attaine vnto this vnion, and intire and perfect conformity with the will of God,we may vnderstand by this, that there is nothing which lets and hinders this vnion and conformity,but only our proper wil, and disordinate appetits , and so consequently the more they shall be mortified and ouercome, the more deare and strait wilt this vnion be , and this conformity with the wil of God.For to ioyne a rough hewen planch, and make it ly euen with an other which is wel smoothed and plained, we must first passe it ouer with the plainer and make it euen; and so in like manner mortification goes perfecting & polishing vs,vntill it make vs fit to be ioyned to God , and applied in all things to his holy will , and therefore the farther we shall proceed in mortifying our selues, the nigher we shall come to vnite & conioyne our selues vnto the will of God,and when we shall once come to be perfectly mortified,we shal then haue attained vnto this perfect vnion and conformity.

From hence proceeds an other good and profit, which we may reckon for the
B 4   third,

third; and that is, that this resignation and entire conformity with the will of God, is on of the greatest, and most acceptable sacrifices, which any man of him selfe can offer to Almighty God. For as much as in other sacrifices, he offers only his goods; but in this, himselfe is offred vp: in other sacrifices and mortifications, he only mortifies himselfe in part, in temperance, modesty, silence or patience, he offers but a part and portion of himselfe; but in this a perfect holocaust, whereby he offers himselfe entirely and altogether to his Diuine Maiestie to be disposed of, in all things as he pleaseth, and when, and how he pleaseth, without any exceptiō, or any reseruation to himselfe; and therfore there is as much difference betwixt this sacrifice, and all other sacrifices and mortifications, as betwixt a man, and those goods which belong vnto him, or the whole of any thing, and any part thereof.

And this God esteems so highly of, that he seems to require nothing els of vs, *Præbe fili mi cor tuum mihi*, my sonne giue me thy harte; as the Royall Eagle seekes no other pray then harts, so the

Prou 23. 26.

the most gratefull and acceptable thing
to God, is this hart of ours, and if you
giue him not this, it is labour lost to present him with any thing besides, for he
regards it not. Neither if we consider it
well, is it so great a thing which he demaunds of vs, when he requires our
harts; seeing that if we who are only dust
and ashes, cannot be satiat or content,
with all those thinges which God hath
euer created, and that our caytiue narrow harts cannot be filled with any thing
which is lesse then God, how can we
thinke to giue God any satisfaction and
content, in affording him but halfe our
harts, reseruing the other halfe vnto our
selues? wee are most grosly abused, if we
thinke our harts can admit of any such
diuision *coangustatum est enim stratum,*
ita vt alter decidat, & pallium breue
vtrumque operire non potest, the hart is
a little and strait bed saith the Prophet
Esay, and is capable of God alone, wherfore the spouse in the Canticles doth call
it her little bed ; *In lectulo meo, quæsiui*
per noctes quem diligit anima mea, in
my little bed I haue sought in the night
him whom my soule dearly loues, and
because

Esay 28.
20.

Gilbert.
Abbas
ser. 1. in
Cât. ap.

Bernar-
in-Cant.
3. 1. becaufe fhee kept her harte fo ftraitned
that no other could lodge in it, befides
her be loued Bridgroom:and who foeuer
fhould feeke to extend his hart fo farre,
as to make roome for any on befides,
would chafe God out of it. And it is of
that, which his Diuine Maieftie makes
Efay. 57.
8. complaint by the Prophet *Efay*, *quia
iuxta me difcooperuifti, & fufcepifti A-
dulterum, dilatafti cubile tuum, & pepe-
gifti cum eis fœdus*, you haue committed Adultery by receauing into the bed
of your hart, any other befides your
fpoufe, and to cloke this your wickednes,
you betray and driue God from you. If
we had a thoufand harts, we were bound
to make tender of them all to God, and
yet we were to conceit we had done too
little,in regard of what we owe of duty
vnto fo great a Lord.

The fourth is, that whofoeuer fhall
haue brought himfelfe to this conformity, will be poffeffed with the perfect
charity and loue of God; and the farther progreffe he makes in it,the greater
and dearer will be his loue of God, and
confequently his perfection, which confifts in this perfect loue and. charity, and
befides

besides that which we haue already said,
may be farther gathered from that which
we are to cōclude with all; seing the loue
of God cōsists not in words, but in effects
and workes : *Probatio dilectionis* (saith
S. Gregory) *exhibitio est operis*, the proofe
of our loue, is the tender of our workes;
& the more hard and painfull to accom-
plish those workes shall be, the more do
they declare our loue and affection: and
so the Apostle and Euangelist *S. Iohn*,
going about to declare the great loue
which God did beare vnto the world, as
also the greatnes of our B. Sauiours loue
vnto his eternall Father: of the first he
sayes: *God so loued the world, as he gaue*
his only begotten sonne to suffer and die
for vs; and for the second our B. Sauiour
himselfe speaking saith : *that the world*
may know how I loue my Father, and that
I doe according as my Father hath com-
maunded me, rise and let vs goe hence, &
the place to which he went, was to the
crosse, to suffer shame, torments & death
for vs. In which he made it sufficiently
appeare vnto the world, that he loued his
Father, in so much as he was obedient to
him in a commaund so hard and rigorous,

Greg. hō
in Euāg.

Ioan. 3.
16.

Ioan. 14
3.

rous. Wherefore we conclude that **our**
loue appeares beft in our Actions, **and**
moft, when they fhall be moft great and
laborious . Moreouer this entire conformity with the will of God, is (as we haue
faid) the greateft facrifice which of our
felues we can offer vp vnto him; & that,
becaufe it fuppofes a moft perfect mortification and refignation, whereby a man
offers vp himfelfe to God, and wholly re-
fignes himfelfe into his hands, to difpofe
of him , in what manner fo euer he fhall
pleafe, then the which there is nothing in
which he can more fhew his loue vnto
him, feeing he freely giues and offers vp
vnto his Diuine Maieftie what fo euer he
hath, as alfo what fo euer he can haue or
may defire, and that with a mind fo li-
berally difpofed , as could he , or had he
more, with the fame willingnes he would
depart with it.

THE

THE IV. CHAPTER.

*That this perfect conformity with the will
of God, is a blessednes and a kind of
heauen in earth.*

W Hosoeuer shall be arriued to this
entire conformity with the will
of God receauing euery thing which may
happen to him, as proceeding from the
hand of God, and conforming himselfe
in all, vnto his most diuine and holy will,
shall haue obteined here on earth a rare
felicity and beatitude, and enioy a wondrous great tranquility and peace, with a
perpetuall ioy and iubily of mind. Which
is that blessednes and felicity which God
Almighties great and faithfull seruāts enioy in this mortall life, for (as the Apoftle says) *the Kingdom of God* (and the
beatitude of this life) *is not meate and* **Ad Rō.**
drinke (nor any other sensuall delight **17. 14.**
and pleasure) *but Iustice peace and ioy in
the Holy Ghost*, this is the kingdom of
heauen on earth, and that Paradice of all
delights which we may enioy in this life,
and which with good reason is called a
beati-

beatitude, since it resembles vs in a certaine proportion, vnto the blessed in heauen: for as in heauen aboue, there is no change nor alteration, but the blessed perseuer alwaies in one being, in the eternall fruition of Almighty God; so also they who are once arriued to this intire and perfect conformity to that, place all their contentment, in the contentment and the will of God; are neuer troubled nor disquieted with any mutation or contrary accident of this present life; in that their harts and wils are so sweetly vnited and conformed vnto the will of God, that the consideration how all is proceeding from him, and how his good will and pleasure is fulfilled in all, makes that pleasing and delightfull to them, which otherwise would be grieuous and sorrowfull. and that, because they desire and loue more the will of their beloued then their owne. Whence it comes that nothing is able to disturbe their peace: for they reioyce and are particularly glad, when they are afflicted, grieued, and despised, as knowing it proceeding from the hand of God, and there is nothing els, which can disquiet them, or bereaue them of

the

the peace and tranquility of their minds.

And this was the cause of that perpetuall cheerfulnes and peace, which those holy Saints, (whom we admire in story) *S. Anthony, Dominicke, Francis,* and others enioyed, as also of that which we read of our B. Father *Ignatius*, and ordinarily see in other great seruants of Almighty God. For do we thinke that these holy Saints had no aduersity? that they had not tentations, and infirmities like vs? that they were neuer crossed with the successe of thinges? without doubt they were, and that farre more then we : for as much as God vses most frequently to try his Saintes, and exercise them in the like accidents. whence therefore comes it, that they remained euer in one state of mind, without any chaunge of countenance, but with a ioy and serenity both in the interior and exterior, so great, as if they had kept perpetuall feast and iubily? The cause was no other then that which we haue already declared, because they were arriued to that degree of perfection, to haue intire conformity with the will of God, and had placed all their delight in the accomplishment thereof, and so the

successe

Lib. 5.c.
5. uitæ.
P. N Ignatij.

succeſſe of euery thing, was their felicity;

Ad Rō.
8. 28.
Mach. 1 2
21.

Diligentibus Deum omnia cooperantur in bonum, non contriſtabit iuſtum quicquid ei acciderit, all labours, tentations & mortifications were conuerted into a delight to them, ſince they acknowledged in them the bleſſed will of God which was all there ioy and contentment. They had already attained vnto the greateſt height of felicity & beatitude, which any on could arriue to in this mortall life, and ſo proceeded in all their actions as if they had been in poſſeſſiō of the glory of heauen. Herupon S. *Catherine of Siena* ſaid

Sancta
Cathari.
de Sien.
en ſes
dialogos

excellently wel, that the iuſt in this world are like our Sauiour *Chriſt*, who neuer wanted the beatitude of his ſoule, how euer great his paines and afflictions were. So likewiſe the iuſt doe neuer looſe that their felicity, which conſiſts in the conformity with the will of God, with how many aduerſities ſo euer they be oppreſt. Seing that there remaines with them ſtil that ioy & contentment which they take in the will of God which is accompliſht in them.

This is a perfection ſo ſublime and of ſo high prerogatiue, as the Apoſtle auouches

it

it to passe all vnderstanding; *Et pax Dei* Ad Phi-lip. 4. 7.
quæ exsuperat omnem sensum, custodiat
corda vestra, & intelligentias vestras in
Christo Iesu, he calls it a peace surpassing
all vnderstanding . for as much as it is a
gift of God so high and supernaturall,
that no humaine vnderstanding by it
selfe, can comprehend how it is possible
for a hart of flesh and blood, to remaine
quiet, at peace, and comforted, in the
middle of those stormes and tempests
raised by the miseries and tentations of
this life; This was notwithstanding to be
be found, in that wondrous bushe which Exod. 3.
Moyses saw, all burning in a flame, and 2.
yet not consumed, as also in that Miracle of the Children, who at *Babylon*
throwne into the fiery furnace, remained
vntoucht in the midst of such a mighty
fier, singing praises vnto God. This is that
which holy *Iob* mentioned in speaking
vnto God, *mirabiliter me crucies* . O Iob. 10.
Lord thou dost torment me after a won- 16.
derous manner, signifying the great paine
and torment which on the one side he
suffred, and on the other the vnspeakable
contentment and ioy, which he receaued
in the sustaining them, seing that such

C   **was**

was the good will and pleasure of his Diuine Maiesty.

Caffian writs of a certaine venerable man, who at *Alexandria*, was incompaſt and hemd in by a ſort of lewd Infideils, who reuiled him with all the iniurious ſpeeches as they could deuiſe ; in the meane time he remained in the middle of them, like a ſilly lambe, ſuſtaining all, and anſwering not a word: they all made their ſport with him , ſtriking and ſhouing him; & doing him a thouſand other iniuries; among the reſt one demaunded of him in mockery , what miracles his *Chriſt* had done? vnto whom he anſwered the miracles which he hath done are, that I in ſuffering all theſe iniuries, and as many more as you can all inuent, do take all patiently , and am neither moued to anger againſt you, nor ſtired vp to paſſion in my ſelfe. This doubtles was a great miracle and wonder, and in him a moſt high, and gainfull perfection.

Aug.lib.
de Gen.
ad lit. in
opere
imper
fect.c.13 The Antients do recount, and *S. Auguſtin* makes mention of it in diuers treatiſes, how that mountaine of Macedonia called *Olympus* is of ſuch ã eminēt height that to the top of it the wind and raine

and

1835660

and clouds haue no accesse; *Nubes exce-* contra
dit Olympus;neither can it be reached by Mani-
the flight of any bird,it being so high that cheos.
it transcends the first and extends it selfe cap.15.
vnto the middle region of the aire; wher- Lucam.
fore the aire is there so pure and rarified l,2.phar-
as the clouds can neither be formed nor salica.
sustained there,they requiring vnto their
being, a thicker and grosser aire : and for
the same reason neither the birds nor men
can be maintained there in life , because
the aire is so subtill and rarified , as it is
not fit to take breath or respire with all;
And thus much we haue from the rela-
tion of those , who went euery yeare vp
to the top to offer certaine sacrifices, ca-
rying with them wett sponges , vnto the
end that applying them vnto their noses,
they might condense the aire, and make
it fit for respiration:where if they chaunced at any time to write in the ashes of
the sacrifice , they should find the next
yeare the Character as entire and perfect,
as when they drew it first , which was a
signe that neither the wind nor raine had
any power there.Behold here that height
or perfection liuely disciphered , vnto
which those are arriued , who haue ac-

quired this entire conformity with the
will of God. *Nubes excedit Olympus,
& pacem summa tenent*, vnto such a glorious height haue they attained vnto such
a happy peace are they arriued aboue all
annoiance either of cloud, swind, or raine,
where no fowle of rapin can come, to
bereaue them of their peace and pleasure
of hart.

S. *Augustin* on these words; *Beati pa-
cifici quoniam filij Dei vocabuntur*, says
that our Sauiour *Christ* hath therefore
pronounced the *peaceable blessed and
children of God*, because there is nothing
in them which resists and contradicts the
will of God, but they conforme themselues vnto it in euery thing, like vnto
good children, who procure in euery
thing to imitate their Father, in both willing and not willing the same with him
in euery thing.

*Aug. li.
i, de ser.
Dom. in
monte
cap. 8,
Mat. 5. 9.*

And this is a point the most spirituall
and of greatest importance of all others
in spirituall life. And whosoeuer shall be
arriued to this to receaue all that comes,
how euer small or great, as proceeding
from the holy hand of God, and conforme himselfe in all vnto his soueraigne
will,

will, so as to haue no other contentment
but the good pleasure of God, and the
performance of his holy will, this man
hath found a Paradice here on earth, *fa-*
ctus est in pace locus eius, & habitatio Psal. 75.
eius in Sion, and, as S. *Bernard* says, may 3. Bern.
sing which all assurance and confidence in senté-
this Canticle of the wiseman, *I haue* tijs Eccl.
sought in all these rest and shall make my 24. 11.
aboad in the inheritance of the Lord:
seing that there he hath incountred with
that true solace, & full and perfect pleasures, which no liuing creature can bereaue him of, *vt gaudium vestrum sit* Ioan. 16.
plenum, & gaudium vestrum nemo tollat 22. & 24.
à vobis. O that we could but once attaine
to this, that all delight might be in the
accomplishment of the will of God, in
such manner as our will might be his and
his contentment ours! O Lord that I had
no other will, then what your blessed
will is, nor any lesse desire of any thing,
but what I knew would be vngratfull to
you, and that your good pleasure, might
be my ioy and comfort in euery thing.
Mihi autem adhærere Deo bonum est, Psal. 72.
ponere in Domino meo spem meam, it is 28.
good, (it is best) for me to adhere to God,

and

and to place my hope in the Lord. Oh
how happy fhould my foule be, to
be conioyned to God in fuch a louing
manner! Oh how bleffed fhould wee
be to be alwaies vnited with him, to make
no account of ought we do or fuffer, but
fo fare forth as we are therein performing the will of God; and from thence
receauing al our fatisfaction and content!
he (fays that all-holy man *) vnto whom
all things are one, who draweth all things
to one, and feeth all things in one, may enioy a quiet mind, and remaine peaceable
in God.*

Thomas
de Kem-
pis li. 1.
de con-
templ.
mundi.
c. 3.

THE V. CHAPTER.

*That contentment is only in God, and
whofoeuer feeketh in it any thing els,
fhall neuer find it.*

THofe who place their contentment
in God and in his diuine will, do
enioy a perpetuall quiet and repofe, in
that being faftned to that firme pillar of
the will of God, they partake of its im-
mutability, and abide allwaies in one
ftate, immobile and firm.: wheras thofe
who

who haue any tye or obligation to the world, and haue placed their harts and contentments thereupon, can neuer enioy any true or lasting peace, since they are subiect to the chaunges of those things vpon which they do rely, and together with them are tost and whirled about. *S. Augustin* doth declare this admirably well, vpon that verse of the Prophet, *concepit dolorem & peperit iniquitatem.* They haue conceiued dolor and brought forth iniquity, saying; *non enim poterit labor finiri, nisi hoc quisque diligat quod inuito non poterit auferri*, there would be no end of griefe and affliction, vntill we came to place our affection vpon that, which against our wils could not be take from vs. For be assured that you shall be alwaies in trouble and disquieted, as long as you affect those things, which are in others powers to bereaue you of.

We read of our B. Father *Francis Borgia* how he hauing conducted the herse of the dead Empresse to *Granada*, where before shee could be interred, he was inforc't for the securing of his conscience and oath, to disclose the coffin to be able to affirme whether it were shee or no,

Aug. in in psal. 7. 15.

Lib. 1 c. 7 vitæ P. N de Borgia.

C 4

no. that he vnueyling her face, & seeing
it so vgly and horribly deformed, as was
inough to stricke affrightment into
those who saw it, was so liuely moued
therwith God at the same instant visiting
his hart and storing it with light to see
the deceits and vanity of the world, that
it conceiued a firme purpose which in
these words he exprest, *I vow vnto thee,
ò my God, I will neuer serue any prince
who can dye againe.* Let vs likewise put on
the same resolution & oblige our selues to
God, to bestow our harts herafter vpon
no mortall thing; nor ought which may
haue end, or which others can bereaue vs
of against our wills: which vnles we do,
we shall neuer be at rest nor quietnes. for
when those things are loued (saith *S. Au-*
gustin) which we may loose, whether we
will or no, we must necessarily remaine
miserably troubled, & afflicted for them
it is naturall vnto vs, not to depart with
that without griefe, which we loued
whilst we enioyed, and the greater our
loue was vnto it, whilst we possest it, the
greater is our griefe when we are berea-
ued of it, and in confirmation of this in an
other place he saith, *Qui vult gaudere de*
                                                    se,

Aug. tra.
24 super
Ioan.

se, tristis eris. If you place your contentment,in such an office or such an imploi-
ment , or are too much affected to any
place, or the like,it lies in your superiours
power at pleasure to depriue you of this
content;and so you will neuer liue a contented life:if you take delight in exteriour
things, or in the satisfying of your owne
desire , all things of this kind are subiect
vnto chaunge; and although they should
remaine in the same state they are , yet
you your selfe would be altered , and be
displeased with that to morrow , which
but to day you passionatly affected ; Of
this the Children of Israell afford vs an
exaple,who when they fed vpon Manna,
were cloyed with it , and demaunded
other meat, when they saw themselues at
liberty, began presently to loue and desire their former bondage , their wishes
euen in sighes, did carry them backe to
Egypt againe , they longed for their fare
of onions and garlicke to which they had
been accustomed, and their supplication
to returne did euen proceed to importunity . you will neuer find content , if
you place it in any of these exteriour
things, *qui autem de Deo vult gaudere*
semper

*semper gaudebit, quia Deus sempiternus
est*; but he who will reioyce in God, and
in the performance of his holy will, shall
haue perpetuall cause for to reioyce,since
God is eternall and aboue all chaunge and
mutation, *vis habere gaudium sempiter-
num*(saith this Saint)*adhare illi qui sempiternus est* , would you haue a ioy and
contentment which should alwaies last,
adheare vnto God and set your hart on
him, who neuer hath an end.

The holy Ghost , doth put this difference betwixt a foolish man,and one who
is wise and holy, *Stultus sicut Luna mu-
tatur , homo sanctus in sapientia manet
sicut Sol*.The ignorant chaunges like the
Moone, which to day is in increase , to
morrow in the wain, to day you shall see
him iocant and merry,to morrow sad and
melancholy,now in one humour presently
in an other,and this because he hath fastned his hart and placed his contentment
in the things of the world, which are still
fading, and euer mutable; wherfore (like
as they say)he daunceth after the musicke
which they make , and his chaunges are
according to their inconstancy.In a word
he is lunaticke and like the sea depen-
dent

Eccles.
27, 12,

dent on the alteration of the moone; but a iust and holy man, remaines alwaies in one state and being like the Sunne, hath no increase nor wain. The true seruant of Almighty God, in all his proceedings is cheerfull and content, he hath placed all his felicity in God, and in the accomplishment of his holy will, which can neuer faile him, nor any creature euer bereaue him of it.

It is reported of that holy Abbot called Deicola, that his countenāce was alwaies composed to smile, and being demaunded the reason, he answered; *Christum à me tollere nemo potest :* happen what may, come whatsoeuer will ; there is no man can depriue me of *Christ.* This holy man had found out perfect and true contentment, since he sought it in him, who could not be wanting to him, nor taken away from him by any one; whom if we will be happy we must imitate. *Exultate iusti in Domino* reioyce ye iust in the Lord. *S. Basil* writing vpon these words obserues, that the Prophet says not, that you should reioyce in the abundance of your temporall goods, neither in any ability, learning, or talent which you haue;

not

Abbas Deicol.

Ps 12.1.
Basilius.

not in your health or ablenes of body;
notin the praise and the esteeme of men;
but that al your delight should be in God,
in the fulfilling of his blessed will, for
this is it alone which is sufficient to satiat
and content vs, all other things hauing
no perfect nor true contentment in them.

S. *Bernard* in one of his sermons vpon
these words of *S. Peter, ecce nos reliqui-*
mus omnia &c.goes declaring of it rarely
well saying *anima rationalis cæteris om-*
nibus occupari potest, repleri non potest
all other things, besides God, may possesse
the hart and soule of man, but satiat them
they cannot, they may prouoke, and set
their appetits on edge, but cannot satisfy
nor take them downe, *Auarus non im-*
plebitur pecunia. Like as the auaricious
(says the wisman) hath a great thirst of
gold; but all which he possesieth can neuer allay nor quench it: so fares it with
the things of this world, which can neuer
satiat our soules and appetits. And *S. Ber-*
nard giues vs the reason , do you know
(saith he) why all the things and riches
of the world can neuer satisfy you? *Quia*
non sunt naturales cibi animæ: since they
are not the naturall food of our soules;
no

Bernar.
Mat. 19.
27.

Ber. tra.
de dilig.
Deo c. 3.
in fine.

no more then aire and wind the sustenance of our bodies : and as we should
laugh, and hold him for a foole who
being ready to die for hunger would by
yawning to receaue the ayre, and Came-
leon-like thinke to nourish himselfe with
it: so (says this Saint) is it no lesse a folly,
to thinke of the reasonable soule of man,
which is a spirit, can be satiat with these
temporall and sensuall things. *Inflari potest, satiari non potest*, it may be puffed
vp, like that other with ayre, but it is
impossible it should be satiat with it; since
ir is a food which hath no proportion to
it, giue to each on its requisit sustenance
corporall food to the body, and spirituall
to the soule; *Panis namque anima, iusti-
tia est ; & soli beati qui esuriunt illam,* Bern. su.
quoniam illi saturabuntur, the bread and illa ver-
naturall nourishment of the soule, is Iu- ba. Ecce
stice and vertue, and they are only happy nos reli-
who hunger and thirst after this Iustice, omnia.
because they shall be satisfied.

S. *Augustin* in his Soliloquies decla- Aug. c.
ring this reason more amply, speaking of cap 30.
the reasonable soule saith. *Facta est capax* soliloq.
*maiestatis tua vt à te solo, & nullo alio
possit impleri,* you haue made our soules,
ô Lord

ô Lord, capable of your diuine Maiefty,
in fuch manner as nothing can fatisfy or
fill them but your felfe. When the chace
or goldworke of a Iewell is made pecu-
liarly for any pretious ftone, there is nothing els which can compleatly fill it, befides that ftone for which it was prepared: as for example the gold indented in
a triangular forme, any Iewel which were
round would neuer fit it: in like manner
our foule is created to the Image & like-
nes of the blefled Trinity, and proportio-
ned and made to receiue nothing els but
God, and therefore it is impoffible that
any thing befides God can fuffice ro fill
it. Al whatfoeuer is contained in this roûd
vniuerfe, is not able to doe it; *Fecifti nos*
Domine ad te, & inquietum eſt cor no-
ſtrum donec requiefcat in te, you haue
made vs, ô Lord, for your felfe, and our
hart enioys no quiet vntill it reft in you.

That common côparifon of the needle
of a dyall, doth aptly ferue for to declare
this better: the nature of this needle (being
once toucht with the loadftone) is, by a
naturall inftinct from God Almighty to
point ftill towards the North, and you
fhall fee it alwaies in an vnquiet motion,
and

Aug. l. 1,
confe.
c. 1.

and neuer refting vntill the point of
it hath reacht the North , when inftantly it ftands quiet and immoueable.
In this manner hath God created man;
with fuch a naturall reference and inclination vnto him as to his North & finall
end, that vntill we haue placed our harts
on God, we fhall like this needle, be neuer at reft nor quiet; This needle as long
as it regards any point of the heauens
which is in motion, neuer finds reft, but
when it lights vpon the North pole,
which remaines euer fixt and immoueable, is ftraight at quiet, and ftands ftill:
fo, as long as we fixe our eyes and harts
on thefe worldly things which decay and
perifh , we fhall neuer find contentment
or repofe; if we place them on God , we
are inftantly at reft.

And this ought to be a great motiue
vnto vs to feeke Almighty God, euen for
our owne fakes and intereft, fince there
is no man , who defires not to liue content . S. *Auguftin* fays *fcimus fratres
quod omnis homo, gaudere defiderat; fed* Aug. fer.
non omnes ibi quærŭt gaudium, vbi opor- 30. de
tet inquiri. We know, my deare brothers, Sanctis.
that all men do naturally defire comfort
and

and content, and feeke after it with all
their harts diligence, by reafon they cannot liue without it ; but all men do not
feeke it there where they ought to do. &
all the felicity or infelicity of man confifts
in the placing his hart and eyes vpon a
true content, or vpon a falfe and deceit-
full on; The Auaricious, the Luxurious,
the Proud, the Ambitious, and the Glut-
tonous man, feeke their contentment and
fatisfaction all ; but the on feekes it in
hording vp riches, the other in purfuit of
honour and dignity, the on in feafting the
other in luxurioufnes , and all in taking
their marks amiffe , and feeking it where
it is not to be found , goe on the way
reuer to arriue vnto it : feeing that all
thefe things , and as many more as are in
the world , are not fufficient to fatisfy a
foule, and put it in a ftate of true felicity.
And therfore fays this glorious Saint. *Quid*

Aug. de
fpirit. &
anima.
cap. 54.

ergo per multu vagaris homuncio quæ-
rendo bona animæ tua , & corporis tui?
Ama vnum bonum , in quo funt omnia
bona; & fufficit: defidera fimplex bonum,
quod eft omne bonum ; & fatis eft , why
,, doft thou rauge abroad filly man, feeking
» good for thy foule and body out of this
　　　　　　　　　　　　　　variety

variety of (worldly) things? loue (God) „
that only good, in whom all other goods „
are comprehended; and it suffices: desire „
that good without all mixture good, „
which is all and solly good;& it is inough. „
It is he alone who can satiat and fulfil the
desires of our harts. *Benedic anima mea*
Dominum, qui replet in bonis desiderium Psal.102.
tuum; may he be praysed blest and glori- 5.
fied for all eternity. *Amen.*

THE VI. CHAPTER.

Wherin is in an other manner declared,
how the only way to arriue to true con-
tentment, is to conforme our selues
with the will of God.

THe glorious *S. Augustin*, writing Aug. tra.
vpon these words of our B. Sa- 73. sup.
uiour (*Quodcumque petieritis patrem in* vcan.
nomine meo , hoc faciam ; whatsoeuer Ioan. 14.
you demaund of my Father in my name, 15.
I will graunt it you) says that no man is
to seeke for rest and peace , by way of
doing his owne will , and obteining that
which he desires; seing it is neither good
nor conuenient for him, and may fall out
perhaps vnto his hurt and ruine: but that
D　　　　he

he is to be refigned, to imbrace willingly
whatfocuer good or better thing God
fhall allot vnto him; and for this only he
is to befeech and petition Almighty God.
Quãdo enim nos delectãt mala, & non de-
lectãt bona, rogare debemus potius Deum,
vt delectent bona, quam vt concedantur
mala, when we find our felues no waies
affected, to the performance of the will
of God, which is the only good, but are
ftrõgly carried away with the defire that
our owne wills be done ; we ought to
make it our petition vnto God, not to
graunt vs that which we defire ; but to
giue vs a taft and fwcetnes, in the performance of his will which is our good, and
moft conuenient for vs. and he alleadges
for this purpofe that which is recorded of
the children of *Ifrael*, in the booke of
Num. 11 Numbers, who becoming weary & euen
4. loathed with the *Manna* which God
fhowred them downe from heauen, defired and begged of God to fend the flefh
to eate, vnto whofe defires he condefcen-
ded, though much vnto their coft : for,
Pfal. 77, *Adhuc efcæ eorum in ore ipforum, & ira*
30. *Dei afcendit fuper eos, & occidit pingues*
eorum, & electos Ifrael impediuit, as yet
the

the meat was in their mouths & the wrath
of God ascended vpon them, the best
pampered of them were slaine, and the
elect of *Israell*, were (mightily) hindered,
God punished them with a grieuous mas-
saker; It is most certaine that that heauenly Māna, which God sent vnto them,
was farre better.thē that flesh which they
desired, and those onions and Garlicke
of *Egypt*, after which they lōged so much;
and therfore they ought not to haue demaunded it of God, but rather that he
would haue rectified their pallat, that
they might haue found gust and sauour
in that heauenly foode; and then there
had been no necessity for them, to wish
for other food, since euery one might
haue found in *Manna* that tast which
he liked best. And euen so, when you lye
vnder the arrest of any passion or tentation, and haue your tast so much depraued, as to find no sweetnes in vertue, no
sauour in any good, but doe lye wishing,
like a sicke and diseased man, for that
which may be hurtfull and preiudiciall
to you, you are not then to gouerne your
selfe according to your owne desire, neither to desire to haue your will accom-

Sap. 16,
20.

D 2

plisht,

plisht, since this were no way to giue you any cōfort, but to sow the seeds of a greater trouble & disquietnes: but that which in such a circumstance you are to desire of God, is that he would salue and heale your pallat, and giue you tast and sweetnes in the accomplishing of this blessed will, which is our good, and most connenient for vs; and so we shall come to obtaine a true peace and content of mind.

S. *Dorotheus* directs vs to it by an other way, or rather declares this in an other manner: he says, that he who in euery thing conformes himselfe vnto the will of God, in such manner, as to make all his owne inclinations readily serue vnto it, is come vnto such a passe as to doe his owne will in euery thing, and to enioy a perpetuall gladnes and quietnes of mind. To declare that which we would procure to say, we will giue an example of this in point of obedience, and make but one labour in dispatch of two affaires. We say commonly to those who desire to enter into Religion, and to make their liues iourny by the way of obedience; you must make account when you are entred into Religion, neuer more to doe your owne

Doroth.
doctrina
9.

owne will againe: and *S. Dorotheus* says
on the côtrary neuer feare it, you may do
your owne will, & that not only lawfully
but alfo holily, & with much perfection.
How is this to be done? *Qui propriam nõ*
habet voluntatẽ, suam ipsius semper facit
voluntatem : that Religious man who is
truly obedient, and hath no felfe will of
his owne, doth alwaies his owne will; becaufe he makes the will of an other his.
Et sic nolentes propriam explere volun-
tatem, inuenimur illam semper exple-
uiffe. do but procure, that your owne will
be the fame with the Superiours, and you
will be doing your owne wil continually,
and that with much merit & perfection.
And fo in conformity to this, I fleepe as
much as I will, becaufe I defire not to
fleepe longer then obedience appoints; I
eate as much as I defire, feeing I require
no more, then that which is allotted vnto me; I pray, I read, I labour as much as
I pleafe, and take vpon me as much pén-
nance as I thinke is neceffary for me, fince
I do all thefe, and in like manner all the
reft, according to the prefcript and will of
holy obedience . And in this manner a
good Religious man, without hauing
any

any inclination of his owne, comes to do his owne will continually. And this is it which makes those Religious, who are good indeed, appeare so cheerfull & ioyfully disposed; for that which reders them alwaies content and glad, is the making the will of obedience their owne.

In this point of obedience consists all the facility, and difficulty of Religious life, and on this depends the ioy and content of a Religious man. If you put but on a resolution, to renounce your owne will, and receaue the will of your Superiour in the place of it, the Religion will be easy and sweet vnto you, and you will liue in it with much content and ioy; but if you nourish a will contrary to the will of your Superiour, there is no liuing in Religion for you. two different wills in one person are incompatible; We see by experience although our will be but one, yet when our sensuall appetit is repugnant vnto reason and to it, how little assurance, and how little rest we haue; and yet this appetit is but an inferiour & subordinate to our will : but what shall we thinke when two equall wils, are striuing in vs for superiority? *Nemo potest duobus*

Mat. 6.
24.,

Domi-

Dominis seruire, no man can serue two
Masters . Now for as much as the difficulty which occurs in Religious life, doth
not consiste in the exercises and labours
themselues, but in the repugnance of our
will , and in the apprehension which our
imagination frames of them ; thence it is,
that we sometimes find its obseruances
more difficill and insupportable. This we
may easily apprehend from the differéce,
which we experience in our selues, when
we are in tentation, and when we are free
from it : for when we are without tentation , all things seeme light and easy to
vs; but when we are assaulted with tentation , or subiected to any griefe or melancholy, that which was wont for to be
easy to vs, is straight conuerted into difficulty, and we thinke we shall neuer be
able to go through it , but that heauen &
earth are come together againe, all as it
were cóspiring to bring vs difficulty. The
difficulty is not in the thing it selfe, since
it is no other then what it was before; but
in our ill disposition of mind . As when a
sickman hath an auersion from his meat,
the fault is not in the meat, which is good
and sauourly; but in the peccant humour
D 4   of

of the ſicke, which makes his food ſeeme vnſauoury and diſguſtfull to him : and it is the like in that which we indeauour to ſay.

And this is the grace and fauour which God doth to thoſe whom he calls vnto Religion, to make it ſweet vnto them to follow an others will. This is the grace of our vocation, with which our God hath preuented vs , with a happines by farre tranſcending theirs, whom we haue left behind vs in the world . For what is it, that affords and giues you this facility, in leauing your owne , and following of an others? who hath plac't in your boſom that new hart, where with you haue in horrour all worldly things, and find ſo much ſweetnes in recollection, prayer, & mortifying your ſelfe ? you brought it not out of the world with you no certainly ; but rather a contrary one , *ſen-*

Gen. 8. 21. *ſus enim, & cogitatio humani cordis, in malum prona ſunt ab adoleſcentia ſua.* It is a gift and fauour of the holy Ghoſt, who like a deare Mother of ours, hath rubbed with aloes and wormwood the treacherous nipples of the world, to wean vs from them, and make them ſeeme bit-

ter,

ter, which nnce wee delicious to vs ; and
honyed the exercises of vertue and Religion, that they might become sweet and
sauoury vnto vs , which before seemed
bitter, and vnsauoury . *Domine qui me*
custodisti ab infantia , quia abstulisti à
me amorem seculi . *O blessed Lord (said*
holy S. Agatha) I render infinite thanks
vnto that deare goodnes of thine which
hath elected, and defended me euen from
mine infancy, and taken away from me
all loue of this wretched world . We are
not to thinke it so great a matter to be
Religious, but it is much, and a great benefit of Almighty God, together with
our vocation to Religiō to giue vs a right
tast and relish of this heauenly *Manna,*
whilst others pallats are longing after the
base sustenance of the garlicke & onions
of Egypt.

I cōsider somtimes with my selfe, how
worldly people, euen from the Lords and
Noblemen in Court, vnto the Grooms
and Footboys of the stable depart with
the freedome of their owne wils for their
particular profit and interest, and put on
the seruill liuery of an other mans; they
eat (as is commonly said) according to
the

Ambro.
psal. 118
octon 4.
super il-
lud . A-
uerte o-
culos
meos ne
videat
vanitatē.
S. Agath

the rate of an others hunger, their fleepe
is meafured by an others watchfulnes, and
they fo aptly cloathe and fit themfelues
with others wills, as it comes to be in only
fafhion with them, and they defire no
other life then it . *Et illi quidem vt cor-*
ruptibilem coronam accipiant; nos autem
incorruptam. What marueile is it , if we
can be delighted and content, with that
manner of regular liuing, which is preferi-
bed vs in Religion, and refigne our felues
vnto that better wil of our Superior; fince
they for a little honour and temporall intereft, fo accommodate themfelues vnto
the wills of others, as it is euen their delight and pleafure for to follow them,
whilft they make night of day, and day
of night . What great wonder is it, I fay,
if we performe as much for the loue of
God, and for the purchaffing of an eternall life? Let vs therfore put on a refolution to make the will of the Superiour
our owne ; and in this manner we fhall
do our owne wils in euery thing, & lead
a life in Religion full of all fweetnes and
cheerfulnes, with a ioy and contentment
moft perfect and fpirituall.

But now to returne vnto our argument,

1. Cor.
9. 25.

ment, and apply all this vnto our prefent
fubiect ; We are to procure to make the
will of Almighty God our owne,& conforme our felues vnto it in euery thing,
and to wil or not will the fame with him
in euery thing; and fo you will come, to
do your owne will continually , and lead
a life full of all content and fatisfaction;
For it is moft euident, that if you defire
nothing els , but what God Almighty
would, your owne will fhall alwaies be
fulfilled : for his will fhall be done , and
confequently that which you defire. This
verity euen *Seneca* was not ignorant of;   Seneca
who faith, that man hath nothing more   in prefa-
high or perfect. thē the knowledge how   tione li.
to fuffer with alacrity all paine and mi-   quæft.
fery, and fuftaine all , as if they were pro-   3. nat.
cured by his owne choice and election:
and euen this much man is obliged to
do fince he knowes it to be the will of
God that it fhould be fo. Oh how happy
fhould we liue , were we but arriued to
that perfection, to make the will of God
our owne, and to bound our defires with
in the limits thereof! and this not only
becaufe by this meanes our will fhould
be fulfilled; but moft of all, becaufe we
                          fhould

should see the will of God accomplisht
in euery thing, whom we do loue so deare
and tenderly. For although we ought to
helpe our selues with that which hath
been hitherto said ; yet we are not to set
vp our rest, vntill we are arriued to place
all our comfort in delighting Almighty
God, and in the fulfilling of his holy wil;
*Omnia quacunque voluit Dominus fecit,
in cælo, & in terra, in mari, & in omnibus abyssis* , God hath done whatsoeuer
he pleased, in heauen and in earth, in the
sea, and in all the deeps; he both can, and
wil do all that he pleases, as the Wiseman
says, *subest enim tibi eum volueris posse*,
& there is nothing which can let or hinder him. *In ditione enim tua, cuncta sunt
posita, & nõ est qui possit resistere eæ voluntati. Voluntati eius quis resistet?*

*Psal. 34.
6.*

*Sap. 12.
18
Ester. 13
9
Ad Rõ.
9. 19.*

THE VII. CHAPTER.

*Of diuers other felicities & profits which
are to be found in this conformity
with the will of God.*

AN other great good and profit in
this exercise is, that this intire conformity with the will of God, is one of
the

the beſt and principall diſpoſitions,which
on our parts we can be prepared with al
to the receauing and in a manner inuiting our bleſſed Lord to beſtow his plen-
tious graces and benefits vpon vs. And ſo
when God had reſolued to make *S.Paul*
of a perſecutour , an Apoſtle and Preacher of his ſauing truth,he preuented and
diſpoſed him by this reſignation. ayming
at him a great light from heauen,which
ſtrucke him from his horſe and opened
the eyes of his ſoule in the fall, inforcing
him to cry out: *Domine quid me vis fa-* Actu 9.6
cere ? Lord what would you haue me
doe ? behould me heer as a little piece of
clay betwixt your hands, mould me and
faſhió me to what ſhape you pleaſe,wher-
upon God made him a veſſel of election,
which might catry and diffuſe his name
through all the world ; *Vas electionis eſt* Act.9.15
mihi, vt portet nomen meum coram gen-
tibus & regibus & filijs Iſrael. We read
of *S. Gertrude* that God ſaid vnto her:
Whoſoeuer deſires that I ſhould make
free repaire vnto them , muſt deliuer o- S.Gertr.
uer vnto me the key of their owne will, refert.
without euer requiring it againe: & ther- Blo cap.
fore our B. Father comends this reſigna- 11. motion nit, ſpir.

P. N. Ig
natius li.
ex 5. spi.
tion and indifference vnto vs, as one of
the best dispositions which we can haue
to the receauing of Gods most exquisit
fauours: and he requires that we should
enter with it into the spirituall exercise,
and he lais vs this foundation euen from
the begining of them, that we should be
indifferet, seuered frō all worldly things,
with affection no more inclining to one
thing then an other, but only desiring
that Gods blessed will should be accomplisht and done in euery thing; and in
those rules or annotatiōs which he giues,
aswell for the directiō of him who giues,
as him who takes the exercise, he says in
„ the fifth of them. It will be of incredible
„ helpe vnto him who takes these exerci-
„ ses, if coming with a great and liberall
„ mind he offer vp himselfe wholly vnto
„ his Creator to dispose of him, and euery
„ thing of his, according to his best pleasure, and in such manner as he may be best
serued by him. And the reason why this
same disposition, is of so great force to
obteine any fauour & grace of Almighty
God, is because on the one side we rid
our selues of all the lets and hinderances
of our depraued affections and desires;
and

and on the other the more confidence
we haue in God, and the more freely and
intirely we refigne our felues into his
hands, in defiring nothing but what may
be beft pleafing to him, the more we
oblige him, to take vpon him the care of
vs, and to be prefent with vs in all our
neceffities.

On the other fide this Conformity
with the will of God, is a moft efficacious
cious meanes to attaine vnto all vertue,
feeing that vertues are not acquired but
by the actes of them. This is the naturall
meanes to attaine the habits of things; and
by this way God Almighty intends to beftow
ftow vertue one vs, whofe pleafure it is
to produce the workes of grace, in a manner
ner conformable vnto thofe of nature.
Exercife your felfe then in this refignation
tion and conformity with the will of
God, and fo you fhall be continually in
the occafion of exercifing all other vertues,
tues, which is the only meanes to attaine
vnto them. Now you fhall haue the occafion
cafion of exercifing humility, now obedience;
dience; at other times Pouerty, Patience,
and fo likewife all other vertues. And in
the meane time, the more you exercife
your

your selfe in this resignation and conformity with the will of God, the more you
shall goe increasing and perfecting your
selfe therin; as also the greater shall your
profit and perfection in all other vertues
be; *Coniunge te Deo , & sustine vt cres-
cat in nouissimo vita tua*, says the Wise
man, vnite your selfe to God , conforme
your selfe in all , vnto his holy will ; an
other version hath *conglutinare Deo*, be
as it were glued vnto him , and made one
with him , and so you will exceedingly
increase and profit in vertue . For this
reason the Masters of spirituall life doe
counsaile vs, (and it is a most good and
profitabla aduice) to single out some one
eminent & Master vertue, in which may
be comprized all the rest, and to bestow
our selues particularly to prayer, and the
whole scope of our examen and other exercises, in the pursuit of it; and that, because attēding only vnto it, we may more
easely attaine vnto it , and hauing attained it, we may be Masters of all the rest.
Now one of the principall things vpon
which we are to cast our eyes , for this
effect , is this resignation and intire conformity with the will of God; and in this

both

Marginal notes: Ecc. 2.3.   Trac. 5. 6. 14. & 15.

both our prayer, and examen will be profitably bestowed, although it were for diuers yeares, yea our whole life long; seeing that in attaining vnto this, we should together attaine vnto all other vertues.

On those words of the Apostle *S. Paul. Domine quid me vis facere?* Lord what would you haue me to do? *S. Bernard* says, *O verbum breue, sed plenû, sed efficax, sed dignum omni acceptione!* O word short, but full, comprehending all, excepting nothing. Lord what is your pleasure that I should do? O short word, but wonderous pithy, but exprest to the life, but efficacious, and worthy of all praise; If you desire therfore a short instruction, and an abridgment of the art of acquiring perfection, behold it here, say alwaies with the Apostle, Lord what would you haue me do? and with the Prophet my hart is prepared, for to do all whatsoeuer you shall require of me, haue this alwaies in your mouth & hart; and your progresse in perfection will be answerable, to the profit which you make in this.

There is yet an other good and profit in this exercise, from whence we may

Act. 9. 6.
Ber. ser. 1. de cõuersione S. Pauli.

Psal. 56. 8. & psal. 107. 1.

E   furnish

furnish our selues with an excellent remedy, against a certaine sort of tentation,
which familiarly vses to offer it selfe vnto vs ; The diuell doth labour somtimes
to disquiet vs, with certaine tentations and
conditionall thoughts , by way of inter-
rogation demaunding of vs; what if one
should say this or this vnto you, how
would you answere him? and in such and
such an circumstance, how would you behaue your selfe ? if such a thing should
happen what would you do ? & the enemy crafty as he is, will present things vnto vs in such a manner, that on which side
soeuer we turne vs, we shall remaine perplext and not dare to venture out , imagining that on either side we shall fall into
the snares: and seeing it is all one vnto the
enemy , whether those things by which
he doth deceaue vs, be true or only apparant, and counterfait , so as he may but
play his prize, and wrest from vs some ill
consent or other, he hath his end , and
takes no further care . To such tentations they say commonly, that there is no
necessity to answere I or no, yea they
affirme that it is better to giue no answere
at all, especially for those persons who are
                                    scru-

fcrupulous, fince it is that which the diuell feekes to hold party with them, and
bring them to defend and proue: for he
is not to feeeke in his replies; and how
brauely refolued fo euer they enter the
fkirmifh with him, they are not like to
come of without a brokē head. But there
occurs to me an excellent and profitable anfwere to put of thefe tētations with
all, which I efteeme to be a farre better
remedy, then the not anfwering them,
and it is that which wee are going to declare ; to wit to euery one of thefe demaunds (deuoutly fhutting of our eyes)
to anfwere if that be the will of God, it is
alfo mine; if God defire to haue it fo, I
defire it likewife ; that which pleafeth
God in it, fhal alfo pleafe me; I referre my
felfe in euery thing vnto his will ; I will
as farre as I may performe my duty in it;
God I hope will giue me his grace, that
I may not offend him in it, but do all according to his holy will. Behold here a
generall anfwere, to giue fatisfaction
vnto all fuch demaunds, and in its gene-
rality it imploys no difficulty, but is rather the more eafy and familiar. For if it
be the will of God, it is beft and moft

conue-

conuenient for me, I may with all affu-
rance.caft my felfe,in vttering that which
hath been faid, into the armes of God
Almighties will and hereby the diuell wil
be fruitrated of his purpofes, and depart
afhamed, and we fhall become ioyfull
and couragious with the victory. And as
in tentations againft our faith they coun-
faile(efpecially thofe who are fcrupulous)
to anfwere nothing in particular, but in
generall to fay; I beleeue and hold all
which our holy Mother the Church
beleeues and holds; fo alfo in this
tentation whereof we fpeake, the beft
remedy is to giue no anfwere in particular,but to haue recourfe vnto the will of
God, which is both good and perfect in
a moft high degree.

THE VIII. CHAPTER.

Wherin is confirmed by fome examples,
how gratefull vnto God, this exercife
is, of the conformity of our wills with
his, and of the great perfection which
is conteined in it.

Cefarius
lib. 10.

C Æfarius relates how there was a
Monke in a certaine Monaftery,
vnto

vnto whom God had communicated a singular grace of working Miracles; in so much as he cured diseased persons, euen with the only touch of his garments or of the girdle with which he girded himself: his Abbot considering this attentiuely on the one side, and on the other obseruing in this Religious no particular notes of any sactity, called him vnto him one day in priuat, and earnestly coniured him, to declare vnto him the reason, why God did worke so many Miracles by him? the holy man ingeniouslv confest that hee knew none; for said he, I fast no more then any of the rest, my disciplines and penances are not exceeding theirs, I spend no more time in prayer, and allow no lesse time to sleepe then any of the rest. All that I can affirme of my selfe is onely this, that neither prosperity doth elate my mind, nor aduersity depresse it, there being nothing in chaunce which can disturbe the quiet of my hart; my soule in all occasions enioyes one tenour of tranquillity and peace, how euer straunge or vncoth they may be vnto my selfe or others. His Abbot wondering ask't him; were you then nothing troubled the o-

dialog.
cap. 6.

E 3   ther

ther day, when that same knight our e-
nemy set fier on our granary, and burnt
our wholl prouission for the yeare ? No
truly, answered the holy man; the content of my soule was no waies touched
with it: for I had long before, committed
all vnto the hands of God: whence it
comes, that I receaue as well prosperity
as aduersity, as well want as plenty, as
equall benefits proceeding from those
holy hands of his. Wherupon the Abbot
acknowledged that to be the cause of the
vertue of working so many Miracles.

Blosius   *Blosius* recounts, how a certaine poore
in appē-   begger, but otherwise leading a holy and
dice ad   exemplar life, being demaunded by a lear-
institu-   ned diuine, how he was arriued to so
tionem   great perfection, answered. I haue taken
spirit. ca.   a resolution, to haue all my dependancy
1. in fine on the diuine will, to which I haue so
wholly confotmed mine owne, that what
soeuer God wils, I also would haue: when
hunger paines me, or the could bites, I
praise Almighty God : be the weather
faire, or rainy or tempestuous, I praise
God still ; whatsoeuer he sends me, or
whatsoeuer befalls me through his permission, be it sweet or bitter, be it vnlucky
                                        or

or fortunat, I am alwaies glad, and re-
ceiue it coming from him; as the greateſt
fauour he could do vnto me; reſigning
my ſelfe with all humility entirely vnto
him: My ſoule hath been able to find no
reſt in any thing, which is leſſe then God,
and now I haue found out my God in
whom I haue eternall peace and reſt.

We read alſo in the ſame *Bloſius* of a
holy Virgin who being demaunded how
ſhee had attained vnto ſo high perfectiō,
anſwered: I haue receaued all troubles
and aduerſities, with a great equality of
mind as comming from the hand of Almighty God, if any one chaūced to trouble or iniure me, I preſently procured to
requite him with ſome ſpeciall benefit, I
haue neuer made my complaint of what
I ſuffered vnto any one, but haue had
mine only recourſe to God Almighty,
from whom I haue preſently receaued
redreſſe and comfort.

Blof. vbi
ſup. & c.
10. !mo-
nil. ſpir.

He writes alſo of an other Virgin of
great ſanctity, who being asked by the
exerciſe of what vertue ſhee had obteined
ſo great perfectiō, anſwered. With much
humility, I was neuer ſo ouerwhelmed
with griefs and oppreſſions of hart, as not

euen to long to suffer farre more **for the**
loue of God. esteeming my selfe vnworthy , of so great graces and fauours as
they were.

Taulerus recounts of a certaine great
seruāt of Almighty God, who had wholly resigned her selfe into his blessed hands,
vnto whose prayers many recommending
the happy successe of their affaires and
businesses:shee denying them vnto none,
would oftentimes forget to pray for some;
and yet notwithstanding, all things suc-
ceeding according to their harts desire,
who had commended themselues vnto
her deuotions. many came to thanke her,
& acknowledge the efficacy of her prayers,whō shee had not so much as thought
vpon; when she blushing at their mistake,
would bid them render all their thanks
to God , for as for her , shee had in nothing furthered their businesses . At last
many coming to her in this māner whom
shee had forgot, she began to make an
amarous complaint to God for giuing
such good successe and dispatch to all
affaires , which were commended vnto
her deuotions, in so much as they came
vsually to giue her thanks for them , for
whom

Taule
rus ser.
1.de Cir-
cumcis.

whom shee neuer had petitioned : vnto
whom her blessed Lord answered , you
must know my dearest, that on that day
when you resigned your wil to me, I gaue
you reciprocally mine; since when , although you should aske nothing in particular, yet whatsoeuer i saw you inclined
vnto, I should effect it according to your
desire.

We read *in the liues of the Fathers* of
a husbandman whose fields and vines,
were far more fruitfull. then any land of
his neighbours there about; who demau-
ding of him how it came to passe. he answered them that it was no wonder, that
his ground did bring forth so good increase. since he had the times and seasons
in his owne hands; wherupon they being
far more astonished the before, ask't him
how that could be. Why said he, I neuer
desire other time or season the what God
pleaseth to send; and because I will , that
which God wills , he giues me that fruit
which I desire.

Seuerus Sulpitius writing the life of *S.*
Martin affirmes of him, that during that
long time which he conuers't with him,
he neuer saw him angry, nor melancholy,
but

in vitis
Patrum.

Seuerus
Sulpi-
tius.

but alwaies cheerfull, and quietly com-
poſed ; and he aſcribes it to this vertue,
which he was eminent in, of receauing
all what euer hapned to him, as ſent vnto
him from the hand of God ; & ſo he conformed himſelfe, vnto his bleſſed will in
euery thing, with a great alacrity and reſignation.

THE IX. CHAPTER.

Of ſome other conſiderations, which may
rēder this exerciſe of conformity with
the will of God, both eaſy and plea-
ſant to vs.

Vnto the end that this exerciſe of the
conformity with the will of God,
may be both eaſy and delightfull to vs,
it is firſt neceſſary that we haue alwaies
before our eyes, that foundation which
we haue laid from the beginning ; to wit
that no affliction or aduerſity can happen
to vs, which hath not paſſed through the
hands of God, being examined and regi-
ſtred by his moſt bleſſed will, which
verity our Sauiour *Chriſt* hath not only
taught vs by word but by example. Whē
he commaunded *S. Peter* the night of
his Paſſion to ſheath his ſword, he added:
                                           Cali-

Cap. 1.
& 2.

Calicem, quem dedit Pater, non vis vt bibam illum? wouldst thou not haue me drinke the chalice which my Father hath sent me? he did not say,the chalice which *Iudas,*& the Scribes & Pharisees had filled out for him,since he knew well that they were only as seruants to administer that draught vnto him, which his Father had set,& that al which they out of their rāco-rous enuy & malice did,was so ordained by the infinit wisdome & goodnes of his heauenly Father,for the redéption of the sinnefull world, and so he answered after-wards to Pilat, when he boasted that he had power to crucify or to deliuer him; *Non haberes potestatem aduersum me vllam, nisi tibi datum esset desuper,* thou shouldest haue no power ouer me , vnles it were giuen thee from aboue , which the holy Fathers explicat: *nisi ex diuina dispositione & ordinatione id factū esset,* declaring thereby, that there is nothing happens but by the disposition and ordinance of God . *S,* Peter in the Actes of the Apostles hath merueilously explica-ted this,in his declaration of those words of the Prophet;*Quare fremuerunt gentes, & populi meditati sunt inania? astite-*
runt

Ioan.18.
11.,

Ioan. 19.
11
Chry. ho
83. in
Ioan.
Ciril. li.
12 c. 22,
in Ioan.
Irē. li. 4.
contra
hereses
c. 34.

Aug.ser.
116.sup:

Ioánem.
Act 4.26
Pſal.2.1.

*runt Reges terræ, & Principes conuene-
runt in vnum aduerſus Dominum,& aduerſus Chriſtum eius* where he ſays: *Cō-
uenerunt enim verè in ciuitate iſta , aduerſus ſanctum puerū tuum Ieſũm, quem
vnxiſti, Herodes & Pontius Pilatus cum
gentibus & populis Iſrael,facere quæ manus tua , & conſilium tuum decreuerunt
fieri .* The Princes and Potentars of the
world aſſembled and were in league together againſt our Sauiour *Chriſt,*to put
that in execution and effect which had
been concluded and decreed,in the con-
ſiſtory of the Bleſſed Trinity : and more
then what had been there determined of,
they could not do . And ſo we ſee that
when God would not haue it ſo, all the
power of King Herod was not ſufficient
to take away his life, when he was yet a
child , and he who maſſacred ſo many
Innocents, could not find out the Infant
whom he ſought;and that, becauſe it was
not his pleaſure then to dye . How often
did the Iewes and Phariſees ſeeke to lay
hands vpon our Sauiour to put him to
death ? once they had him on the very
edge of the mountaine on which their
Citty was built, to throw him headlong
                                    downe,

downe and the holy Ghospells says: *ipse autem transiés per medium illorum ibat;* he made his way securely through the midst of them. because it was not his pleasure then to dye. that kind of death, and therfore they had no power to procure it him: an other time they would haue stoned him, and had euen lifted vp their hands to let them fall in showres of stones vpon him. & he did no more but mildely expostulat with them, saying; *Multa bona ostendi vobis ex patre meo, propter quod eorum opus, me lapidatis?* I haue shewed you many good workes, of my Fathers part, for which of them do you now stone me? he would not permit thē, nor giue them leaue to discharge their stones vpon him; *Quia nondum venerat hora eius;* because his houre was not yet come. But when the houre indeed in which he had resolued to dye was come, then they could execute what he had decreed to suffer, becaufe then he would haue it so, and gaue them leaue to do it: *hæc est hora vestra & potestas tenebrarŭ,* he told them when they came to apprehēd him, I was daily with you teaching in your Téple, and you haue not taken me,

Lucæ 4. 30.

Ioan. 10. 32.

Ioan. 17. 30.

Lucæ 22. 53.

becaufe

because as then my houre was not come, but now it is, and therfore come, behold, heere I am he ; What did not *Saul* do? (who was a figure of this) what diligence vsed he not, what ftratagems to get *Dauid* into his hands? A King of Iſraell againſt a priuat man . *Vt quærat pulicem vnum*, as *Dauid* ſaid in ſearch of a ſilly flea , and yet with all the diligence he could vſe , he could neuer intrap him, which the holy ſcripture notes, and giues the reaſon of. *Non tradidit eum in manus eius* , becauſe God would not deliuer him ouer vnto his hands; & this is all.

Reg. 26. 20, & ca. 24. 15.

1. Reg. 25. 14.

S. *Cyprian* therefore on theſe words, *& ne nos inducas in tentationem* , doth well obſerue, that in tentations and aduerſities, all our feare , deuotion and attention, muſt only haue God Almighty for their obiect ; ſeeing that neither the diuel nor any perſó, can do vs any harme, vnles God firſt do giue them faculty.

Cypr. ſerm. de oration. Domi- nica. Mat. 6.

Secondly although this verity , pondered attentiuely, hath great force & efficacy for to conforme vs in al things vnto the will of God; notwithſtanding we are not here to make a ſtay, but we muſt proceed forwards, to an other ſubſequét point,

Doroth. doctr. 13 Hil c. 29. de orat. idem di- xit Do-

point, which the holy Saints do generally mino. 5.
note. & that is; that we ought to perſwade Gert. re-
our ſelues, that al things proceeding from fert Bloſius, cap.
the hand of God, are alſo ſeruing to our 11. mo-
good and profit. The torments of the nil. ſpiri.
damned are proceeding from the hand of
God, but not for their profit and amendment, but for their puniſhment: but the
paines and afflictions, which God in this
life ſends to any one, be he righteous or a
ſinner, we ought to haue that aſſurance
and beliefe of his infinit mercy & goodnes, that they are al directed for our greater good, and as the meanes and helpes
moſt proper and neceſſary, vnto our ſal-
uation. And *Iudith* when ſhee ſaw her
people in ſo great affliction and diſtreſſe,
beſieged and vexed by their enemies, ſaid:
ad emendationem & non perditionem no- Iudith.
ſtram eueniſſe credamus, beleeue aſſu- 8. 27.
redly, that theſe miſeries and afflictions
are ſent vnto vs by God for our amendment and not for our perdition, we may
well aſſure our ſelues, of ſo good and
louing a will as Gods, who tenders vs ſo
dearly, that it inclines to reſolue of nothing concerning vs, which is not good,
and the beſt, and moſt expedient for vs,
like

like as herafter we shall more amply declare.

Thirdly, that this verity may be to our
greater profit, & be made vp to the com-
petency of an efficacious meanes, to helpe
vs to a perfect conformity with the will
of God, it is not inough that we vnderstand in specie only that all things are
proceeding from the hand of God, and
that we belieue it in grosse and generall,
because it is taught vs by faith, or els
perhaps we haue read or heard so much;
but it is necessary, that we put this beliefe in practise, the better to arriue vnto
an experimentall knowledge of it in such
manner, as to receaue all things which
happen to vs, as if with our owne senses
and eyes we did perceaue our Sauiour
Christ in this manner speaking to vs: Here
my sonne I send thee this; it is my pleasure that for the present, thou shouldst
do or suffer this, or that other thing. For
by this meanes it would be a thing most
easy and pleasant to vs, to conforme our
selues vnto the wil of God in euery thing,
since it is most certaine, that should our
Sauiour *Christ* personally appeare vnto
vs and say.; behold my sonne, see this is
that

that which I defire of you; I would haue
you to fuffer this paine or ficknes at this
time for my fake ; it is my pleafure to
make vfe of you, in this or the other office: it is moft certaine I fay , that we
fhould vndertake it moft willingly, euen
our whole liues long, were it a thing of
the greateft difficulty in the world, and
efteem our felues highly honoured, and
happy men, that God would vouchfaffe,
to ferue himfelfe with vs, and we fhould
gather only from his commaundingit,
that it were the beft and conuenienteft
thing of all others for our faluatiõ, without doubting in the leaft kind therof.

Fourthly we ought to reduce this exercife to practife, both in our prayers and
other exercifes, by deluing and finking
deepe into this rich mine of fo fatherly
and particular a prouidence as God hath
of vs, to the end that we may the better
know how to make due vfe of fuch an
inexhauftable treafure, as we fhall goe declaring in the following Chapters.

F   THE

THE X. CHAPTER.

*Of Gods fatherly and particular proui-
dence of vs, and of the filiall confidence which we ought to haue
in him.*

AMong other the great riches **and**
and treasures which we enioy, who
are in the Catholike Church, one of the
greateſt is Gods fatherly and particular
prouidence of vs; it being moſt certaine
that there is nothing can arriue vnto vs,
which hath not firſt paſſed and been recorded by the hand of God. And ſo the
Prophet ſays. *Domine vt ſcuto bonæ vo-*
luntatis tuæ coronaſti nos , thou haſt en-
uironed and defended vs, ô Lord, with
that good will of thine , as with a ſheeld
of defence , we are round incompaſſed
with this good will of God, in ſuch manner as nothing can come vnto vs which
paſſeth not firſt by it : and therfore there
is nothing which we are to feare ; for he
wil let nothing paſſe, but that which may
be for our greater good . *Quoniam ab-*
ſcondit me in tabernaculo ſuo, in die ma-
lorum

Pſal. 5.
13.

Pſal. 20.
5.

lorum protexit me, in abscondito taber-
naculi sui. The Prophet Dauid affirmes,
that God hides and preserues vs, euen in
the most secret of his Tabernacle, and
shelters vn vnder his wings: and says yet
more. *abscondes eos in abscondito faciei* Psal. 30,
tua, our Lord doth hide vs in the most 21.
hidden part of all his face, which are the
eyes, in whose apples he hath lodged vs,
and so an other version hath, *in oculis fa-*
ciei tuæ. God hath made vs the very apples of his eyes, to verify that which is said
in an other place ; *Custodi me vt pupil-* Ps. 16.8.
lam oculi. qui tetigerit vos, tangit pupil- Zach. 2.
lam oculi mei. We are warrented vnder 8.
his defence and protection as the apples
of his eyes, and they are the words of
God: whosoeuer touches you, shall touch
me in the sight of mine owne eyes. Can
thereby imagined a thing more rich,
more pretious, or more worthy of all
esteeme then this?

O that we could but maturely apprehend and penetrat this verity ! how de-
fenc't and fortified should we find our
selues? how assured, how comforted should
we be, in all our labours and necessities?
If here in this world one haue but a Fa-

ther riche and mighty and one of the
deereſt fauourits of a King;what cōfidēce,
what aſſurance hath he in the ſucceſſe of
all his buſineſſes , knowing that the fauour, authority and protection of his Father will not be wanting to him ? how
much more reaſon haue we to be confi-
dent and aſſured, whilſt we conſider that
we haue him for our Father, in whoſe
hand is all the dominion of heauen and
earth? and that nothing can arriue vnto
vs, which paſſeth not firit by his paternall
hands?if a ſonne can repoſe himſelf vpon
the confidence and aſſurance of his Fathers fauour ; how much more confidence ought we to haue in him, who is
more our Father then all other Fathers
beſides, and in compariſon with whom,
there is none deſerues the tender name of
Father: for there are no bowells of loue,
which may be compared with the loue of
God to vs,which ſurpaſſes by infinite degrees all the loues which euer earthly Fathers were ſenſible of , we may well aſſure our ſelues that whatſoeuer ſuch a
Father ſends vs, is for our greater vtility
& good;ſeeing that loue which he beares
vs in his only ſonne , permits him to doe
nothing

nothing els then to procure the good of
him, for whose loue onely he deliuered
ouer his sonne vnto the torments of the
crosse . *Qui etiam proprio filio suo non* Ad Rŏ.
pepercit , sed pro nobis omnibus tradidit 8. 32.
illum, quomodo non etiam cum illo om-
nia nobis donauit ? says the Apostle *S.*
Paul. he who hath not spared his only
sonne, but hath deliuered him ouer(vnto
death) for all of vs, how can it be,but he
hath giuen vs with him all other things?
he hath giuen vs the most he could, and
will he deny vs any little thing ? Now if
all men ought to haue such confidence in
God Almighty ; how much more Religious men, whom he hath receaued particularly for his owne, and giuen them
both the spirit and hart of sonnes indeed,
inuiting them to abandon & forsake the
Fathers of their flesh and blood , and to
make choice of him for their only true
Father? with what hart, what fatherly tē-
dernes shall God loue such as these? what
care, what prouidence shall he haue of
them ? *Quoniam pater meus & mater* Psal. 26.
mea dereliquerunt me: Dominus autem 10.
assumpsit me , a happy choice you haue
made of such a deare Father , in place of
those

those parents, **whom you haue departed**
with you may now with more reason and
greater confidence say . *Dominus regit*
me, & nihil mihi deerit, God hath taken
vpon him the charge of me , the care of
me, and all that belongs to me, and I fhall
want for nothing. *Ego autem mendicus*
fum & pauper, Dominus folicitus eft mei,
I am(t'is true) a begger needy and poore,
but God is folicitous and carefull for me.
who would not be comforted with this?
nay who would not euen melt away in
the loue of fuch a God? Oh who, are you,
ô Lord, who haue taken vpon you the
charge of me, and haue fo intenfe a care
of me, as if in heauen and earth you had
no other creature to gouerne but me
alone! Oh that we could but delue and
make paffage deepe inough into this fo
vifcerall, fo paternal loue, prouidence and
protection which God Almighty hath
of vs!

From hence is begotten in the faithfull
feruants of Almighty God , a moft familiar and filiall confidence in him, which
is fo exceffiue in fome , that there is no
child in the world who confids fo much
at all affays in the protection of his Father,

Pfal. 22.
1.

Pfal. 39.
13.

ther, as they in God, feeing they know
right well that the bowells of his affectió
to them, is more then either of Father or
Mother, which vfes to be the tendereft of
all; and fo the Prophet *Efay* fays . *Nun-* Efaȳ 49.
quid obliuifci poteft mulier infantē fuum, 15.
vt non mifereatur filio vteri fui? & fi illa
oblita fuerit , ego tamen non obliuifcar
tui . ecce in manibus meis defcripfi te.
muri tui coram oculis meis femper : can
a mother forget her owne child, fo as not
to haue pitty of the fonne of her wombe?
and if fhe fhould forget, yet will not I forget thee. for behold I beare you coppied
out in my hands, and your walles are alwaies before mine eyes: as much as to fay
I do carry you euen in the palmes of my
hands, which do prefent you alwaies before mine eyes , for to defend and keepe
you. and he declares as much by the fame
Prophet with an amorous comparifon,
qui portamini à meo vtero, euen as a wo- Efa. 46.
man great with child, doth carry her in- 3.
fant in her wombe, and is all in all vnto
it, both lodging, bearer, wall, and nurtri-
ture; euen fo faith God I beare you in my
bowells. And with this confideration the
feruants of God do liue in fuch affurance,

and

and esteeme themselues so well prouided
for, so safe against all chaunces, that they
are neuer troubled or disquieted with any
variety or accident of this life, *& in tem-*
Ier. 17.8. *pore siccitatis non erit sollicitum*, the
hart of the iust says the Prophet *Hieremy*
is neuer subiect to commotion, or losse of
the rest & quietnes, for the diuers chaunces
and successes of things: seeing they are assured, that nothing can happen to them
without the will and priuity of their
Father; and of his excessiue loue and
goodnes they are most secure; as hol-
ding for certaine, that whatsoeuer arriues
them is for their greater good, and all
which on the one side he takes away fro
them, he will restore on the other with
aduantage and vsury.

From this confidence so familiar and
filiall, which the iust haue in God, is begotten in their soules that so great peace
tranquillity & security which they haue,
conformable to that of *Esay*, *& sedebit*
Esa. 32. *populus meus in pulchritudine pacis*, *&*
18. *in tabernaculis fiducia, & in requie opu-*
lentà, & my people shall rest in the beauty
of peace, and in the Tabernacles of confidence, and in a riche repose. Where the
Pro-

Prophet moſt fitly and aptly conioynes peace and confidence together, becauſe the one is proceeding from the other, for he who hath his truſt and confidence in God hath nothing to feare or to be troubled at, as hauing God to warrant and ſecure him. And this is that which the royall Prophet ſings, *in pace in idipſum* Pſal. 4. 9. *dormiam & requieſcam, quoniam tu Domine ſingulariter in ſpe conſtituiſti me,* in peace in the ſelfe ſame will ſleepe and reſt, becauſe thou ô Lord haſt ſingularly ſettled me in peace, and aſſured my life vnder the hope of thy deare mercy.

Neither doth this filiall confidence produce peace only, but it accompanies it with a great ioy and gladnes, *Deus autem ſpei* (ſays the Apoſtle S. *Paul*) *re-* Ad Rō. *pleat vos omni gaudio, & pace in creden-* 15. 13. *do, vt abundetis in ſpe & virtute Spiritus Sancti,* the God of hope fill you all with ioy, and peace in your beliefe that you may abound in the hope and vertue of the holy Ghoſt. This firme beliefe of ours, that God knowes what he doth, and doth all for our good, is cauſe that we feele not thoſe tumults troubles & thoſe anguiſhes, which they experience who
　　　　　　　　　　　　　　　　only

only looke with eyes of flesh and blood,
vpon the chaunce of things ; but rather
extraordinary gladnes and delight,in extraordinary chaunces:& the more a man
shall haue of confidence,the more abun-
dant shall his spiritual ioy and gladnes be:
for the more he shall confide and loue,
the greater shall his assurance be,that the
issue of all things will be to his auaile:
neither is it possible that he should otherwise perswade himselfe, or els hope lesse
from the exceeding goodnes, and infinit
loue of God.

This renders the Saints so vndaunted
and assured, in the midst of all their afflictions, so as they haue no dread of men,
of diuells, beasts, or any thing; as knowing assuredly that without the permission
of the will of God, they cannot so much
as touch them: and so *S. Athanasius* reports of B. *S. Anthony* that whē one time
among the rest,the diuells presented thē-
selues in most fearfull shapes,and hideous
formes vnto him,of wild and cruel beasts,
as of Lyons, Tygers, Bulles,Serpents and
Scorpions,all compassing him about,and
terrifying him with their claws , teeth,
horns,stings, roaring, and fearfull hissing,

Athana,

so

ſo as it ſeemed they would preſently deuour him : what did the Bleſſed Saint?
but laugh't them all to ſcorne: and told
them; if you had any vallour, you would
come but on at once , to fight againſt a
ſingle man as I am ; but by reaſon that
you are cowardly , and that God hath
depriued you of your might , therefore
you come ſuch a rabble together of you,
that your number at leaſt may make me
affeard, when your forces came not . If
God hath giuen you any power ouer me,
behold me here , deuour me; but if you
haue no permiſſion for to do it , why do
you make all this ſtir for nothing ? from
whence we may clearly perceaue , that
the great peace and courage, which this
holy perſon found within himſelfe, in this
occaſion , was proceeding only from the
well conſidering that they could do no- Greg. li.
thing without the will of God , and the ₃. dial. c.
conforming himſelfe vnto that bleſſed ₁₆ refert
will . We haue diuers other examples of mile ex-
this kind, in the Eccleſiaſticall hiſtory, and emplū.
we read the like of our B. Father S. *Ig-* Li. ₅. vitę
natius, in the fifth booke of his life: and nat: c. ₉.
in the ſecond, it is recounted , how once & lib. ₂.
as he ſailed towards Rome, there roſe cap. ₅.
ſuch

such a fearfull tempeſt, that the Maſt
being ſplit by the violence of the wind,
and moſt of the Cables and tacklings,
ſheard and broke, all the Paſſengers being
in a mighty feare, and almoſt dead with
the expectation and the dread of death,
only he in ſo great a feare and danger (as
he confeſt himſelfe) was ſcarcely moued
to any thing, beſides a tender feeling and
ſorrow, that he had not ſerued God, ſo
truly and faithfully as he ought; and for
any other thing, it neuer touch't the confidence of his mind; *quia venti, & mare
obediunt ei,* for he knew that the winds
and ſea were obedient vnto God, and
without his will and permiſſion would
not lift vp a waue to ſwallow any one.
Let vs likewiſe ſtudy, (the grace of God
ſuppoſed) to arriue vnto this familiar and
filiall confidence in God, and to this aſſurance and tranquillity of mind, by this
exerciſe of the conformity with the will
of God, deluing by the meanes of prayer
and conſideration, & ſinking deeply into
this moſt rich mine of Gods ſo fatherly
prouidence of vs, I am moſt certaine
that nothing can happē to me, & that neither the diuels nor men, nor any creature,
                                          can

Math. 8.
27.

can do more vnto me, thē God giues way to and permits: and in his holy name let that be done, I do not refuse it, neither desire any thing but purely the will of God.

We read of *S. Gertrude* that neither daungers, nor tribulation, neither temporall losse nor any hinderāces, no not so much as her owne defects and faults could euer obscure that constant and secure confidence which shee had in the most gracious mercy of Almighty God, she belieuing most assuredly that all aswel prosperity as aduersity would by that diuine prouidence be conuerted into good, and our Lord once said vnto this virgin: The assured cōfidence which a man hath in me, belieuing me vndoubtedly both to be able and willing to assist him faithfully in all occasions, doth euen pierce my hart, and offer such violence vnto my mercy, that I cannot be wanting vnto such a creature, for the increase of his merit, and mine owne delight to see him so intirely dependant on me : neither can I otherwise choose but fauour him, for hauing so free and cofident recourse to that which I am, and which I am able to do : and he

vseth

Blos. c. 11. mon. spirit.

vseth this forme of speaking, like to one who were transported & as it were with fond loue. It is recounted of *S. Mech-tilda*, that our Sauiour said vnto her. It is most gratefull vnto me, that men do con-fide in my goodnes and presume of my fauours towards them. for whosoeuer doth humbly put his trust, and firmely belieue in me, I will both in this life be gratious to him, and after his death re-ward him aboue his merits. The more one belieues & piously presumes of my good-nes towards him, the more euen to an infinite proportion shall he obteine of me; seeing it is impossible for a man not to re-ceiue of me that, which he hath hoped for and holily confided to obteine: and ther-fore it is most profitable for a man, to promise the most vnto his hope, and to belieue my promises to him. And to the same *Mechtilda*, desirous to know what we were chiefly to belieue of his vn-speakable goodnes, our Lord answered, belieue with an assured faith, that I will receaue thee after thou art dead, as a Fa-ther would do his best beloued child; and that neuer any Father did so faithfully deuide his inheritāce with his only child,

as

(marginal note:) Blosius vbi sup.

as I will communicat both my selfe and all I haue with thee, whosoeuer shall firmely belieue this of my goodnes, with an humble charity, shall be happy aboue all beliefe.

THE XI. CHAPTER.

Of diuers passages and examples of the holy Scripture, which may helpe vs much to obteine this familiar and filiall confidence in God.

IT will be good for vs first of all, to put before our eyes the frequent custome of those ancient Fathers, to attribute vnto God, all things which happened to them, by what meanes or way soeuer they arriued. In the two and fortieth Chapter of Genesis, the holy Scripture recounts, how *Iosephs* brethren, whilst they were returning towards their countrey with that prouision of corne which they had bought in *Egypt*, in opening their sacks (as they baited at an Inne to prouander their beasts) did find each one in the mouth of his sacke, the mony, which they had disbursed for their corne (which

(which *Ioseph* had cōmaunded his steward to reſtore in that manner vnknowne
to them) they perceiuing this and being
much troubled cryed one vnto an other;
Quidnam eſt hoc quod fecit nobis Deus?
what is this, which God hath done vnto
vs? where we are to obſerue, that they
did not ſay, this is ſome plot laid for vs,
there is ſome practiſe in it, or the ſteward
through his negligence hath left the money in our ſacks; neither, perhaps he ment
to beſtow it on vs in Almes; but they aſcribed it vnto God ſaying, what is this
which God hath done vnto vs? in it acknowledging that as the leaſe of a tree
could not be ſhaken but by the will of
God, ſo alſo that could not happen but
by the ſame prouidence. And when *Iacob* remoued with all his family into *Egypt*, *Ioseph* with all his children went to
viſite him, who being demaunded by his
Father what children thoſe were? anſwered: *filij mei ſunt, quos donauit mihi Deus
in hoc loco*, they are my children whom
God hath beſtowed vpō me in this place;
& the like anſwer *Iacob* gaue when meeting with his brother *Eſau*, and he demaunding of him what children thoſe
were

Gen. 42.
22.

Gen. 48.
9.

were which he had brought with him,
he answered, *paruuli sunt quos donauit* Gen. 33.
mihi Deus, they are little ones whō God 5.
hath bestowed vpon me, and presenting
him with certaine things he said. *Suscipe*
benedictionem quam attuli tibi, & quam Gen. 33.
donauit mihi Deus tribuens omnia , re- 11.
ceaue this present (which he calls a bene-
diction of God, whose euery gift is a benefit) receaue it (said he) which I haue
brought for you , and which God hath
bestowed vpon me, who is the distribu-
ter of euery thing. Also when *Dauid* all
incens't with rage and passion was on his
way to ruine the house of *Nabal* , and
Abigail meeting him with her presents
and prayers assuaged his fury, *Dauid* said; Reg. 25.
Benedictus Dominus Deus Israel, qui mi- 32.
sit hodie te in occursum meum , ne irem
ad sanguinem . Blessed be the Lord God
of Israell, who hath sent thee to day to
meet me, that I might not go forwards
vnto blood and to the slaughter of the
house of *Nabal.* as if he had said, you are
not come of your selfe , but God hath
sent you vnto the end that I might not
sinne, I acknowledge the benefit from
him, vnto him be praise and thanks therfore.

fore. This was the common ftile among thofe aunciēt Fathers,which we ought to make ours by imitation.

But to come neerer to the matter; the **Gen.;37.** Hiftory of *Iofeph*,which we haue touch't in paffing , is no leffe ftraunge, then feruing to our purpofe; whom his brothers out of enuy (that he might not come to rdigne ouer them, and be their Lord according to his dreame ,) fold into bondage vnto certaine marchants : and the fame meanes , which they ferued their turnes withall to prouide that he might not come to raigne ouer them,God made vfe of to effe&t that which his diuine prouidence had defigned; which was, both to make him Lord ouer them , and all the land of *Egypt* . And fo the fame *Iofeph* affirmed vnto his brothers,when difcouering himfelfe vnto them, they were euen loft in the feare and amazement of fo wonderous an euent, *Nolite pauere,* **Gen. 25.** *nec vobis durum effe videatnr,quod ven-* **5.** *didiftis me in his regionibus : pro falute enim veftrà mifit me Deus ante vos in Ægyptum,premifitque me Deus vt referuemini fuper terram, & efcas ad viuendum habere poffitis .* be not affraid neither

ther let it seeme vnto you a hard cafe,
that you did fell me into thefe coun-
tries: for God for your (good and) fafty
hath fent me hither before you into *E-
gypt*: God hath fent me before, that you
might be maintained vpon the earth, and
be prouided with victuals to fuftaine
your liues, together with all the people
of *Ifrael.* It is God faid he who hath fent
me, *non veftro confilio, fed Dei volun-
tate huc miffus fum*; It was not your
doing, but the prouidence of God; *Num
Dei poffumus refiftere voluntati? vos co-
gitaftis de me malum, fed Deus vertit illud in bonum, vt exaltaret me; ficut in
prafentiarum cernitis, & faluos faceret
populos multos*, who can refift the will of
God? you imagined euell againft me, but
God conuerted it all to good, that he
might exalt me, like as you fee at this prefent, and worke the fafty of many people: And who is there who hereafter will
not confide in God? who fhall feare any
more the malice of men, or the worlds
aduerfities? When they fhall know that
all is forefeen by God; & that he vfes the
fame meanes, which they inuent to trouble and perfecute vs, for our aduance-

Gen. 50.
19.

G 2   ment

ment and our greater good? *Confilium*
meum ſtabit, & omnis voluntas mea fiat,
ſays God by the Prophet *Eſay.* go which
way you will, you haue your choyce, but
ſo, as at the end whither you will or no,
you muſt arriue thither where God
would haue you go, who makes vſe of
your meanes vnto that end.

Eſa: 46: 10.

S. *Chryſoſtome* conſiders yet an other
particular in this Hiſtory, ſeruing for our
preſent purpoſe, treating how *Pharaos*
cupbearer, after he was reſtored vnto his
office, for two whole yeares neuer had
thought of *Ioſeph* his Interpreter, although he had moſt earneſtly cōmended
himſelf vnto his memory, to beſeech Pharao for his deliuery. Do you thinke, ſaith
this ſaint, that this his forgetfulnes was by
chaūce? No aſſure your ſelfe, but ſo reſolued vpon & decreed by God, intēding to
await the conueniency of time, to deliuer
Ioſeph out of priſō vnto his greater glory
and aduancement, for if the Cupbearer
had been mindfull of him, it had been an
eaſy matter for him, conſidering his authority, to haue work't vnder hand his
deliuery ſo, as none ſhould euer haue ſeen
or hard of him, but God intended not to
                                    haue

Chri. hŏ.
63. ſuper
Geneſ.
Gen. 40.
23.

haue him so deliuered, but in such manner as might gaine him honour and authority; permitting the other to be forgetfull of him for two yeares together, that the dreame of *Pharao* might chaũce in the interim, when at the instance of the King of himselfe, compelled by necessity he might be deliuered from prison with that glory and Maiesty, to be made ruler ouer the whole Land of Egypt. God knowes well saith *S. Chrysostome* like a cunning artizã, how long the gould must be trying in the fier, and when t'is fittest time to take it out.

In the first booke of Kings we read an other example in which the prouidence of God, euen in little & particular things is perceaued most clearly. God told the Prophet *Samuel* that he would shew vnto him, that man who was to be King of *israel*, vnto the end he might ánoint him, and said, *hac ipsa horà quæ nunc est, cras* *mittam virum ad te de terra Beniamin,* 1. Reg. *& vnges eum Ducem super populum meũ* 9. 16. *Israel*, to morrow at this very hower I will send vnto thee the man whom thou art to annoint for King, & this was *Saul*; whose manner of sending was this; The

asses

aſſes of his Father were gone aſtray, and
his Father ſent him for to ſeek them out:
he tooke a boy with him, and ſought all
vp and downe, but could heare no newes
of them ; whereupon *Saul* was in mind
to returne home againe, by reaſon it was
late , and his Father might be fearfull
what was become of them ; but the boy
was of opinion that they ſhould by no
meanes returne , vntill they had found
them out: there is a man of God here
hard by , ſaid he (meaning the Prophet
Samuel) let vs haue recourſe to him, and
without doubt he will tell vs newes of
them. Hereupon they go to find *Samuel*
out , and at their arriuall God ſaid vnto
him ; *Ecce vir, quem dixeram tibi; iſte
dominabitur populo meo*, this is he whom
I told you I would ſend; this is the man
you muſt annoint for King . O ſtrange
and wonderfull iudgment of God Almighty! his Father ſent him to ſeeke after his ſtrayed beaſts , and God ſent him
to *Samuel* to be annointed King . What
difference is there betwixt the deſignes
and pretenſions of men, and God ? How
farre was *Saul* and his Father from any
ſuch thought, that he was then going to
be

be annointed and confecrated King? and
fo how farre are you and your Father &
fuperiour oftentimes , from imagining
that which God intends to do. From that
which you thinke leaft of, God Almighty drawes forth his owne ends . No , no,
the beafts were not loft but by the will
of God , neither was it by chaunce that
Saul was fent by his Father to feeke the
out, neither that he could not find them,
nor the counfaile of the boy to go to the
Prophet *Samuel* to heare newes of them,
but all was fo ordained and defigned by
God , who vfed thofe meanes to fend
Saul vnto *Samuel* , that according as he
had premonifhed him , he might annoint
him King . Your Father, when he fends
you to ftudy at one of the Vniuerfities, or
beyond the feas, intends to bring you vp
to learning , and thereby to make you a
way vnto fome dignity wherby you may
honourably liue hereafter; and he de-
ceaues himfelfe, for God fends you thither to incorporate you into his owne
houfe, and make you Religious. *S. Au-*
guftin when he went from Rome to Mil-
lan, and alfo Symmachus the Gouernour
of the Citty who fent him thither, did
                      G 4   thinke

thinke the caufe of his going was to teach
Rhethorick there, but there was no fuch
matter; for God fent him thither that *S.
Ambrofe* might conuert him and make
him Catholike.

Let vs confider a little the fundry vocations of men, and the particular and expreffe waies, and ftraunge paffages, by
which God leads feuerall men vnto Religion; for doubtles it is a thing defer-
uing all admiration to fee, that had it not
been for fuch a toy or trifling thing,
which hapned to you, in fuch a circum-
ftance, you had neuer been Religious: and
now that thing was expreffly ordained &
fo ordered by God, to the end to bring
you to Religion; which in paffing ought
to be reflected on by thofe, whofe minds
are oftentimes troubled and tempted to
call in doubt whither their vocations
were from God or no, fince they haue
been brought into Religion, by fuch in-
tricat waies as we haue mentioned; which
is no other then an illufion of the enemy,
enuious of that ftate in which you are,
fince there is nothing more ordinary to
God, then to ferue himfelfe of fuch vn-
likely waies, vnto that end which he pretends

tends of his greater glory, and your greater vtility and good; and of this we haue many examples in the liues of Saints. God ordained not your iourney to feeke out the beafts . *Nunquid de bobus cura eſt Deo?* But he would lead you by that way vnto a kingdom, *feruire Deo regnare eſt.* 1. **Cor.** 9. 9.

When the Prophet *Samuel* afterwards was fent from God , to checke *Saul* for his difobedience in not wholly ruining *Amalec* as God had commaunded him, the Prophet hauing fharply reprehended him, and turning his backe for to depart, *Saul* tooke him by his garment to ftay him, and defire him to pray for him and reconcile him vnto God againe; and the text fays , that the peece of *Samuels* garment which *Saul* laid hold vpon, toar of, and remained in his hand . Who would not thinke it a very chaunce that the garment of the Prophet fhould be rent and torne? either becaufe that *Saul* held faft and pulck't him hard , or that the Prophets garment was lightly rent , becaufe it was old and worne : who I fay would not imagine this rather, then that it was fo difpofed of by the particular prouidence of God ; to fignify that *Saul* was 1. **Reg.** 15. 27.

was deuided from his kingdom, and depriued of his crowne for his offences,and
yet this was it which *Samuel* said, to
Saul, when he saw what was happened;
*scidit Dominus regnum Israel à te hodie,
& tradidit illud proximo tuo meliori te,*
the Lord (by the diuision of my garmēt)
giues thee to vnderstand,that to day the
kingdom of Israel is rent from thee,and
deliuered vnto thy neighbour a better
man then thou.

In the same first booke of the Kings,
is recounted how *Saul* once held *Dauid*
and his people so besieged, *in modum co-
rona*, that *Dauid* euen despaired of esca-
ping his hands: being in this distresse,
there arriues in al hast a Post in the Campe
of *Saul*, bringing newes that the *Philistims* had made impression on his Country, ransacking and spoyling all, wherupon *Saul* to make head against that
daunger which did most concerne him,
was inforced to breake vp his siege, and
lead his forces against the *Philistims*,and
so *Dauid* escap't. This enterprize and in-
uasion of the *Philistims* was no waies
casuall, but a kind of stratagem of Almighty God, by that meanes to deliuer

Dauid

1. Reg.
23. 26.
1. Reg.
29. 6. &
cap. 30.

Dauid from his enemy.

An other time the Princes or *Satrapæ* of the *Philiſtims* would needes expell *Dauid* out of their Army, and effected ſo much, as their King *Achas* commaunded him to his houſe, although otherwiſe he ſtood well affected towards him, and was delighted in his company . *Sed Satrapis non places.* this ſeems to haue been done only to pleaſe the *Satrapæ,* & an vnlucky chaunce for him; but it happened otherwiſe, and that which they intended vnto his miſchiefe , was directed by the particular prouidence of God vnto an other end: for *Dauid* being returned vnto his houſe , found that the *Amaleks* had ſet fier of *Siceleg* a towne of his, and had led away into captiuity, all the woemen and children , *à minimo vſque ad magnum,* and among the reſt the woemen of his owne houſhold ; whereupon he follow's them vpon the ſpure, ouertakes, defeats them, and recouers all the pray, and priſoners againe, euen to a man. Which he could not haue done, had not the *Satrapæ* expelled him their Army : and vnto this end did God direct their counſaile, how euer they had diſpoſed of it for an other end.

end. In the Hiſtory of *Eſther* this particular prouidence of God is alſo cleerly to be ſeene, euen in very ſmall and particular accidents, in that his ſo miraculous deliurance of the Iewiſh Nation, from the cruell ſentence of King *Aſſuerus*: as that *Vaſti* ſhould be reiected & *Eſther* choſen for Queen, a Iew by nation, the better and with more intereſt thereafter to intercede for them. It ſeemes that *Mardocheus* by meer chaunce came to haue notice, and to detect the *Eunuches* conſpiracy againſt the life of King *Aſſuerus*, and that the King on night ſhould haue no liſt to ſleepe, & to paſſe away the tediouſnes of the night, ſhould cauſe the Chronicles of the time to be fetch't and read, and that they ſhould light iuſt vpõ that place, where the ſeruices of *Mardocheus* were mentioned: but nothing of all this did happen by caſualty, but all was ſo diſpoſed by the profoũd iudgmẽt of Almighty God, and his particular prouidẽce, which had choſen thoſe meanes for the deliuery of his people; & ſo *Mardocheus* ſent word to *Eſther* when ſhee durſt not aduenture to ſpeake vnto the King, alledging for her excuſe that he had not called for her. *Quis*

nouit

no nit vtrum idcirco ad regnum veneris, Efter. 4.
vt in tali tempore parareris? who knows 14.
but you haue been therfore chofen vnto
the dignity of Qneen, that you might be
ready in fuch a time **as this** , to afford vs
helpe and fuccour.

The holy Scripture and the holy Ecclefiafticall Hiftories are full of the like
accidents, the better to teach vs to afcribe
all chaunces vnto God, and receaue them
as proceeding from his diuine hand for
our greater commodity and good. In
the booke of *S. Clements* reueus, we
read a moft remarkable Hiftory feruing
for our prefent purpofe ; Whilft *S. Pe-*　Clemẽt.
ter had *Simon Magus* hotly in purfuit at l. recog-
Rome , Saint *Barnaby* eonuerted Saint nitionū.
Clement to the Chriftian faith, who hauing recourfe vnto Saint *Peter*, declared vnto him the progreffe of his con-
uerfion , and befought him to add his
helpe , vnto the better inftructing of
him in the Mifteries of his beliefe .
Saint *Peter* told him , that he came
moft oportunely, for (faid he) to morrow is appointed for a publique dif-
putation , betwixt *Simon* the Magi-
cian and my felfe , where being pre-
　　　　　　　　　　　　fent

sent you may both see and be satisfied in
that which you desire : whilst they were
yet in speaking, in comes two of *Symon
Magus* disciples, sent from him vnto *S.
Peter* to desire that by reason of some
vrgent affaires of his, the disputation
might be for some two or three daies differd. *S. Peter* told them that he was content. They departing, *S. Peter* perceaued
S. Clement sensibly waxing sad, and melancholy ; and demaunded of him what
the matter was? to whom *S. Clement* replyed; Father I must confesse, that it is a
cause of much affliction to me, to see this
disputation respited, which I so much
desired to haue been to morrow . hereupon hapned a thing worthy to be obserued in a thing of small importance: for
S. Peter tooke him by the hand, and dis-
cours't at large vnto him on this subiect,
saying amongst many other things. Behold, my sonne, when any thing chaunces
among the heathens, otherwise then they
desire , they become straight waies troubled ; but it becomes vs who know that
God directs and gouernes all , to be in
continuall quiet and repose : and vnder-
stãd, sonne, that this is so hapned for your
greater

greater good ; for if the disputation had been to morrow, there had passed many things aboue your vnderstanding, which now in the meane time I will so informe as you shall receaue both much content and profit, when the day of disputation comes.

I will conclude with a domesticall example, which is recorded in the life of our B. Father; in which appear's most apparently this diuine prouidence wherof we speake : and it is concerning the departure of *S. Xauerius* towards the east Indies. The meanes by which he came to be designed for that expedition are most worthy of consideration. Our B. F. *S. Ignatius* designed for that mission , *F. Simon Rodriguez*, & *F. Nicholas Bobadilla : F. Simon* as that time was much crazed with a Quartane Ague , yet notwithstanding without delay he embark't himselfe for *Portugall, F. Bobadilla* was aduertised by letter that he should leaue *Calabria* and repare presently to Rome: he came, but so weakned with the Iourney and those extreeme wants which he had suffered vpon the way, and withall so ill disposed in one of his leggs , that it

was

Lib. 2.c. 16 vitæ P N. Ig. & in vita P Fran- cisci Xauerij.

was neceffary he fhould remaine fome-
time vnder cure after his arriuall to
Rome,and *Don Petro Mafcaregna's* haft
calling away for *Portugall*,*S.Ignatius* of
neceffity was to take a new refolution,
(the Embaffadour ftill vrging for an o-
ther Father)and fubftitute (by happy aduenture) *S.Xauerius* in *Bobadilla's* place; It might feem that by reafon *F.Boba-
dilla* was named for that Iourney and
not *S.Xauerius* , and that he was only,
becaufe of the Embaffadours neceffity
of departure , fubftituted into the others
place,that his defignement for that expe-
ditiō was by meer hazard thought vpon,
but there was no chaūce in it,but only the
particular prouidence of God,which had
determined to make him the glorious
Apoftle of thofe Eafterne parts;& moreouer when they were arriued in *Portugall,* the *Portugezi* confidering the great
profit which they did , entred vpon a refolution to detaine them both there; neither could they be fo wholly drawne
from it , as not to keepe the one , whilft
the other fhould be fuffered to goe on his
voyage to the Indies . Looke here how
things feeme to goe by chaunce : neuertheles

theles vnto God there is nothing casuall: in the end, the expedition to the Indies fell vnto *S. Xauerius* lot, becaule the will of God had so disposed of it, as a thing the most conferring to his glory, and the saluation of so many soules. Let men proiect and designe things as they pleafe, and take that way to effect them, as they fancy best; but God will make vse of thofe meanes which they inuent, to put his owne ends in execution, and order all as shall be most expedient, and to his greater glory.

Besides thefe examples and others the like which the holy fcripture affords vs, and which we daily fee and experience afwell in our felues as others, it is requifit that we proceed by the way of prayer, and confideration, to confirme and imprint in our hearts this happy cōfidence. Neither are we to impofe an end vnto this exercife; vntill we fenfibly perceaue in our hearts this familiar and filiall confidence in God; And be aſſured that the greater this your confidence shall be, wherby you caft your felfe (as it were) into the armes of God, the more and greater ſhal your fecurity be, and on the

contrary,you shall neuer arriue vnto true
peace and quietnes of mind, vntill you
haue attained this filiall cõfidence,seeing
that without it, there is no thing so slight
and little,which hath not force to dismay
and trouble you . Let vs therfore resolue
to cast and commit onr selues with all
speed into the hands of God,and to place
our assurãce in him;following that counsell of the Apostle *S. Peter. Omnem soli-*
citudinem vestram proycientes in eum,
quoniam ipsi cura est de vòbis, casting all
your solicitude in him , because he hath
care of you, and the Prophet says . *Iacta*
super Dominum curam tuam , & ipse te
enutriet, cast all the care of your selfe
vpon God and he will nourish you . O
blessed Lord you haue tendred me so
much as to deliuer ouer your selfe for
my sake without any reseruation, into
the hands of those cruell tormenters, for
to do with thee whatsoeuer their strangly
ingenious malice could inuët, *Iesum vero*
tradidit voluntati eorum, what wonder
is it then, if I do put and resigne my selfe
intirely into those not cruell,but deare &
charitable hands of thine, for to do with
me whatsoeuer thou shalt please,when I
am

1. Petri.
5.7.Psal.
54; 23.

Lucę 23.
25.

am most certaine that thou wilt do nothing but what may be best , and most
conuenient for me. Let vs become iointe-
partners in that contract which our Blessed Sauiour made with S. Catherine of
Siena . Our Lord at sundry times in-
deared this Saint vnto him with most
sweet priuacy, inriching her noble soule
with many high graces and fauours, a-
mong the rest one and a most particular
one was, that one day appearing vnto
her he said , *filia cogita tu de me & ego
cogitabo continenter de te,* my daughter
do thou thinke of me , and I will haue
perpetuall thought of thee . O blessed
accord! ô happy exchaunge! ô rich gaine
of our soules. This bargaine God is ready
to make with euery on of vs: do but lay
aside the thought of your selfe and the
solicitude of things ; and the more you
shall forget your selfe to thinke and confide in God, the greater charge and care
shall God Almighty haue of you . Who
is there who would not with all his soule
accept a condition so delicious and auail-
able, as the Spouse in the Canticles glo-
ries to haue made with her beloued. *Ego* Cat.7.10
dilecto meo & ad me conuersio eius. I to

my beloued and his regard is to me.

THE XII. CHAPTER.

How great profit and perfection it is , to apply prayer vnto this exercise of the conformity with the will of God, and how we are so long to descend vnto particulars vntil we arriue vnto the third degree of the said conformity.

Rusbroc
in fine
operum
suorum

I Ohn Rusbrock a very learned & spirituall man, writs of a certaine Virgin who in rendring an accoūt of her prayer vnto her Ghostly Father a great seruant of Almighty God , and a man of high contemplation with earnest desire to be instructed by him, told him, that her exercise in her prayer, was on the life and passion of our Sauiour Christ , and the profit which she reaped from thence, was the knowledge of her selfe, and of her passions and defects, as also a sorrow and compassion for the paine and sufferance of our Sauiour Christ, her Confessor told her , that all this was good , but yet on without much vertue might be liuely toucht with tendernes and compassion

of

of the death and paſſion of our Sauiour
Chriſt,like as we ſee the naturall loue and
affection which one beares an other,doth
make him haue a deepe reſentment of
his friends miſery and aduerſity.The Virgin then demaunded of him,whether the
daily deploring of our ſinnes,were a true
deuotion or no? he anſwered it was good,
but not the perfecteſt , ſeeing that euill
naturally brings with it a hatred of it , a-
gaine ſhe asked him , whether it were a
true deuotion to thinke often on the
paines of hell, and the glory of the Bleſſed?he anſwered t'was likewiſe good but
as farre from being the beſt as the former
was, ſeeing that nature its ſelfe by a certaine inſtinct doth commonly abhorre
and fly from all paine and torment, and
loues and ſeekes after that which may
bring vs to content and glory;as when you
ſee but the picture of ſome faire & pleaſant Citty, you deſire preſently to inhabit it. This did exceedingly grieue the
holy Vigin, and left her much diſconſo-
late and ſad in that ſhee knew not which
way ſhe might beſt apply her exerciſe of
prayers, to be moſt pleaſing to Almighty
God . Not long after there appeared to

her an Infant of exquisit beauty, to whom
when shee had related the cause of her
sadnes, adding withall it was so great that
none could comfort her. The Child. did
tell her she should forbeare to say so, since
he himselfe both could and would comfort her; therfore go (said he) vnto your
Ghostly Father and declare vnto him,
that true and solid deuotion doth consist
in the abnegation and contemning of
ones selfe, as also in an intire resignation
into the hands of God, aswell in aduersity as prosperity, in being straictly vnited by loue to God in euery thing. The
Virgin with ioyfull cheer went presently
vnto her Ghostly Father, to informe him
of all this, who no sooner heard her but
he answered . this this is that indeed, to
which you are to apply your prayer, seing
that heerein consists the true charity and
loue of God, and consequently our profit
and perfection, It is recounted of an o-
ther Virgin, that our Lord tought her
to insist long time together vpon these
words, *O Lord your will be done one*
earth as it is in heauen, and we read of
S. Gertrude that inspired by God Almighty shee repeated without any inter-
mission

Refert
Blos ca.
11.mon
spirit.

miſſion, thoſe words of our Sauiour. *Not* Lucæ 22 *my will* (ò *Lord*) *be done* , *but thyne*, 42 three hundred ſixty fiue times together, and ſhe vnderſtood that it was a deuotion moſt gratfull to Almighty God. Let vs then imitate theſe examples, and directing all our prayers vnto this end, go forward couragiouſly in this exerciſe . Now that we may the better, and with greater profit doe it, we are to preſuppoſe two things. The firſt is, that this exerciſe is of greateſt neceſſity in time of aduerſity, and whē we haue any difficulty to ouercome, vnto the conqueſt whereof is required a conflict againſt fleſh and blood: for in theſe occurrances there is greateſt need of vertue , and in ſuch times as thoſe the loue which we beare vnto God Almighty doth more manifeſtly appeare. Euen as a King in time of peace by obliging his ſoldiers by his liberality doth ſhew the affection which he beares to them, and they in the time of warre in fighting & dying for him, do ſhew the loue and loyall reſpect which they haue to him . So in the time of ſpirituall ioy and conſolation the King of heauen giues vs to vnderſtand how dearly he tenders vs, and we in the

H 4 time

time of defolation & aduerfity, do more
fhew forth our affection vnto his feruice,
then we are able to do whilft we are in
comfort and profperity . Mafter Auila
fays excellent well that to render thanke
to God in time of confolation is common vnto all , but to bleffe and praife
him when we are oppreffed with tribulation and aduerfity , is only proper to
the good and perfect,and a moft harmonious muficke to the eares of God . And
he adds that in the midft of aduerfity
only to fay . I render you thanks ô Lord,
bleffed be God or the like, is of more
worth & merit then thoufands of thanks
and benedictions in time of profperity,
and in this fenfe the holy Scripture com-
pares the iuft vnto the carbuncle ; *Gem-*
mula carbunculi in ornamento auri, becaufe that this pretious ftone giues greater luftre by night then in the fhining
day ; fo in like manner the faithfull and
true feruant of God Almighty fhines and
fhewes forth more clearly what he is, in
the cloudy night of tribulation , then in
the bright funne fhine of profperity.And
therfore the holy Scripture praifeth holy
Toby fo much,for that he although God
                                                per-

M. Auila
to. 2. ep.
fol. 20.

Eccl. 32.7

Tob. 2.
14.

permitted him to fall into sundry calamities, and laſtly had depriued him of
his ſight yet neuer proceeded in his ſadnes
againſt Almighty God, nor remitted any
thing of his former fidelity and obediéce
to his Diuine Maieſtie, but he remained alwaies immoueable rendring equall
thanks to God his whole life long, aſwell for his blindnes as for the faculty of
ſight, as holy Iob in his affections had 　Iob 1.21
done before. This ſaith S. *Auguſtin* is
that which we are to indeauour to imi-
tate, *vt in cunctis idem ſis, tam in proſpe-*　Aug. ad
ris, quam in aduerſis, that as well in proſ-　fratres
perity as aduerſity we remaine alwaies　in Heré.
the ſame. *Sicut manus quæ eadem eſt, &*　ſer. 4.
cum in palmam extenditur, & cum in
pugnum conſtringitur: Like as the hand
is alwaies the ſame, as well when we ſpan
it out as when we clutch our fiſt; ſo likewiſe the ſeruant of Almighty God ought
alwaies to be at quiet in the interior of
his ſoule, how euer he may ſeeme to the
exterior ſhew, to be perplext and ſorrow-
full. And if it be true which is reported
of Socrates, that in the greateſt diuerſity
of fortune, he was alwaies one, and that　Socrates
he was neuer obſerued to exceed a mo-　refert
Cicero.
dera-

deration in his mirth or sorrow. *Nec bilariorem quisquam nec tristem Socratem vidit, æqualis fuit in tanta inæqualitate fortunæ vsque ad extremum vitæ*, what extraordinary thing were it in vs, who are both Christians and Religious men, to indeauour to aspire to a perfection vnto which a Heathen had arriued before vs.

Secondly we are to know that it is not sufficient to haue this conformity with the will of God in Generall, seeing it will be no hard matter to attaine it so: for who is there that will not say, he desires that the Diuine will be performed in euery thing; and both the good and bad say in there *Pater noster*, euery day, *your will be done on earth as it is in heauen*, but it is necessary that we consider it in precifer manner, and descend vnto those particulars which might cost vs most paine and difficulty should they arriue vnto vs, and not to rest vntill we had facilitated euery one of them : We are not to remaine (as they say) carrying our launce at randome without putting it in
our rest; and alwaies in daunger of being cast from our conformity with the will
of

of God, as soone as any vnexpected difficulty comes and bids vs battaile; but we
are to make head againſt them of our
owne accord.

Neither are we to content our ſelues
with this, but we are to inforce our ſelues
to paſſe onward ſtill , vntill we come to
find taſt and cordiall delight. that the wil
of God is accompliſhed in vs, although it
be in matter of paine ſorrow & diſeſteem,
which is the third degree of this conformity; for this is likewiſe deuided into ſun-
dry degrees ; the one more ſublime, and
perfect then the other: although chiefly
they may be reduc't to three, in the ſame
manner as the Saints haue diſtributed the
vertue of patience . The firſt is when a
man doth neither accept of , nor deſire
thoſe things which go aceompanied with
paine, but rather ſhuns them , yet ſo as he
had rather vndergoe them, then to commit any ſinne to be deliuered from them;
this is the loweſt degree and of cōmaūd-
ment . in ſo much as although a man in
his miſhaps be ſenſible of paine griefe and
diſcontent, although he ſigh and grone
whilſt he isſicke , and cries out through
the vehemency of his griefe, and bewailes
the

the loſſe and death of friends , yet with
all theſe he may ſtill haue conformity
with the will of God. The ſecond degree
is when a man (although he doe not deſire that any harme ſhould chaunce vnto
him, neither makes choice of it) notwithſtanding when it is once hapned to him,
doth willingly imbrace and ſuffer it, becauſe it is the good pleaſure and will of
God: and this ſecond degree , ſurpaſſeth
the firſt, in that a man in ſome ſort hath
a liking and affection to ſuffer diſcom-
modity and paine for the loue of God,
and proceeds ſo farre, as to deſire it, becauſe it is Gods pleaſure it ſhould be ſo.
The firſt degree ſupports theſe things
with patience, the ſecond implies beſides,
the ſuffering them promptly and with
willingnes; The third is when the ſeruant
of Almighty God , out of the great loue
he beares our B. Lord, doth not only accept of, and ſuffer moſt willingly whatſoeuer paine and affliction which he ſhall
ſend him , but alſo is longing for them,
and reioyceth in them becauſe he knows
them to be the will of God . And ſo *S.*
Luke writs of the Apoſtles . *Ibant gau-*
Act.5.41 *dentes a conſpectu concilij, quoniam digni*
habiti

habiti sunt pro nomine Iesu , contume-
liam pati, after they were most ignomi-
niously whipt , they went reioycing out
of the presence of the councell , for hauing been esteemed worthy to suffer cō-
tumely for the name of Christ , and the
Apostle *S. Paul* says. *Repletus sum con-*
solatione, superabundo gaudio , in omni **Ad Cor.**
tribulatione nostrà, I am filled full with **7. 4. .**
consolation, and do abound with ioy, in
al our tribulation, chaynes and aduersity.
and for this reason he prayseth the He-
brews writing vnto them . *Et rapinam*
bonorum vestrorum cum gaudio suscepi- **Ad Hębe**
stis , cognoscentes vos habere meliorem **20. 34.**
& manentem substantiam, you haue receaued ioyfully the losse of your (temporall) goods as knowing your selues to
haue better and more lasting riches. Vnto
this must we indeauour with the grace of
God to arriue , to beare with ioy and
gladnes all tribulations and aduersities
which may happen to vs as, *S. Iames*
counsels vs in his Canonicall Epistle ;
Omne gaudium existimate fratres mei, **Iaco. 1. 2.**
cum in tentationes varias incideritis ,
esteem it deare brothers for the complet-
est ioy of all , when you shall fall into
sundry

sundry tentations; The will and contentment of God ought to be vnto vs a thing
so pretious and sweet, that it should be
sufficient to conserue and sugar all bitter
chaunces which may happen to vs; all
the miseries and disgusts of the world,
should become sweet and delicious vnto
vs; only because it is the good pleasure, the
will of God; and this is it which *S. Gre-*
gory says, *si mens in Deum forti inten-*
tione dirigatur, quidquid tibi in hac vita
amarum sit, dulce æstimat, omne quod af-
fligit, requiem putat, transire & per mor-
tem apetit, vt obtinere plenius vitam pos-
sit, if our mind were once directed to
God with a strong intention, it would
esteeme all that were bitter in this life,
for sweet, all that were afflicting vs it
would account for rest, yea it would euen
long to passe by death it selfe, for to obteine a more full and perfect life.

Greg. li.
7. mor.
c. 7.

S. Catherine of Siena in a certaine
Dialogue which shee hath left written
of the consummat perfection of a Christian, says that among other things which
her deare spouse our Blessed Lord had
tought her, one was, that shee should
build vp her selfe a chamber of repose,
which

S. Catha.
de Sena.

which should be round about vaulted
with the will of God, and that there she
should inclose herselfe and make perpetuall abode, neuer going out, or stiring
foot or hand, or casting a looke out from
thence, but alwaies remaine recollected
in herselfe, as the bee in the hiue, or the
pearle in its shell, and although that in
the beginning perhaps this habitation
might seeme too narrow and retired, notwithstanding shee should soone find it of
a wonderfull extent; in so much as without going out of it, shee might recreate
her selfe among the eternall mansions of
the Blessed, and make greater profit in a
few daies there, then shee could do without in a long space of time. Let vs likewise doe the same, and make this our
continuall exercise, *Dilectus meus mihi,
& ego illi*, my beloued to me, and I to Cant. 2.
him, in these two words we haue inough 16.
to entertaine our selues for our whole liues, and therfore we ought to haue them
alwaies in our mouths and hearts.

THE

THE XIII. CHAPTER.

*Of the indifferency and conformity with
the will of God, which Religious men
ought to haue, in going and remaining in any part of the world, where
they may be disposed of by Obedience.*

TO the end that we may make more
profit out of this exercise of the cō-
formity with the will of God, and put
in practise that which we haue said, we
will go declaring in particular some principall points in which we ought to exercise our selues; and afterwards descend
to certaine other Generall heads, which
appertaine to all. And now we will begin
with those particular things which are
conteined in our constitutions, since it is
most consonant to reason that a Religious man, should chiefly in their obser-
uance shew forth the vertue and Religion which he hath, and afterwards each
on may apply this doctrine vnto other
things of the same kind, either in his Religion or his state of life.

7. p. Cŏst.   In the seauenth part of the constitu-
c. 1. §. 1.   tions

tions our B. Father treating of Missions whic his on of the principall functions of our Instſtut, says that those of the Society are to be indifferent to go, and make their aboade in any part of the world where soeuer obediéce shall send thē, either amóg Christians or Infidels, either to the Indies, or among the Hereticks: and concerning this, those who are professed do solemnely make a fourth vow of particular obedience vnto the Popes Holines, to go readily and willingly without alledging any excuse, vnto any part of the world where his Holines shall send them, without demanding any temporallities either by themselues or others, for their charges of their iourney on the way, or for their maintenāce when they are arriued there; but that they will go either by horse or foot, with money, or without it, begging and lining on almes as it shall seeme beſt vnto his Holines. And our B. Father declares in the same place that the end and intention of making of this vow was to come more nearer to the will of God, for as much as the firſt Fathers of the Society being for the moſt part of diuers nations and prouinces, and not knowing in what

margin note:
c. 1. exā.
§. 5. & 5.
p. conſt.
c. 3. §. 3.
& C & p.
6. c. 2. §.
13. & 1,
& p. 7. c.
1. §. 3. &
E. 7. p.
conſt. c.
1. §. 1. &
B.

part of the world to imploy their labours, so as they might be best pleasing to Almighty God, whether among the faithfull or Infidells, to arriue to a certaine knowledge of the will of God, they made this vow to his Vicar heare on earth, to the end that he might dispose of them throughout the world, according as he should iudge it to be most requisit for Gods greater glory. But those of the Society, saith he, ought in no wise to intermedle themselues, or procure to be sent, and abide more in one place then an other, but they are to remaine wholly indifferent, leauing the free and intire disposition of themselues in the hands of their Superiors, who gouerne them in the place of God, as may be most for his seruice and greater glory.

And that we might perceaue what an absolute indifferency and readines to go vnto any country of the world, where holy obedience might dispose of vs, our B. Father requires; we read in his life, that F. Iames Laynes once said vnto him that he felt a great desire in himselfe, to go vnto the Indies to procure the saluation of those blind Infidels, who were lost for

want

Lib. 5.c.
4 vitæ P.
N. Ignat.

want of Euangelical labourers. to whom
our B. Father anſwered that for his part
he had no ſuch deſire , and being ask't
the reaſon , he ſaid , becauſe that we in
hauing made a vow of obedience to his
Holines, to go vnto any part of the world
where he ſhall ſend vs for the ſeruice of
Almighty God , ought to be intirely indifferent, and not to haue any inclination
more to on place then to an other;and he
added more ouer if I did perceaue my
ſelfe as you inclined , to go vnto the Indies, now, I ſhould beſtow all my indea-
uours,to bend my inclination to the contrary , that ſo I might arriue to that perfect indifferency and equality , which is
required to the obteining the perfection
of obedience.

Notwithſtanding we doe not ſay that
the deſires which we may haue of going
to the Indies, be either ill, or imperfect,
for they are ſo farre from that, as they
are both good and holy , and as ſuch , it
is good to propoſe and preſent them to
our Superiors whenſoeuer our Lord ſhall
pleaſe for to inſpire them , and ſo our B.
Father, in the ſame place ſayes that the 7.p.cōſt.
Superiors with good reaſon may be much c.2.lit. 1.

com-

comforted when such desires are proposed vnto them, by any of their charge,
seeing that they are most commonly the
signes, that such are called vnto it by Almighty God, and so they come to be disposed of with greater sweetnes and more
gentlenes:but we haue said it vnto the end
that we might perceiue the readines and
indifferency which our B.Father requires
of vs, to go and remaine in what part of
the world so euer; seeing that he would
not so much as haue vs affected more
then ordinary vnto a mission so laborious and so much importing the seruice
of Almighty God, as that; and that vnto
the end that our inclination to any particular thing , might not set any barre betwixt vs and that promptitude and indifferency which we ought to haue to any
other thing, or place, besides vnto which
Obedience might thinke fit to send vs.

From hence there may be some con-
sequences drawne forth, which may helpe
vs better to comprehend this same . The
first is, that if the desire of going for the
Indies , should be occasion to him who
doth conceiue it, of failing in any point of
this redines and indifferency vnto any
                                    other

other thing, which obedience might appoint him, that then it is not good, but an imperfection: if I were taken with so great desire, and weare so set vpon going to the Indies or els where, that it should disquiet me, and be the occasion that I should remaine with lesse contentment either heere or in any other place where obedience should dispose of me, and that I did not discharge with that willingnes those present functions in which I were imployed, neither performed them with due application, by reason my eyes and thoughts were fix't vpō that other thing; then it is most apparant, that such desires are neither good, nor proceeding from God Almighty, since they are impediments vnto his will, and God cannot be contrary to himselfe: as also because the desires and inspiratiōs of the holy Ghost, do not vse to go accompanied with trouble and disquietnes but with a profound peace and tranquility. And this is one of the signes which the masters of spirituall life do giue, to know whether our inspirations and desires be proceeding from God or no.

Secondly it followes from hence that

he

he who fhould haue an vniuerfall difpofition, both prompt and indifferent to
tranfport himfelfe into any part of the
world, or to performe any thing which
obedience fhould prefcribe, although he
felt in himfelfe no fuch particular inclination as others haue of going to the In-
dies.or any other country remote.or neer,
hath no reafon to trouble himfelfe ther-
fore.feeing that he is no waies in the wor-
fer ftate, but rather the better difpofed, it
being fuch a difpofition as our B. Father
requires of all the Society, to haue of our
parts no affection or particular defire,
more vnto one thing then an other;but he
would haue vs in a difpofition anfwerable
to the tongue,of a ballance which inclines
no more to on fide then an other; and of
this fort are many, or according to my
opinion the greater part . Our B. Father
had taken a deliberation once to fend F.
Natalis in a certaine miffion, and to proceed in it with the more fweetnes,he defired before to know his inclination . F.
Natalis by letter anfwered him, that for
his part he was inclined to nothing, but
only to this, to haue no particular inclination of his owne, and this difpofition
                                    our

our B. Father esteemed for the best of all,
and the most perfect: and that with good
reason . for that other seems only to be
fastned to one thing alone, but this with
his indifferency is imbracing all whatsoeuer may be commaunded him , and is
prepared & disposed with an equall mind
vnto all alike; and for as much as God regards only the heart and will of a man,
which before him. is as much as the worke
it selfe, therfore this ready will for all, is
as acceptable to him as the execution of
all would be.

And to declare this more fully , if any
one who were tepide, pusillanimous or
vnmortified , should haue no desire of
going to the Indies, by reason of his want
of courage and resolution, to leaue those
commodities which here he imagins himselfe to haue , or to be in the way of obteining, or els because he hath no will, to
expose himselfe to those many labours
which there he must vndergoe, in this
man I say such a disposition is selfe loue
and imperfection, but one who forbears
not to desire it , out of any fainthearted-
nes, or lesse will and courage to vndertake
those labours, and others yet more pain-
I 4   full

full for the loue of God , and saluation
of soules, but onely becaufe he is vncer-
taine whether it be the will of God to
difpofe of him that way , or in any other
thing, and is in himfelfe both ready and
prepared to performe any thing which he
fhall know to be the will of God , and
would go for the Indies or England or
any other place if he fhould chaunce to be
fent, with as prompt and good a will, and
perhaps better then if himfelfe had re-
quefted and defired it; and that becaufe
then he fhould haue more affurance that
he did not his owne will in it , but purely
the will of God. There is no doubt , but
this mans difpofition were better and
more perfect , and fuch as thefe the Superiors neuer doubt, to difpofe of, either
to the Indies, or any other place.

But to returne to the principalleft point
of all, our B. Father requires that we
fhould all remaine with an equall indifferency & refignation to remaine as willingly in on place as an other, to go as readily to this country as to that , and that
no refpect of corporail health fhould be
fufficient to take vs from this indifferency . It is faid in the third part of our
Cóftitutions, that it belongs vnto our vo-

cation and Inftitute , to go and remaine
in any part of the world, where the greater feruice of God and the greater good
of foules may be hoped for; but yet if it
fhould be found by experience that ones
health were much impaired, and that the
aire and Climat did not agree with him:
that then the Superior might confider
whether it were better that fuch an one,
fhould be difpofed of to an other place,
which might be more agreable to his
health, and where he might with more
profit imploy himfelf vnto Gods feruice,
and the good of foules; Neuertheles it is
declared exprefly, that the difeafed perfon , is in no wife to demand to be remoued, or to fhew himfelfe to haue any inclination therunto but to leaue all the care
of it, to his Superiors . *Non tamen erit*
ipfius infirmi, huiufmodi mutationem po-
ftulare , nec animi propenfionem ad eam
oftēdere, fed Superioris cura id relinqui-
tur. It is no little thing, but a point of high
confequence which our B. Father, requires of vs ; feing that each one, is to
be refigned and mortified, not only in not
demanding to be remoued , but alfo in
not fhewing themfelues to haue any inclination therunto, although they fhould

continue ill difpofed and fi ckly all their liues. So that for as much as concernes our miffion to the Indies, or among the Hereticks, each one, as we haue faid, may freely propofe his inclination and defire, fo as it be with indifferency and refignation: but in this point of health, there is not permitted any liberty, either to aske our remouall or to fhew our felues inclined therunto, which is much more then the other; only it is permitted, that if any one finde himfelfe fick or ill difpofed, he may propofe to the Superior, his ficknesse and indifpofition, with his difability to difcharge his functions, and thus much we are obliged to do by Rule; but hauing once propofed it, we are to do nothing more, it belonging only to the Superior to aduife, if fuppofing he be fo ill difpofed, it were not fitter to fend him to fome other place, where by recouering his health he might be enabled to do more; or whether it were not to Gods greater glory, that he fhould ftill remaine in the fame place, although he performed not fo much or perhaps nothing at all, for this concernes him nothing. Euery one is to fuffer himfelfe to be guided by his Superior,

perior. who in the place of God hath the
difpofing of him, and to efteeme what fo
euer he fhall ordaine , to be the beft, and
moft confering to the feruice of Almighty
God. How many are there who only to
get their liuing do liue here and in other
places which are moft contrary to their
health ? how many are there who paffe
the feas to the Indies and Turky for a litle
gaine , and put not only their health but
alfo their liues in daunger ? What great
matter is it then if we (who are Religious)
do fo much for God, and for obedience,
as thofe of the world do, to gather wealth
together ? And if it fhould occurre vnto
your mind, that you could do fomewhat
in an other place, or perhaps very much,
and that there where you are your health
is impairing, and your labours nothing,
do but remember that for all this, it is
better for you to remaine there in doing
nothing fince it is the will of God , then
to haue your owne will in being remoued
to any other place, although you fhould
doe neuer fo much; and conforming your
felfe with the will of God, who for the
prefent requires fo much of you, for caufes
which he knows beft, and which it is not
expe-

expedient you should know.

In the Chronicles of the Order of S. Francis we read how S. Francis gaue leaue to Brother Giles, to go where he would, and to liue in whatsoeuer Prouince or Couent he pleased, leauing him to his owne free election as being one whom he knew of great vertue and sanctity, but the holy man, had not liued fower dayes in this manner & freedome, but he found the tranquility and peace of his soule sensibly diminished, and in lieu thereof a great disquietnes and perturbation in his mind; whereupon he went to S. Francis againe and desired him with much earnestnes, that he would appoint him to liue in some certaine place & Couent, and not leaue him any more vnto his owne free choyce, assuring him that he could find no rest nor comfort, in such a wild and vnlimited obedience; Good religious men ought to haue no peace and contentment in performing their owne wills, and so consequently to haue no desire to remaine and dwell in this Colledge or in that, in this or the other Prouince, but they are to expect vntill holy obedience do take them by the had,

and

and difpofe of them, according as fhe
pleafes, as knowing that fuch is the will
of God, in which they are only to take
all pleafure and content.

THE XIV. CHAPTER.

Of that indifferency and conformity with
the will of God, which Religious men
are to haue, concerning thofe offices &
functions in which obedience fhall im-
ploy them.

WE ought likewife to haue this indifference & refignation, wher-
of we haue fpoken, in all thofe functions
and offices, in which we may be imployed
by obedience: we perceaue well how
many and diuers thofe offices and functions are in a Religious Order, and
each one in particular is to go confidering
of them, vntil we haue brought ourfelues
vnto an indifferency for all, Our B. Father fays in the conftitutions, and we haue
it likewife in our Rules, that in exercifing
abiect and humble offices, we are more
readily to accept of thofe, from which
we

we haue the greateſt auerſion, if it ſhould
be inioyned vs to exerciſe our ſelues in
them, we haue moſt need of reſignation
and indifferency, in point of theſe meaner
and abiect offices, by reaſon of the naturall repugnance which we haue againſt
them : and therefore he doth more, and
ſhewes a greater vertue and perfection,
who offers himſelfe vnto God to performe theſe offices, then he who ſhould
make choyce to do more high and honourable ones. If one who had a great
deſire to ſerue ſome nobleman, ſhould preſent his ſeruice in ſuch manner vnto him,
as to remaine all his life his drudge or la-
kie, if he ſhould thinke it fit, it is moſt
apparant that he ſhould do more, and declare a greater will to ſerue that nobleman, then one who ſhould make offer of
himſelfe, to be his Gentleman of the horſe
or ſteward of his houſe; ſince this is rather
to demaund a benefit, then preſent his
ſeruice: and moreouer, the others affection
to his ſeruice would appeare the more, if
offering himſelfe vnto thoſe humble offices, he had ſufficient tallent to perfor̄me
more honourable ones. And it is euen ſo
in Religion, if you ſhould offer vp your
                                        ſelfe

felf to God, faying ô Lord I defire to ferue
you in quality of Preacher, or Diuinity
Mafter, the matter were not much, feing
thefe high and honourable offices, vfe for
themfelues to be fought after and defired,
and therfore you declare in this no great
defire of feruing God ; but when you
offer your felfe to ferue all the daies of
your life in the houfe of God, in côtemp-
ible & bafe offices, repugnant vnto fenfe,
then you doe giue a teftimony indeed of
the great defire you had to ferue almighty
God, and this defire would be the more
gratefull & meritorious, the more fit and
able you were for the difcharge of higher
functions. And this were enough to ftire
you vp to the defire of humble and abiect offices and to feeke after them, efpecially feing indeed that in the houfe of
God there is no office which is vile and
abiect: for (as they fay commonly) if in
the pallace of an earthly King there is nothing accounted bafe, but his title enno-
bleth all, and there is great account made
of feruing him in the meaneft quality, how
much more ought we to efteeme of all
things belonging to the feruice of God, to
ferue whom, is properly to raigne?

S.

S. Basile to stire vs vp vnto the affe-
ctionate loue of humble and abiect offices, sets the example of our Sauiour before our eyes, who as we read in the holy
scripture, did imploy himselfe in the like
offices, as in washing the feet of his Apostles, and not only in that, but also for a
long time together in seruing his most
holy Mother and S. Ioseph, being subiect
and obedient vnto them in all whatsoeuer they commaunded him: *Et erat sub-
ditus illis.* From the twelfth yeare of his
age vntill he was thirty yeare old, the holy
scripture makes no other metion of him,
but only this, that he was subiect vnto
them; which the holy Fathers considering do excellent well infer, that in that
time he serued and helped them in many
lowly and humble offices, as considering
their pouerty we may piously imagine. *Ne*
dedignetur facere Christianus quod fecit
Christus, let not a Christiā & much lesse a
Religiousmā, thinke much & disdaine to
do those things which Christ hath done:
since the sonne of God hath not refused
to imploy himselfe in these contemptible
offices for the loue of vs, let not vs make
any difficulty to be exercised in them, for
the

the loue of him although we should continue in them all our liues.

But to come nearer yet vnto our purpose, one of the principall reasons, and
powerfulst motiues which should incite
vs to accept with great readines what-
euer office obedience should impose vpon
vs; is to consider that it is the will of God,
because as we haue said heretofore, it
ought to be all our comfort and consolation in all our imploiments, that we performe the will of God in doing them:
this is that alone which ought to suffice
and content a soule; it is the will of God
that for the present I should do such a
thing: behould now you know the pleasure of God, and are not to seeke after
any thing besides, seing there is nothing
better or more sublime then the will of
Almighty God; Whosoeuer should go on
in this manner, would not esteeme it to
import any thing, whether they enioyn-
ed him this, or that to do, or imployed
him in an eminent or abiect office, since
there would be no difference vnto such
an one.

S. Hierome relates an example very
fitly seruing for this present subiect, he

sayes that visiting those holy Mōks who liued in the desert, he saw one whom the Superior had commaunded (both for his owne aduancement in perfection, as also to giue an example of obedience vnto the younger sort of Religious) to carry twice a day, a mighty stone three miles, vnto no other end, and for no other profit, but to obey and mortify his proper iudgment, and this had he already done for eight whole yeares together. This saith S. Hierom would appeare vnto those who do not know the true value of the vertue of obedience, and haue not attained vnto this purity and simplicity, but are yet of proud and hauty minds, but a childish thing, or an idle action, and they would demaund of him, how he could indure to be so imployed by obedience, and euen I my selfe (saith this Saint) did question him and desire to know what motions he felt within his heart, whilst he was performing this; and the blessed man answered him, I am as content and glad when I haue executed this, as if I had done the most high and important thing as they could haue commaunded me: and S. Hierom sayes that this answere did so

liuely touch him, that from that time forwards he began to lead the life of a Religious Monke . This is to be a Religious
man indeed , and to lead an anſwerable
life vnto their ſtate , not to regard what
the exterior action is, but to make the will
of God our pleaſure & delight, which we
performe in doing of that acte: and ſuch as
they , are thoſe who profit and go ſen-
ſibly forwards in vertue and perfection,
ſo as euen to make it their liues ſuſtenãce
to do the will of God , wherewith they
are nouriſhed as with the very fatnes of
the corne. *Et adipe frumenti ſatiat te.*

But ſome one perhaps will ſay , for my
part I ſee well enough that it is a thing of
great perfection , to doe the will of God
in euery thing, and that in euery office in
which they do imploy me , I may performe his holy will , but neuertheleſſe I
would willingly be applied & ſet to more
important things , and be executing the
wil of God in ſuch functions as thoſe;
and this is to be wanting euen in the firſt
principall, ſeing that really it is nothing els,
then to deſire that God ſhould do your
will, and not to indeauour to accompliſh
his. I am not to preſcribe any law to God,

K 2 neither

neither to seeke to bring him to consent
vnto that which seemes best to me, and
is most to my desire, but I ought to follow that which God Almighty shall ordaine and thinke the best, and accommodate my selfe to that which he desires concerning me. S. Augustin saith excellent well: *Optimus minister tuus est,
qui non magis intuetur hoc à te audire
quod ipse voluerit, sed potius hoc velle
quod à te audierit*, he is thy best seruant
ô Lord, who doth not looke to haue
thee commaund him that which he desires, but who rather desires that which
thou shalt commaund; and the holy Abbot Nylus said: *Non ores vt fiant quæ
fieri velis, sed potius ora sicut orare di-
dicisti, vt fiat voluntas Dei in me*, do
not pray; that that should be done which
thou desirest, but rather desire as our B.
Lord hath instructed thee to pray, that
the will of God be (alwaies) performed
in thee.

Which point is worthy to be conside-
red, as one very profitable, and vniuer-
sally seruing for all chaunces and contrary
accidents which may happen to vs. We
ought not to determine and choose in
what,

what, and how we will indure and suffer, but God alone, it belongs not vnto vs, to make choyce of those tentations, with which we are to be proued, or to say. Oh if it were any other tentation then this, I would not care, but this is such an one; as I can no waies indure. If that paine which we haue, were that which we did desire, it would be no paine vnto vs; If you desire indeed to be pleasing vnto Almighty God, beg of him to conduct you by that way which he best knowes and pleaseth, and not by that which you your selfe desire: and when our Lord doth send you that which you haue most auersion from, and should be most sorry to vndergo, then if you conforme your selfe vnto his will, you imitate most neere our Sauiour Christ, who said vnto his heauenly Father, not my will, but thine be done and this is to haue an intire conformity with the will of God, to make him an absolute oblation of our selues, that he may doe with vs whatsoeuer he shall please, when, and in such manner as he shall please, without any exception, contradiction, selfe iudgment, or reseruing any thing. Blosius recoūts how the holy

K 3   Virgin

Virgin S. Gertrude did once out of her
compassion pray for a certaine person,
who (as shee heard) did with great impatience complaine, that God had sent
her certaine afflictions which were lesse
conuenient for the good of her soule, vnto whom our Sauiour answered: tell that
party for whom thou prayest, that seing
there is none can obteine the Kingdome
of heauen, without suffering at least some
crosses and afflictions, that shee had best
choose, and declare what afflictions shee
should thinke most profitable for her, and
when God should send her those receaue
them patiently, by which words of our
Lord, and the manner with which they
were deliuered, S. Gertrud vnderstood
that it was a most daungerous kind of
impatience, for one to desire proudly and
peruersly to make choyce themselues of
that which they would suffer, saying
forsooth that those afflictions which are
sent them by God Almighty are lesse fitting for the good of their soules, and more
then they can sustaine; seing euery one is
to assure himselfe, that whatsoeuer God
doth send him or permits to happen to
him, is most conuenient for him, and for
                                    such

such he is to welcome it both with patience and conformity with the will of God. And as you are not to make choice of those tentations and afflictions which you are to vndergoe but to receaue all which shall be sent you, as proceeding from the holy hand of God, vnderstanding them to be the most conuenient for you, so likewise are you to be as farre frō making your owne election of those offices and functions which you are to be employed in, but are to receaue all which obedience shall appoint as cōming from the hand of God, and perswade your selfe that it is the only thing which of all others is most expedient for you.

There is added moreouer vnto this, a very spirituall point, which teacheth vs to be so resigned vnto the will of God, and to liue in such confidence and assurance of his paternall goodnes, as not so much as to desire to know in what manner God shall please to dispose of vs: Iust as there are some Noblemen in the world who trust their stewards so farre as not to know themselues what their owne reuenues are, or what they haue in the house, which is a signe of their great confidence

K 4   in

in them, and so the Patriarch Ioseph affirmeth that his Master did with him,
ecce Dominus meus, omnibus mihi tra-
ditis, ignorat quid habeat in domo sui
behould, my Master hauing deliuered
ouer all into my hands, doth not know
himselfe what he hath in his owne house;
in like manner also that Religious man
declares his confidence in God to be great
indeed, when he desires not so much as to
know, how God shall be pleased for to
dispose of him, but saith, I am in a good
hand, and that is enough for me; *in ma-*
nibus tuis sortes mea, in that I am most cō-
tented and assured, and more then that I
haue no need to know.

Concerning those who aspire to higher
degrees, places and functions, perswading
themselues that they should more profit
their neighbours by them and aduance
the seruice of Almighty God, let them
assure theselues that they are farre deceaued if they thinke they doe it out of zeale
of Gods greater seruice and the good of
soules, for it is farre otherwise; they are
caryed away only with the zeale and the
desire of honour, of their owne esteeme,
and priuat commodities and because such

an

an office or function is most agreable to
their owne desire and inclination, therfore they seeke after it with so much earnestnes, which may clearly be perceaued
from hence: if you were a secular in the
world, or a single man, it seemes it might
become you for to say, this is better then
that other, and affords more profit for
the good of soules, and therfore I desire
to imbrace this and to let that alone, seing
that I suffice not to the discharge of both,
but in Religion there is no leauing one
thing for an other, but it is necessary that
both be done, here we are to Catechise as
well as to preach; to teach Grammer as
well as Diuinity, and this is only the point:
if you will keepe aloft, and do nothing
but the most high and eminent things, an
other of necessity must abase himselfe and
do those meaner ones, and if you had but
the least humility in you, you should rather desire that those high & glorious fu̅-
ctio̅s should be co̅ferred vpon some other
man, & ought to perswade your selfe, that
he would discharge them better then you
could do, and with more fruit, and lesse
danger of vanity.

For this cause and diuers other. Our B.
Father

Father S. Ignatius, hath left vs an excel-
cellent leſſon, which he hath ſet for the
foundation of elections in thoſe his three
degrees of humility, where the third and
the moſt perfect is, that when two things
do preſent themſelues vnto vs, both e-
qually making for the ſeruice and glory
of God, one ſhould make choyce of that,
in which he might haue a greater occaſion of being contemned and ſcorned,
therby to imitate more nearly the life of
our Sauiour Chriſt, who for our ſakes
was content to be deſpiſed and had in no
account. In which there is yet an other
great good to be conſidered; which is, that
in theſe humble and abiect things, our
proper intereſt is leſſe by farre, and a man
hath no reaſon for to ſeeke himſelfe, or
cauſe to feare his becoming vainly proud,
which daunger goeth alwaies accompanied with thoſe higher and more reſplen-
dant offices; In humble and abiect offices,
we can alwaies iointly exerciſe humility
and charity, and they afford humility its
proper nouriture, with thoſe ſlight acts
which are exerciſed in them, but in more
higher functions, charity without daunger of humility canot be exerciſed, which
                                    ought

ought alone to be a sufficient reason why
they were not only to be desired, but rather with great feare to be auoided by vs.

THE XV. CHAPTER.

Of the conformity which we are to haue
with the will of God, touching the di-
stribution of Tallents, and naturall
guifts.

E Very one is to be well content, with
those Tallents which God hath cō-
municated to him of vnderstanding, wit,
sufficiency, and other parts which God
hath bestowed vpon him, and not to be
troubled and afflicted if he haue not so
much ability as an other, nor so many
good parts, or be not so fit for great and
high imployments, it is a thing of which
we all stand in need, for let vs graunt that
one makes greater shew, and seemes in
some certaine things to excell and haue
the preeminence of others, notwithstanding they haue some wants or other sufficient to abash and humble them, where
in they haue need of this conformity. And
therfore it is good for to go well prepared,

red, for the Diuell most commonly assaults vs in nothing more. In time of your studies when you see one of your Concurrants grow excellent, that he disputes and argues learnedly and well, you shall be ouertaken perhaps with a certaine kind of enuy, which although it arriue not to make you sorrow for your brothers good (for that were expresly the sinne of enuy) notwithstäding shall bring you at the last, vnto a certaine sadnes and melancholy, to see an other get the start of you, with his fine wit, and your selfe cast behind, not being able to keepe pace with him, or shew your head amongst the formest of them, this I say wil make you droope and conuerse with them confounded and ashamed, whence you will fall into languor & weary somnes, and be moued with a tentation to giue ouer your studies, and perhaps sometimes to take leaue of your Religion if you be not well grounded in humility, as diuerse haue giuen a lamentable experience. An other thinks to become eminent, and to surpasse all others of his course and to be famed for the best scholler throughout all the country: who when he sees all his dreames and hopes to be come to nothing, becometh so shamed,

difcouraged and mortified, as the Diuell
who is neuer wanting to fo faire occafiõs
perhaps will put him in the head, that he
fhall neuer recouer the difgrace, nor be
rid of his melãcholy, as long as he tarryeth
in Religion, and this tentation is no new
but a very ancient one.

We read an exãple of this kind in the
Chronicles of the Order of S. Dominicke,
& it is of Albertus Magnus, who was the
Mafter of S. Thomas of Aquin. The faid
Albertus when he was a little child, was
very deuout vnto our B. Lady, and recited
certaine prayers vnto her honour euery
day, he afterwards by her fauour & inter-
ceffion being but fixteẽ yeare old, was ad-
mitted into the Order of S. Dominicke,
whõ (as it is faid) in thofe his tender yeares
being applyed to his ftudies his wit was
but reafonable or rather indeed he was
wholly dul and vnfit for learning, & being
among others who had liuely & excellent
wits, he was fo difcouraged with the fmall
profit which he made, that this forrow of
his, being cloily followed with a ftrõg tẽ-
tatiõ, did put him in fuch dãger, as he was
vpon the point of cafting of his habit: he
being in this diftreffe of toughts, was wõ-
                                    droufly

derouſly helped by a certaine viſiõ, foras
he ſlept one night, he imagined that he
had reared a Ladder againſt the Monaſtery walls and was going out and leauing
the order when climing vp he ſaw fowre
venerable Matrons ſtanding on the top,
of whom one ſeemed to be miſtriſe of the
reſt, and when he was come cloſſe by the,
one of thoſe Matrons ſhou'd him backe
againe and would not permit him to go
out of the Monaſtery ; notwithſtanding
he aduentred once againe, and being euen
at the top, the ſecond ſerued him as the
firſt had done, and when the third time,
he aſſayed to get vp againe, a third of
thoſe Matrons demaunded of him, why
he had ſuch deſire to leaue the Monaſtery, vnto whom he anſwered, with a
face al bluſhing with ſhame, becauſe Lady
I ſee my companions of the ſame courſe
with me, to profit in the ſtudy of Philo-
ſophy whilſt I ſpend my time and labour
all in vaine, which ſhame grieues me
ſo much as it makes me reſolue to leaue
my Religion, vnto whom the Matron
ſaid, pointing him vnto the fourth of
them, behould this is the Mother of God,
and Queene of heauen, vpon whom we
                                          with

with reuerence do attend, comend your
felfe to her, and we with our intreaties
will fecond you, that fhe would intercede
vnto her B. Sonne for you, vnto the end
that he would beftow vpon you, a witt
fo docile as might render you fit to go forwards in your ftudies; which Albertus
hearing was wondrous glad, and being
conducted vnto our B. Lady by this Matron, fhe receaued him gratioufly, and demanded of him what he defired and wi-
fhed for with fo much earneftnes? he anfwered, fome degree of excellency in Philofophy, which was the ftudy to which
he then attended, although he comprehended nothing of it. Whereupon the
Glorious Virgin anfwered, be of good
cheere and courage, and ftudy well, and
I will affure you, you will become an eminent and learned man in the fcience of
Philofophy, but to the end that you may
know, faid fhee, that it is a donatiue only
of my fauour, and not attained by any naturall parts, or induftry of your owne,
fome time before you dy, you fhall come
to forget whilft you are in your publique
lecture, all the learning which you had
before. With this vifion was he greatly
                                    com-

comforted, and from that time he profited so greatly in his studies, not only in Philosophy but also in Diuinity & knowledge of the holy Scriptures, as nothing can better witnesse then those works which he hath left behind:& three yeares before his death, as he was actually teaching at Collen, he wholly lost all memory of euery thing which belonged to learning, remaining as ignorant, as if he had neuer in his life so much as knowne the first rudiments of any Science; & it may be also that it is so befalne him, in punishment of his want of indifferency, & conformity with the will of God, in point, of that tallent and sufficiency which he had bestowed vpon him. Howeuer, he then remembring the vision which he had at that time when he was minded to haue forsaken his Religion, did publikely before all his Auditors declare what had passed, and therupon taking his leaue of all, he retired himselfe to his couent and there spent the residue of his time in prayer and contemplation.

Now that we our selues may not fall into this danger, it is necessary that we go preparing our selues before; and there is

no better preparatiue then a deepe humility,for such a difficulty as this proceedeth
only from the want of it,when you cannot indure to be accounted the worst and
last of all your course.If one should come
afterwards and let you vnderstand, that
you were to study no more, and that you
were to breake of your course , and all
those proiects which you had fancied to
your selfe; and in the meane time you
should see your Companions go on with
their Diuinity , and become learned and
famous preachers : here now without
doubt were need of profound humility,
and a great resignation to the will of God.
And this tentation comes to be renewed
againe after your studies are done , when
you will not want such thoughts as these
to be working vpon you againe: why am
not I so learned,and in as high place as he?
why am not I an excellent Preacher?why
haue not I such a grace in setting my self
forth, and in discourfing as this or the o-
ther hath? wherfore am not I imployed in
important businesses , and why do they
make so little account of me?and the like
is to be said of those who are not schol-
lers, for you shall haue them busied with

L   such

such thoughts and tentations as these. Oh
that i were a scholler? that I were a Priest
and had but learning to be profitably im-
pl.yed in the helpe of soules, and sometimes it may fall out that such a tentation
as this, may bring you to such straits as to
in danger the losse of your vocation, and
perhaps your saluation too. as the lamentable falls of others do testify.

This is a generall doctrine, and euery
on may apply it to his owne state of life,
and therfore it is necessary for euery one
to conforme himselfe vnto the will of
God in being content with that Tallent
which he hath receaued from God, and
that state of life which he hath placed
him in, without desiring to be more, then
what God Almighty hath ordeined him
for to be. S. Augustine vpon these words
of the psalme. *Inclina cor meum in testi-*
monia tua & nō in auaritiam, incline my
hart vnto thy testimonies & not to auarice, says that this was the begining & root
of all our euil, since our first Parents in hauing a desire to be more then God had
made thē, & to haue more thē he had bestowed vpon thē, came therby to fall from
that state in which they were, & to loose

all

all that which God had imparted to thē.
The Diuell laid before their proud desires this baite ; *Eritis sicut Dij scientes
bonum & malum,* you shall be like Gods
hauing knowledge of good and euill, and
therby deceaued them, and wrought their
destruction ; and this vice we inherit of
them by succession, being egged on with
a desire of diuinity , and a kind of folly
and madnes to be greater then we are; and
for as mnch as the Diuell had so good successe in tempting our first parents with it,
therfore hath he been so busy euer since
to enkindle vs with the same, and set our
desires on fire, of becoming greater thē it
is Gods pleasure we should be , without
suffring vs to be content with those Tallents which we haue, and that condition to which we were borne and bred.
And therfore saith S. Augustin doth the
Prophet desire of God , that he would
giue him a heart free from all proper interest and faithfully inclined vnto his will
and pleasure , and not to his owne profit
and commodity : he sayes that by auarice
is to be vnderstood all sort of particular
end, or gaine, and not only the couitious-
nes of wealth, and it is this which S.Paul

affirmes

1. ad Ti.
6. 10.
affirmes to be the root of all euill , *radix omnium malorum cupiditas.*

Now that we may attaine to this ir dif-
ferency, & disposition of conform ing our
selues vnto the will of God, and conten-
ting vs with those talents which he hath
bestowed vpon vs, as also with that state
and degree in which he hath placed vs it
is sufficient to know that it is the will of
God ; *Hæc autem omnia operatur vnus*
1. Cor.
12. 10.
*atque idem Spiritus diuidēs singulis prout
vult.* Saith S. Paul vnto the Corinthians,
all those things are the worke of one and
the same spirit , who giues euery one his
share according as he pleaseth; The Apostle doth vse this Metaphor, which vpon
Tract. 4.
c. 4.
an other occasion we haue borrowed; and
it is deriued from a humaine body , he
sayes that euen as God hath disposed and
apted the members of a body , euery on
according as he liked best, where the foot
complains not , that it was not made the
head , neither the hand . because it was
not made an eye , so is it likewise in the
body of the Church, frō which the body
of a Religion differs not. God hath disposed of euery one , in that place and office
which is best pleasing to him, neither are
they

they ſo ordained only by chance, but by his ſingular wiſedome and proui-dence. If God therefore be pleaſed to haue you a foot, it is no reaſon, you ſhould ſeeke to be a head; if God haue or-dained you only for a hand, you do not wel in aſpiring to be an eye. O how deepe and high are the iudgments of Almighty God! and who is there who is able to comprehend them? *quis enim hominum* Sap. 9, *poterit ſcire conſilium Dei?* O Lord all 13. things what ſo euer, are proceeding from you, and you are to be praiſed in euery thing; you know what is requiſit to be-ſtow on euery one, and it belongs not to vs to iudge, and be inquiſitiue to know the cauſe why one hath leſſe conferred vpon him then an other, how know you what would become of you, if you had a wit, and great abilities? how know you if you had an excellent talent in preaching, and your Sermons were followed with a great applauſe whether it would not be the cauſe of your vtter ouerthrow as it hath been of diuers others, who therby haue become proud and exorbitantly vaine? the learned (ſaith that holy man) Thõ. de take delight to be ſeene, and to be eſtee-Kempis.

med

med for such: if you with that pényworth
of vnderstanding which you haue, and
halfe pennyworth of learning which
you haue scraped together, with that mediocrity or leſſe then mediocrity of yours,
can be ſo vainly glorious to eſteeme ſo
highly of your ſelfe as to compare and
perhaps prefer your ſeife to others, and
to take it heinouſly that you are not imployed in this or the other thing, and are
not promoted aboue ſuch & ſuch an one:
what would you do were you excellent
indeed, and had extraordinary partes a-
boue the reſt ? The ant gets wings & flies
vnto its coſt, and ſo perhaps ſhould that
honour you deſire, proue to your greater
loſſe; Aſſuredly had we but eyes to ſee, &
were not deceaued by looking through
thoſe falſe lights, we ſhould render infinite
thankes to God, for hauing diſpoſed of
vs in a ſtate ſo vile and abiect, and not
beſtowed vpon vs thoſe excellent parts
and great abilities: and we ſhould ſay with
that holy ſeruant of his: O Lord I eſteeme
it for a ſingular benefit, not to haue thoſe
many qualities, which might make me
honoured and praiſed by men. The Saints
were not ignorant of that great danger
which

which goes accompanied with preeminency and excellency, and therfore they haue not only not fought after them, but alfo fhūned and ftood in feare of them, by reafon of the great perill there was in them of lifting men vp to pride,& throwing them headlong into ruine and perdition . *Ab altitudine diei timebo*, & this rendred them fo acceptable to God. who more dearly affects his feruants which are humble,then the great;O if we could but once throughly perfwade our felues, and truly vnderftand that all befides the doing of the will of God , is but deceit and folly ! that we could but place all our contentmĕt in pleafing of God Almighty! If you in hauing leffe learning, and perhaps none at all, neither capacity for any, are more pleafing vnto God , wherfore are you fo defirous to be learned ? why doe you wifh for more knowledge and better partes? if there were any motiue to make you couet it , it fhould only be to ferue God more faithfully,and to content him in a more abfolute manner : now if God can be better ferued by you, vnlearned , and without this great fufficiency, wanting thofe tallents and extraordinary

L 4   parts,

parts, as it is moſt certaine he can , ſince
it is he alone who hath ordained it ſo,
why are you afflicted with it ? wherfore
deſire you to be that , which God is not
pleaſed to haue you & which is no waies
fit or conuenient for you? Thoſe riche &
ſumptuous ſacrifices of Saul were nothing
pleaſing to Almighty God , becauſe they
were not conformable to his will: and he
is as little pleaſed, with your haughty and
high deſires. Our being famous preachers
and learned men, confers nothing to our
good, nor helpes to our progreſſe in vertue and perfection, neither our being en-
dowed with rare partes, and hauing deepe
inſight in obſcure and lofty things; but
only in performance of the will of God,
and in the diſcharging well thoſe things
which we haue to doe , and profitably
imploying that tallent which we haue receaued ; and therfore we ought not to
ayme at any higher thing , ſince this is
that only which God requires of vs.

To explicate this the better, the compariſon which they bring of players, is not
impertinent, where a man receaueth not
his ſhare according to the dignity of that
part which he doth acte , but according
to

1. Reg.
13, 10 &
c. 15, 21.

to the goodnes of his action, whence it is,
that if he who played but the drudge
haue performed it better then he who
acted the part of the Emperour, he shall
haue more applause of the spectators, and
be thought worthy of a greater share by
all equall Iudges; Eué so. that which God
esteems meriting reward & praise in this
mortalllife of ours (which is but as a Co-
medy quickly past, and would to God it
were not a Tragedy so metimes) is not the
part which we play, the one a Preacher,
the other Superior, this Sacristan or Por-
ter; but the well performing of their parts:
and therfore if the lay brother act his
part better vnto the life, then the Preacher or Superior, he shal be more esteemed
by God, & merit more applause, honour,
& recompence. And as it is ordinary with
the players, that he who acts in Comicke
excellent well, as the Esquire errant or
Country clowne hath no grace, or person
for to acte a King, and yet notwithstanding he is held an excellent actor: so you
perhaps are no waies fit to make a Superior or a Preacher of, and should performe
with good satisfaction the office of a
Ghostly Father or Coadiutor. God
knowes

knowes well how to fit euery actor with
his part, and appoint each one that office
which he can do the best. *Vnicuique se-*
cundum propriam virtutem , our Lord,
says the holy Euangel, diftributs his gifts
and tallents refpectiuely to the ability of
euery one, and therfore one man is not
to defire the part , or tallent of an other
man, but all are to indeauour to performe
that part well which is a appointed them,
and imploy to beft aduantage that tallent
which they haue receaued , and keepe a
cleere account, and fo they fhall come to
pleafe God Almighty the beft, and be re-
warded with greater recompence.

THE XVI. CHAPTER.

Of the conformity which we are to haue
with the will of God in time of ficknes.

S Ickneffe is as well a guift of God as
health , and fent vs , by him for our
tryall, correction, and amendment, as alfo
for diuers other commodities and profits which are proceeding from it; as the
knowledge of our infirmity, the difcouery
of our prefumption, our riddance of the
loue

loue of worldly things, and of the con-
cupiscences of sensuality, the deading and
diminishing in vs, the forces of the flesh
our Capitall enemy, and giuing vs to vnderstand that the place where we liue is
not our owne country, but like an Inne
which we haue taken vp in manner of
passengers and wretched bannish't men,
and diuers other commodities besides; &
for this reason the wiseman hath said, *in-*
firmitas grauis sobriam facit animam,
grieuous infirmity makes an vnderstanding soule, and therfore we are to conforme our selues as well vnto the will of
God in sicknesse as in health, and receaue
it when soeuer God shall please to send it
vs, as proceeding from his holy hand. One
of those ancient Fathers said vnto his Dis-
ciple who was sicke; my sóne be not grieued at your infirmity, but on the contrary, render hearty thanks to God Almighty for it; for if you be iron, this is a
fire for to take of your ruste, if you be
gould, this is a fire to try you: to render
thanks to God when we are sicke, is an
acte of great vertue, and worthily besee-
ming a true Religious soule.

Surius relats in the life of S. Clare, how
that

that for eight and twenty yeares together
shee was afflicted with grieuous infirmities, in all which time her patience was so
inuincible. as she was neuer heard, to vtter
any complaint , or vse any murmuring
speeches in those her violent fitts but shee
continued alwaies thinking and praising
God : and in her last sicknesse when shee
was so tormented, as for seauenteen daies
together she could not eate one bit, Fryer
Reginald her Ghostly Father, comforting
her and exhorting her to patience in so
long and dolorous a martyrdome as shee
suffered in so much sicknesse and infirmity ; shee answered , neuer since I haue
been acquainted with the grace of my
Lord Iesus Christ , through the intercession of S. Francis his humble seruant, hath
any sicknesse, seemed hard vnto me, any
paine grieuous , or any penance sore and
troublesome . In this kind also is the life
of Saint Liduuine admirable and of great
example, as also giuing great courage
and comfort vnto those who are sicke;
who for eight and thirty yeares together, was oppressed with most grieuous
and extraordinary diseases and paines.and
for thirty yeares could neuer rise from
that

that poore couch on which she lay, or su-
steine her selfe on her feet . in all which
time , our Sauiour visited her with high
and singular fauours.

But for as much as diuers particular
reasons, do vse to present themselues, vnder the colour and shew of greater good,
vnto the hinderance of this indifferency
and conformity , it is requisite that we
solue and answere them. And first, some
one may say,for my part it is all one to me
whether I be sicke or well, only that
which troubles me is that I feare I am a
burthen to those of the house,& a charge
vnto the Religiō: vnto this I answere,that
this is nothing els then to condēne the Superior & those of the house,of wāt of charity & litle resignation to the will of God;
the Superiors are vnderstood to be arriued to that perfection,to receaue all as cōming from the hand of God, and to conforme thēseluesin all vnto his blessed will,
and so if God be pleased that you should
be sicke, & that one should be imployed in
nothing els then in tēding to the recouery
and the care of you;they are likewise well
content, & as you beare that crosse which
God hath sent you,so do they likewise sustaine,

ftaine,that which God would haue them beare with great conformity.

But you will reply, I fufficiētly fee in this point,the great charity of the Society,and nothing troubles me , but to thinke how much profit I could make in ftudying, preaching.& hearing confeffions, & how I cannot imploy my felfe in any of thefe, by reafon of my ficknefle. Vnto which S. Auguftin anfweres excellent well, faying that we know not whether it were better to do that which we pretend or no, and therfore are to propofe nothing vnto our felues aboue our capacity,and if afterwards we can execute that which we defigned,we are not to reioyce becaufe that which we intended & defired is brought to paffe, but becaufe in it,the will of God is done: and if that which we ordeined be not effeded , we are not therfore to be troubled and loofe our peace of mind, feing that *æquius eft vt nos eius , quam vt ille noftram fequatur voluntatem* , it is more reafonable that we fhould followe Gods will , then he ours. And glorious S. Auguftin cōcluds with an admirable fentence . *Nemo melius ordinat quid agat, nifi qui paratior eft, non agere, quod di-*
uina

minà posestate prohibitur, quàm cupidior agere quod humanà cogitatione meditatur, there is no man doth better dispose of what he would do, then he who is readier to do nothing that the diuine authority may forbid, then desirous to do that which in his owne thoughts he intends. We are then to determine and dispose of things with such indifferency, as to be alwaies prepared to conforme our selues vnto the will of God. if by any chance our pretensions might be crossed; and so we should neuer be grieued or troubled, if through sicknes or any other casualty, we could not bring that to passe which we had purposed, although the thing in it selfe were of neuer so great consequence for the good of soules. Master Auila writing vnto a Priest visited with sicknesse saith wondrous well : doe not consider so much what you could do if you were well, as how pleasing you should be to God, in being well content for to be sicke, and if you seeke purely the will of God (as I suppose you do) what matter is it, whether you be sicke or well seing that his will alone is all our good?

S. Chrisostom saith that holy Iob did

merit

Iob. 1.21   merit more and did please God more in
this . *Sicut Domino placuit , ita factum
est, sit nomen Domini benedictum,* it is so
falne out, as it hath pleased God , be his
name (euer) blest, and in conforming himselfe in all his miseries, sufferings and that
lothsome Leprosy which God sent him,
vnto his holy will , then in all the Almes
and good workes which he did whilst
he was in health and full prosperity: and
so in like manner you shall please God
more by following his will whilst you
are sicke, then in all which you could do
if you were well. S. Bonauenture says the
Iob. 1.21 same; *Perfectius est aduersa tolerare pa-*
Bonau.   *tienter, quàm bonis operibus insudare,* it
de grad is more perfection to suffer aduersity pa-
virt.c.24.
& lib.de tiently, then to performe good works ne-
perfect. uer so earnestly , God can well be with-
Relig. c. out both you & me for any profit which
37. hoc he intends vnto his Church, *ego dixi Deus*
refert ex
Diuo   *meus es tu , quoniam bonorum meorum*
Gregor. *non eges,* he is pleased for the present to
preach vnto you , in sicknesse , and re-
psal. 15. quires that you should learne patience &
2.   humility out of it , commit all to God,
he knowes best what is most expedient
for you , and you are wholly ignorant of
it

it your selfe , if we were to desire health
and corporall forces for any cause , we
ought to desire it the better to imploy our
selues in the seruice of God , and to be
more pleasing to him ; If then our Lord
is pleased more, and had rather haue me
exercised with sicknesse, and in suffering
patiently the paine of my disease, his will
be done, it is the best for me, and most .
conuenient.S.Paul the Apostle and Prea- A&. 28,
cher of the Gentils was by the permission 30.
of God.deteined two yeares in prison, in
a time when the primitiue Church had so
much need of him , it is not much then
for you, if God doe keepe you two mo-
neths, or two yeares, or all your life if so
he pleases inthrald vnto some sicknesse,
who are farre from being so necessary in
the Church of God, as was that glorious
Apostle S. Paul.

Others there are , who when they are
disabled by sicknesse, or long and continuall infirmity , to liue according to the
community , but are inforced to accept
of particularities are much troubled and
disquieted,scarcely esteeming them selues
Religious men, and thinking euery one
disedified with them , in seing their ex-

traordinary fare and manner of life, and
especially if their disease be such as ex-
tendeth not to the exterior shew, when
their sicknesse is only knowne to God &
themselues, and their particularities and
exemptions knowne to all; to these I answere that it is a good and laudible consideration, and you haue iust cause to haue
resentment of it, but so, as not to cease
in point of your sicknesse to conforme
your selfe vnto the will of God, and to
make your benefit of a double merit, by
conforming vour selfe on the one side entirely with the will of God, in all those
indispositions and infirmities which he is
pleased to visit you withall, and on the o-
ther by a great desire, as farre as shall be
possible vnto you, to performe and exercise your selfe in all the functions of your
Order, in being heartily sorry, that you
cannot be imployed in that which others
do, and in this manner besides the merit,
of induring sicknesse, patiently and willingly, there is place in this second point
of meriting as much as those who are well
and lusty, and actually imployed in all
those exercises.

3, Augu.   S. Augustin in his 62. sermon de tempore

pore, treating of the obligation which each one had vnder mortall sinne to fast time of lent, coming to speake of those who were infirme, and vnable to fast, says that it is sufficient for such as those, to eate at least with interior griefe and sorrow, sighing and lamenting that whilst others fast, they are not able to beare the company, like as a valiant souldier, who hauing been wounded in fight, hath more affliction and griefe that he cannot go to field, to do some acte worthy the seruice of his King, then paine and anguish to be vnder the Chirurgions launce. Euen so it is with good Religious men, when they are sicke, who are more troubled & grieued that they cannot performe the exercises of the Religion with the rest, then at the torment of their owne disease. But in fine neither that, nor any other thing, is to be a hinderance to our conformity with the will of God in our infirmities, but we are to receaue them, as presents directed vnto vs, from his owne hands vnto his greater glory, & for our greater good and benefit,

S. Hierom recounts how a certaine Monke beseeched holy Abbot Ioannes

Hieron. in vit. Patrum.

M 2   an

an Egyptian by nation, to cure him of a
violent feuer which much tormēted him,
vnto whom the bleſſed Saint anſwered:
rem tibi neceſſariam cupis abijcere, vt
enim corpora nitro, vel alijs huiuſmodi
lineamentis abluuntur à ſordibus, ita ani-
mæ languoribus alijsque huiuſmodi caſti-
gationibus purificantur, you deſire to be
rid of a thing which is very needfull for
you, for euen as we clenſe the filth of our
bodies, with ſope and lie, ſo by infirmities & the like chaſtiſements are our ſoules
made cleane and purified.

THE XVII. CHAPTER.

How we are not to repoſe our truſt in Phi-
ſitians and Medecins, but only in Al-
mighty God, and are to conforme our
ſelues vnto his will, not only in ſickneſſe
but alſo in all other things which doe
accompany it.

T Hat which hath been ſaid of ſickneſſe, is likewiſe to be vnderſtood,
in matter of all other things which during our ſickneſſe are accidentall to vs, S.
Baſil touching this matter hath left vs an
excel-

excellent document, saying that we so
ought to make vse of Phisicke and Phisitians, as in the meane time to place no
trust in them, as King Asa did, whom the
holy scripture therfore reprehends: *Nec in*
infirmitate sua quæsiuit Dominum, sed
magis in medicorum arte confisus est, he
hath not sought after God so much as in
his infirmity, but hath rather trusted to
the skill of the Phisitians, we are not to
attribute to them, either our recouery or
remaining still infirme, but ought to fixe
our hope only on God, who sometimes, is
pleased to restore vs so our health, by Phi-
sicall meanes and sometimes suffers vs to
receaue no good by it, and therfore saith
S. Basil although we haue neither commodity of Phisitian nor his drogs, yet are
we not to dispaire of recouering our
health, seeing that our Sauiour Christ as
the holy Scripture testifies, sometimes
cured diseases by his only will, as that
Leaper who said vnto him, *Domine si*
vis potes me mundare, Lord if you will
you can make me cleane, and our Sauiour answered, *volo, mundare;* I will, be
cleane, at other times he did apply certaine things, as when he made clay with

Basil. in
reg. Fu-
sias dis-
putat. 55

2. p. 16.
12.

his spittle, and annointed the eyes of the
blind with it, commanding him to go
wash himselfe in the poole Siloe: at other
times againe he would leaue the sicke in
their infirmities, and not suffer them to be
cured although they euen wasted their
whole substance in procuring helpe at the
Phisitians hands : so in like manner God
sometimes restores vs to our health againe,
without helpe of Phisicke , by only willing it; at other times he sends it vs by the
meanes of Phisitians, and sometimes notwithstanding the consult of Doctors and
applying of many soueraine remedies,
God will not recouer you, to teach vs to
confide our whole trust on him , and to
lodge no hope in any humane helpe. As
King Ezechias did not attribute his cure
vnto that lump, of figs which Esay applyed to his impostume , but only to Almighty God , so must not we acknowledge the recouery of our health , to any
medecine or Phisitians, but to God who
cures all our infirmities. *Etenim neque*
herba , neque malagma sanauit eos, sed
tuus Domine sermo qui sanauit omnia,
for neither hearbs nor plasters haue hea-
led them, but thy word ô Lord the generall

4. Reg.
20. 7.

Sap. 16.
12.

rall cure of all, neither when we are not cured, are we to lay the fault on the Phisitians, but acknowledge God in it, whose will is, to leaue vs in our sicknesse, and afford vs no redresse: so likewise, when the Phisition is ignorant of your disease, or is mistaken in his iudgment of it (which is an ordinary thing euen with those who are best skil'd and practised, and in the behalfe of honourable persons) you are to accept of this mistake of theirs, as also any negligence or fault of the Infirmarian, as a thing expresly so ordeined by God, and therfore by no meanes ought to say, your feauer is returned vnto you againe, through an others fault or want of taking heed, but you must receaue all as sent vnto you from the hand of God, and say it hath pleased God that my feauer should increase and that such an accident should happen to me, for it is most certaine that how euer in regard of those who are to tend you and looke vnto your health a fault may be cōmitted, yet notwithstanding vnto God it is a premeditated thing, vnto whom nothing is by chāce or casuall. Do you imagine it an accidentall thing, that the Swallous flying

M 4   ouer

ouer Tobies head, fhould dunge into his
eyes, and depriue him of his fight? affuredly it was not, but done with deepe refolution, and by the particular will of Almighty God, to giue vs therby an exāple
of patience in him, equall to that of holy
Iob, and fo the facred Scripture teſtifies:

Tob. 2.
11. *hanc autem tētationem ideo permifit Dominus euenire illi, vt pofteris daretur exemplum patientæ eius ficut & Sancti Iob,*
and the Angell faid vnto him afterwards.

Iob. 12.
15. *Quia acceptus eras Deo neceffe fuit vt tē-
tatio probaret te ,* God hath permitted
this tentation for your proofe and tryall.

Abbas
Stepha-
nus re-
fert e-
tiā Do-
rot. do-
ctri. 7. We read in the liues of the Fathers
how Abbot Stephen being ficke, his cō-
panion would needes make him a cake,
and thinking to bake it with good oyle,
he miftoke & made it with lintfead oyle,
which is exceeding better , and fo gaue it
him to eate, Stephen hauing tafted of it,
eate a litle and put away the reft , without faying any thing. An other time he
baked him an other in the fame fafhion,
and hauing brought it him, when he faw
he would not eate he tooke a peece of it
himfelfe, to prouoke him vnto an appetite , and tafting of it faid, pray Father
eate,

eate, the cake is very good, but finding
the bitternes of it, and his miftake with
great affliction of mind he cryed out and
faid : I am a butcher and murtherer of
men. wherupon the good Father anfwered : fonne doe not trouble, nor difquiet
your felfe, if God had not been pleafed
that you fhould miftake the one oyle for
the other, it had neuer happened. We likewife read of diuers other Saints, who fuffred with great patience and equality of
mind, the cures which others prefcribed
them for their ficknefles, although they
knew them wholly contrary to the nature of their difeafe and in this manner
are we to beare the faults and negligen-
ces.afwell of the Phifitian as Infirmarian,
and neither complaine of the one, nor lay
the blame vpon the other.

It is a circuſtance in which a mans vertue is difcouered and feene the beft, and
therfore a whole houfe is edified, by feing
a ficke Religious man, take all that comes
with an equall countenance, and with
the fame cheerfulnes, as cõming all from
the bleffed hand of God, and ſfuffering
himfelfe to be ruled by his Superiors and
the Infirmarian, as if the remembrance
                                    and

and care of his owne selfe concearned him
nothing, S. Basil saith, you haue trusted
your Superior with your soule why therfore do you not trust your body to him?
you haue put your eternall wellfare into
his hands, why do you not aswell commit
vnto him your temporall health, & seing
our rule doth exempt vs at that time, frō
the solicitude of our body, and cōmaunds
it also, why do we not make vse & great
account of a priuilege so much to our aduantage and behofe? On the contrary,
the sicke Religious man who is too scru-
pulous of his health, who is to exact and
precise in euery thing which is admini-
stered to him, and in the manner of taking it, and the time, and who if all things
be not done as he would haue them, can
lightly complaine of it, and murmure at
it too, disedifies very much all who conuerse with him.

Cassian.
li. de in-
stitut.re-
nūt. c 7. Cassian says excellent well that the
infirmity of the body is no waies hinde-
ring the purity of the mind, but much
conferring to it, if men but make their
vse of it as they ought: but take heed saith
he, that the infirmity of the body, doth
not passe vnto the soule, if any one so be-
                                        haue

haue himſelfe as to make vſe of the occaſion of his ſickneſſe, to do what he thinks beſt, and is not tractable nor obedient; this mans corporall ſickneſſe hath extended it ſelfe vnto his ſoule, and the Superior will haue more to doe, to prouide remedies for this ſpirituall diſeaſe then for his corporall. A man for being ſicke, is not to ceaſe and neglect to appeare and to be Religious, neither to imagine, that he is not obliged as then by any rule, and that he is to make it his only care, to looke vnto the recouery and cheriſhing of himſelfe, without once minding his ſpirituall progreſſe, or looking after it. He who is ſicke (ſaith our B. Father in the Conſtitutions) is to indeauour no leſſe in time of his ſickneſſe, to edify others by ſhewing his humility and patience then whilſt he was in health. **§.** Chriſoſtome on theſe words of the Prophet : *Domine vt ſcuto bonæ voluntatis tuæ coronaſti nos,* ô Lord you haue crowned vs as with a ſheeld of your good will, diſcourſing how during the courſe of this life, there is a continuall fight, ſays that therfore we are alwaies to haue our weapens in hand, as well thoſe who are ſicke, as thoſe who are in health.

Et

Reg. 50. Sūmarij

Chriſoſt. Pſa. 5. 13.

Et ægroti & sani: morbi enim tempore,
huius maximè pugna tempus est , quando
dolores vndique conturbant animam ,
quando tristitia obsidèt, quando adest dia-
bolus incitans , vt acerbum aliquod ver-
bum dicamus , but this fight (saith he) is
hottest in time of sicknesse , when torments on all sides do molest the soule,
when we are incōpas't with sadnes,& the
Diuell is ready at hand, to incite vs to vtter some impatient word,or to be immoderate in making of our moane , which
Seneca likewise confirmes saying, that a
Seneca. valiant and couragious man hath as faire
epist.78. an oportunity to exercise his forces well
in bed , in suffring sicknes, as in the field
in battaile against his enemies ; And therfore the wiseman says that a patient man
is better then a strong: *melior est patiens*
Prou.16. *viro forti ,* and he who hath the mastery
32. of himselfe,then a Conquerour of Citties:
& qui dominatur animo suo , expugna-
natore vrbium,

THE

THE XVIII. CHAPTER.

Wherin that which hath been said is con-
firmed by some examples.

WE read of the holy Virgin S. Gertrud, how that one day our Sauiour Christ appeared vnto her, bringing
in his right hand, health, and his left sicknesse, and bid her choose whether of the
shee would, vnto whom shee answered,
inclining vnto neither of his hands) that
which out of my whole hart I desire Lord
is, that you would haue no regard vnto
my will, but that your good pleasure in
all may be fulfilled.

It is recounted of a certaine person,
much deuoted to S. Thomas of Canter-
bury, how he (being afflicted with a grieuous sicknes) had recourse vnto his Pa-
trons shrine, where begging with great
feruour his holy intercession for the recouery of his health, the B. Saint heard
his petition, and obtained it him, wher-
vpon he returning, began to consider attentiuely with himselfe, whether it were
not more for his soules good, that he
                              should

Blo.c.18
monili
spir.

should still be sicke, and not being able to resolue himselfe, he returned againe vnto the sacred shrine, and there renewing his prayers againe, he beseeched the Saint, to obteine for him of God that which should be most expedient for his saluation, when presently his sicknes returned vnto him againe and so he passed the rest of his dayes, taking great comfort and content therin, as in a thing the most conuenient for him.

Surius in the life of S. Vedastus Bishop, doth bring an other example of the like nature, of a blind man, who vpon the day of the translation of this holy Prelats body, had a great desire to behould his holy reliques and consequently to recouer his sight againe: when on the instant he obtained of God that which he wished with so much earnestnes, and saw that which he desired so much, and casting his eyes vpon himselfe, he made it his petition vnto God againe that if the sight of his eyes might be preiudiciall to the good of his soule, that it might please him to leaue him blind as he was before, and hauing made this prayer, his former blindnes closed vp his eyes againe.

Surius.

S.

S. Hierom writs now S. Anthony being inuited by S. Anastasius Bishop of Alexandria to confer his helpe vnto the resisting and confuting of the Hereticks, had conference with one Dydimus who came to visit him, an excellent scholler, but wanting his corporall sight, this Didymus discoursing rarely well of the holy Scripture in so much as S. Anthony euer praysed to admiration the excellency & sharpnes of his wit, was demanded by the Saint whether he were not agrieued, that he wanted his corporall eyes, Dydimus was ashamed to answer, at the first, vntill being vrged by him a second and third time, at last he brought him to cofesse ingeniously the sorrow of his mind: when S. Authony said vnto him. I wonder much that a wise man as you are, should grieue the want of that which flies pismires and ants enioy, and not rather reioyce in the possession of that, which only vses to be imparted to Saints and Apostolical men. Where out we may learne saith S. Hierom that it is farre better to see with the eyes of the soule then of the flesh.

Fryer Ferdinand de Castile in his Chronicle of the Order of S. Dominicke recounts

Hier. ep. ad Castr. cæcum.

Cro. or. Præd. 1. p. li. 1 c. 49.

Croni.
ord.Pre.
1.p.l.1.
c.49.

counts how S. Dominicke during his a-
boad at Rome went often to vifit a certaine holy feruant of Almighty God, who
liued in clofed betwixt fower walles, in
a Tower of S. Iohn Laterans port. whether fhee had retired herfelfe, which holy
woman was afflicted with a moft horrible
infirmity, fhe was called Bona, and her
name was very fignificant to expreffe her
life, vnto whō God had tought the great
perfection in goodnes & fanctity, to take
pleafure in aduerfity, and to find repofe
euen in death it felfe; fhee fuffred grieuous paine and torment in her breafts;
which were almoft eaten vp with the Cā-
cer and the flefh conuerted into crawling
worms, and yet this life of hers which
would haue been to any other the greateft of all torments, was vnto her the occafion of thanking God the more, and exercifing admirable patiéce; S. Dominicke
who viually heard her confeffion and ad-
miniftred her the B. Sacrament, feeing her
on the one fide fo afflicted and infirme,
and on the other fo eminently vertuous,
did beare her fingular affection, and on
day after he had confeft and communicated her, he had a great defire, to fee her fo
her-

horrible and loathsome soare whose only
light was enough to affright and startle
any heart, which not without some difficulty, he obteined but when shee opened
her breast, and the Saint saw on the one
side foule matter, the festred canker and
the crawling worms, and on the other
her wondrous patience and cheerfulnes,
he could not choose but haue great compassion of her, but notwithstanding being
more desirous of that soare of hers, then
of all the treasors of the world, he desired her with great instance to bestow one
of those wormes vpon him, which he
might keepe as a pretious relike of hers,
the holy Saint would not graunt him his
request, vnles he first promised to restore
it backe againe, for shee tooke such pleasure in seing herselfe in that manner eaten
vp aliue, that if any of those worms cha-
ced to fall from her breast vnto the
ground, shee would take it vp, and lay it
in its place againe, on this condition shee
did giue him one with a foule blacke
head, and of a mighty sise, S. Dominicke
had scarsly receaued it in his hand, when
it changed into a riche and orient peale
his companions wondring at it would haue

perſwaded the Saint to haue kept it ſtill,
but the holy ſoule aſked it earneſtly a-
gaine, and ſhee no ſooner had it reſtored
vnto her, but it turned into a worme , as
it was before, and ſhee repoſed it in her
breaſt againe , where it had been bred,
and nouriſhed before; thereupon S. Dominicke praying for her , and bleſſing her
with the ſigne of the holy Croſſe, left her,
and went his wayes, but he was not gone
downe the ſtairs of that Tower wherin
ſhee liued , when thoſe cancorous and
wormy breaſts of hers, fell from her, and
ſound fleſh by litle and litle ſwelling in
their place, within ſhort time ſhe was entirely cured, and remained; declaring vnto
all that wōdrous miracle, which God had
wrought in her by means of his holy ſeruant S. Dominicke.

   In the ſame Chronicle is likewiſe recounted, how Fryer Reginald whilſt he
was ſuing to S. Dominicke, to take the
habit of his order and his entrance into
the Religiō was concluded of, was forced
to keepe his bed , through the violence of
a continuall feauer, which the Phiſitians
iudged to be mortall. S. Dominicke toke
his ſicknes much to hart, and prayed vnto
                                          God

God continually for his health, the sickman likewise no lesse solicitous for his
owne health, did with great feeling and
deuotion inuocate the helpe of the glorious Queene of heauen : whilst both of
them, were iointly directing all their
prayers vnto this end, the B. Virgin entred the chamber of the sicke encompas-
sed with a most resplendent light, accompanied with two blessed Virgins which
seemed to be S. Cecily and S. Catherine
Martyas, who attended on the glorious
Virgin vnto the bed where the sicke Religious lay, whom as a Queen, and soueraigne Mother, and Mother of pitty shee
comforted and said: what doe you desire
that I should doe for you? I am come on
purpose to heare your petition, present it
to me, and I will graunt it you . Wher-
vpon Reginald much troubled and aba-
shed, transported with so diuine a vision;
was in great perplexity what he should
do, or say, when one of those holy Virgins of her traine, to free him from his
anxiety said vnto him, commit your selfe
entirely into her hands, for shee knowes
better what to bestow vpon you, then
you to aske, the sickman tooke this coun-

N 2   sell,

fell, which was giuen him with so much prudence and discretion, and answered in this manner to the B. Virgin; Glorious Lady I require nothing of you, but like as one who hath no other will, then what is yours, doe remit my selfe entirely vnto you and resigne me ouer into your blessed hands. Hereupon the B. Virgin extending of them forth, and taking from her Virgins an oyle which they had brought for that effect; annointed him with it, in the same manner as they vse to those who are annealed, and the touch of her sacred hands, had such excellent force, that he was presently deliuered from his feauer, and restored to as perfect health, as if he neuer had been sicke: and what is yet more strange; besides this so great benefit of his corporall forces, he receaued in his soule a farre more singular one, in that he was neuer from that houre forwards in any place, time or occasion touched in his person whilst he liued on earth, with any sensuall or dishonest motion.

Hist. Ecc.
p. 2. l. 6.
c. 2. We read in the Ecclesiasticall History, how among other men who flourished in that age, one *Beniamin* was of great renoune

noune and fame vpon whom God had
bestowed the gift, of healing all diseases,
with no other medicines, then the bare
touch of his hand, or with chaffing them
only with a little oyle, and praying ouer
them. This holy man, together with this
great grace and priuiledge of restoring
health to others, was so miserably vexed
with the dropsy himselfe, as he came to
be so mightily swolne, that he could not
go out of his cell, without vnhinging the
dore to make him larger passage, and in
this manner continued he in his cell for
eight months together vntill he dyed; sit-
ting on a wide settle, and curing many diseases of other men, with out so much as
once complaining or being troubled, that
he could not apply a remedy to his owne,
and those who pittied him, he comforted,
and said pray vnto God for my soule, and
take no thought for my bodies infirmity,
which euen when I was well, did serue
me to no vse.

In, *Pratum spirituale* there is made Pra. Spi-
mention of a certaine Religious Monke, rit. c. 10.
who was named *Barnaby*, this hauing a
great splinter of wood, as he went vpon
the way, runne vp into his foot, would not

draw it out, nor suffer it to be cured for many dayes, that he might haue more occasion to suffer for the loue of God, and he said vnto those who came to visit him, the more the exterior mā suffers & is mortified, the more the interior mā is strēgthned and enabled.

Surius
in vita
S. Pachomij.

Surius in the life of *S.Pachomius* writeth of a certaine Monke called *Zacheus*; who although he had the falling sicknesse, did notwithstanding neuer remit any thing of his accustomed abstinence of feeding only with bread and shalt, neither did he omit any of those ordinary prayers which the others Religicus who were in health did vse to make, but was still present and assisting at mattins and all the other howers. All the time which he had vacāt from his prayer he imployed in making matts, baskets and cords, and he had so galed his hands, with drawing bulrushes and the stalks of hempe, that they were alwaies rawe and full of chaps, at night before he gaue himselfe to sleepe, he vsed to meditate vpon some point of the holy Scripture, and afterwards making the signe of the holy Crosse, ouer his whole body, he would repose himselfe, vntill

vntill the hower of Mattins, vnto which
he would rise with the first, and be present at all the other howers, as hath been
said, and this was the distribution of time,
& the ordinary exercise of this holy sicke
Religious man; It chanced that a certaine Monke came once to visit him and
seing his hands so sore and full of chaps,
he told him that if he annointed them
with oyle, he should allay the paine and
smart of them, *Zacheus* was swayed by
his counsell and anointed them with oyle,
but the paine did not only not asswage,
but it increased excessiuely more, in so
much as he was inforced to go to *S. Pa-
chomius* to declare his griefe vnto whom
the Saint answered: do you imagine sonne,
that God doth not see all our infirmities
and that he cannot cure vs if he please?
Wherfore then do you conceiue that God
doth it not, but suffers vs to be afflicted
as much as seemes good to him, but only
to induce vs to leaue all care of our selues
to him, and in him to repose all our confidence? besides it makes for the good and
profit of our soules, he augmenting afterwards our reward and eternall recompence in an infinit proportion to these

short and petty sufferings, which he sends
vs here: which *Zacheus* hearing his soule
was stroken with a liuely sorrow and he
said Father forgiue me, and pray to God
for pardon of this sinne of mine, of hauing so litle confidence and conformity
with his holy will, and hauing a desire so
immoderate to be cured: and being departed from *S.Pachomius* he entred vpõ
a rigorous course of penance for so light
a fault, fasting a whole yeare together,
without receauing any sustenance, but
only euery second day, and that in litle
quãtity, accompanied with many teares.
This so remarkable an example *S.Pacho-
mius* vsed afterwards to recount to his
Religious, to incourage them vnto per-
seuerance in paine and labour, as also to
stire them vp to confidence in God, and
to correct in themselues the smallest
faults.

THE

THE XIX. CHAPTER.

Of the conformity which we are to haue
with the will of God, aswell in death
as life.

WE ought moreouer to symbolise
with the will of God, aswell to
dy, as to liue, although this point of death
is of it selfe the hardest of all, according
to the saying of the Philosopher: *omnium* Arist. 3.
rerum nihil morte terribilius, nihil acer- Ethico-
bius, death is the most terrible and bitte- rum c.6.
rest thing of all: neuertheles vnto Religious men this difficulty is either for the
most part none at all, or much facilitated;
they hauing already passed ouer the one
halfe of the way, and almost all, seing that
one of the first & principall causes which
renders seculars so loth to die, and so ap-
paleth them when that hower doth ap-
proach, is because they are to leaue their
riches, the honours pleasures recreations
and delights, which here they did enioy,
together with their parents, friends wife
and children, which vseth not a litle
to afflict them at that hower, especially
                                    when

when they haue not been well prouided
for; Now Religious men haue long since
freed themselues of all these things, and
therfore they cannot be grieued nor troubled for thē. When a tooth is well cleared
and separated from the gummes, you may
plucke it easely out, but if you go about
to draw it out, without first loosing it
from the flesh, it will cost you excessiue
paine; In like manner a Religious man,
who is seuered from his friends of flesh &
blood, and free from all worldly things,
is not agrieued at the article of death to
leaue them all, since he had freely and
with merit before giuen ouer all part in
them, at his first entrance into Religion;
not expecting to depart with them at the
hower of death, as worldlings do, who
then mnst leaue them whither they will
or no, neuer without great sorrow and
griefe; and oftentimes without all merit:
they rather leauing their possessors, then
they who did possesse them, leauing thē.
And this is one of the fruites which they
do reape who leaue the world to enter in
to Religion. And S. Chrisostom excellent
well obserueth, that vnto those who liue
in the world, and are as it were inchained
to

to the riches, paſtimes, delights and plea-
ſures of this life death is exceſſiue bitter
and greeuous; conformable to this ſentence of the wiſeman : *O mors quàm a-* Eccl. 41.
mara eſt memoria tua,homini pacem ha- 1.
benti in ſubſtantijs ſuis.O death how bitter is thy memory,vnto a man who hath
ſet vp his reſt in his owne poſſeſſions;and
if the memory only of death, be ſo bitter
vnto them , what will it be when they
come to taſt of it ? But death is no whit
bitter to a Religious man , who hath already acquitted himſelfe of all , but rather on the contrary pleaſant and delightfull , as being an end and concluſion of
all his paines and labours,and as a paſſage
only to receaue the premium and reward
for all that which here he left and abandoned for God Almighties ſake.

   An other principall thing, which vſeth
in this article of time, exceedingly to af-
fiict worldly people , and render death
terrible and fearfull to them, is , ſaith S, Ambro.
Ambroſe , an ill aſſured conſcience and de bono
want of diſpoſition, which hath,or ought c. 8.
to haue no place in a Religious man,
ſeing that his whole life is nothing els
then a continuall preparation vnto death;
                                        It

It is recounted of a holy Religious man
that when the Phifition aduifed him to
prepare himfelfe for death, he anfwered,
euer fince I haue taken the Religious habit, my whole exercife hath been nothing
els; an exercife befitting euery Religious
man . A Religious ftate of life doth of it
felfe put vs in that difpofition which our
Sauiour requires of vs againft his comming . *Sint lumbi veftri præcincti & lu-*
cernæ ardētes in manibus veftris, let your
loynes be girded and your lights burning
in your hands. S. Gregory fay that by the
girding of the loynes, chaftity is denoted,
& by the burning lights which they were
to haue in their hãds, the exercife of good
works , both which do fhine forth moft
particularly and bright in a Religious
ftate , and therfore he who is a good Religious man hath no reafon to be affraid
of death.

Where we are to note one thing feruing much vnto our purpofe , which we
haue touched in paffing once before, and
it is that one of the moft certaine pre-
fumptions which we haue of a good and
pure confcience ftanding right with God,
is to be wholly conformable to the Diuine

Luc. 22.
35.

Greg. hõ
13. in E-
uang.

Tract. 2.
c. 5.

uine will in that which concerneth the
hower of death, expecting it with ioy
and cheerfulnes, like one who awaited
his spouse for the celebration of his heauenly nuptialls: *Et vos similes hominibus* Luc. 12.
expectantibus Dominum suum quando re- 15.
uertatur à nuptijs. And on the contrary, it
is no good signe when death doth bring
anxiety to any; and when in pointe of it,
a man is not well resigned vnto the
will of God. They vse to bring certaine
similitudes to declare it the better, to vs:
do you not obserue with what peace, and
how quietly the sheepe goes to the Butchery without bleating, or making any
the least resistance; this example the holy
Scripture vseth in speaking of our Sa-
uiour: *Tanquā ouis ad occisionē ductus est,* Isa. 53. 7.
he was led like a sheepe vnto the slaugh- & Act. 8.
ter: but vncleane beasts do nothing els but 32.
cry, and keepe a struggling when they
are to be killed. And this is the difference
betwixt the good, who are signified by
the sheepe, and the bad and carnall men,
represented by those other beasts. The pri-
soner who is condemned to dy, is stroke
to the heart, at euery opening of the prison dore, as fearing the officers are then
                    com-

comming to take him from the prison to execu-ion, but he who is innocent, and expects to be acquitted by the Iudge, is glad euery time he heares the turning of the key, as hoping that they come to set him at liberty. In like manner the wicked when he heares the noise and stirring of the bolt of death, when sicknesse oppresseth him, when his fits redouble, is in great dread and feare, seing he hath a cauterized conscience, which makes him stand in dread that euery thing is messenger of death, and comes to carry him downe to the eternall fire of hell; But he who is not pricked with these stings of conscience, receaueth comfort from it, as knowing his liberty to be intended by it, and that he is to depart vnto eternall rest, and to a pleasure that neuer shall haue an end. Let vs do then as becomes good Religious, and we shall not only find no difficulty in conforming our selues vnto the will of God, concerning the hower of death, but also reioyce in it, and beseech God with the Prophet, to deliuer vs from this prison. *Educ de custodia animam meam,* lead my soule out of this prison, S. Gregory on these words of holy Iob: *Et be-stia-*

Psal. 141. 8.

stias terræ non formidabis, iustis namque Greg. li.
initium retributionis est ipsa plerumque in 6. moral.
obitu securitas mentis, saith that to haue c. 16.
this cheerfulnes, this rest, this security of Iob. 5,21
conscience in the hower of death, is a beginning of the recompence of the Iust,
and that they begin as then to taft a drop
of that delicious peace, which shall afterwards like a mighty riuer ouerflow their
foules, and therby already relish their happines: wheras on the contrary the wicked
in that article begin to haue an essay of
their hell and torment, through those
pangs and remorses which they feele as
then.

So as it is a happy signe to desire death
and to reioyce in it . *S. Iohn Climachus* Climac.
and *S. Ambrose* esteeme him worthy of c. 6.
great praise, who euery day expects to dy,
and him to be no lesse then blessed and
a *Saint* , who euery hower wisheth for
death, and so we see that those holy Pa-
triarchs of the old Testament had the
same desire, accompting themselues no
other then Pilgrimes and strangers on
the earth , and to haue here no setled bi-
ding place: *Confitentes quia peregrini &* Ad hebr.
hospites sunt super terram, as *S. Paul* hath 11. 14.
admi-

hath admirably well obserued . *Qui hæc
dicunt , significant se patriam inquirere,
and therby they gaue sufficiently to vnderstand , how much they desired to be
free from this banishment. and this was the
reason why the Royall Prophet sighed.*

Psal. 119.
5. *Heu mihi quia incolatus meus prolonga-
tus.* Woe is me that my soiourning is pro-
longed , and if those antients Fathers ex-
pressed themselues to be all of this desire,
in such a time when the gates of heauen
were shut, and when they could not haue
present accesse vnto it; how much more
are we to wish for it now heauen is opened , and the soule pure from sinne goes
directly to enioy Almighty God?

THE XX. CHAPTER.

*Of some reasons and motiues which may
induce vs holily to desire a lawfull
death.*

VNto the end, that we may better
and with more perfection conforme
our selues vnto the will of God, as well in
life as death, we will set downe some motiues and reasons which may induce vs to
desire

desire to dy, as our better choyce: the
first reason which we may haue to wish
for death, is to decline the labours which
are incident to this life; seing that the wiseman saith. *Melior est mors quàm vita*   Eccl. 30
amara, death is better then a bitter life.   17.
We see worldly people for this cause often to desire to dy. and beseech it of God,
and they may do it and not sinne in it;
seing that in fine the calamities of this life
are so numerous and great, that to auoid
them, it is lawfull to desire to dy; One of
the reasons which the Saints giue why
God sends so many afflictions to man, is
because there should not be to straight an
affiance betwixt the world and him; that
he might not so passionatly affect this life,
but that we should bestow our whole
heart and loue vpon the other; & sighing
after it, *Vbi non erit luctus, neque dolor*   Apoc.21
erit vltra, when there shall be no plaints,   4.
nor any griefe no more. *S. Augustin* saith
that our Lord hath pleased out of his infi-   Aug. ser.
nit goodnes & mercy, that this life should   37. de sã-
be but short, & quickly at an ẽd, since it is   ctis qui
so troublesom; & that the other which we   est 1. in
hope for should be eternall, to the end   festo õ-
that the paine should endure but a while,   niũ SS.

and the icy and contentment for euer
more. S. *Ambrose* saith, *tantis malis hæc*

Ambr.
fer fuper
c. 7. Iob.
to. 2.

vita repleta eft , vt comparatione eius,
mors remedium putetur effe , non pæna,
this life is replenifhed with fo many euills,
as in regard therof , death is accompted
a remedy and not a paine , as feruing to
bring to end, fo many miferies and calamities . It is true notwithftanding that
worldly people do often finne herein
through their impatience, with which
they do receiue aduerfities, and in their
manner of demaunding of God to dy,
with plaints and difcontents ; but fhould
they require it, peaceably and with due
fubmiffion faying : O Lord if you fhall
pleafe to take one out of thefe miferies,
that time which I haue liued fufficeth
me ; I haue no defire for to prolonge my
dayes; they fhould commit no finne in
doing it.

Secondly one may defire to dy, and
this with more perfection , that he might
not fee the troubles and perfecutions of
the Church , and the continuall offences
which are committed againft Almighty
God, as we fee the *Prophet Elias* to haue
done ; who behoulding the perfecution
of

of *Achab* & *Iezabel*, how they diftroyed
the Altars, and murthered all the Prophets of the true God, and for the fame
caufe were in purfuite of him, enkindled
with a zeale of the honour of God, and
confidering himfelfe not able any waies
to remedy it, he retired himfelfe into the
defert, and fitting downe vnder a tree: *Pe-*   3. Reg.
tiuit anima fua, vt moreretur & ait, fuf-   19. 4.
ficit mihi Domine, tolle animam meam,
neque enim melior fum quàm patres mei,
he defired for his foule to dy, and faid, it
fufficeth me ô Lord, take my foule, for
I am not better then my Fathers (were) I
haue liued long enough ô Lord, take me
out of this life, that I may not fee fo many
euills and offences, as are committed a-
gàinft thee. And that valiant Captaine
of the people of God, *Iudas Machabeus*
faid: *Melius eft nos mori in bello, quàm*   1. Mach.
videre mala gentis noftræ & Sanctorum,   3. 39.
it is better for vs to dy in warre, then to
fee the euills of our people & the Sainds,
and he vfed this motiue to exhort and en-
courage them to fight. We read in the
life of S, *Auguftin*, that the *Vandals* paf-   Auguft
fing out of *Spaine* into *Africke*, and wa-
fting all, fparing not man nor woman,

Clergy

Clergy or secular, neither children nor
old age, a came at last to lay downe their
siege before *Hippo* where he was Bishop,
with a mighty Army beleagering it about.
S. Augustin seing so great affliction, the
Churches without Clergy, Citties vnin-
habited, priuate houses destitute, wept bitterly in that old age of his, and assem-
bling the Clergy he said vnto them: I haue
prayed vnto God to deliuer you from
these dangers, or to giue you patience, or
lastly to take me out of this life, that I
may not liue to see so many calamities; the
last of these three God hath granted me,
and presently he fell sicke in the third
month of the siege, of that disease wherof afterwards he dyed. And we read in
the life of our B. F. *S. Ignatius* an other
example almost like to this. This is a perfection proper vnto the Saints so to resent
the calamities of the Church, and the sinnes which are comitted against the Maiesty of Almighty God, as rather to desire to dy, then indure the sight therof.

There is yet an other reason, both excellent good, and of great perfection to
desire to dy, and begge it at the hands of
God, which is that we may be free and

Lib. 4. c.
16. vit. S.
P. Ignatij

RO

no more subiect to offend him , for it is
most certaine , that so long as we are in
this life, we can haue no assurance from
falling into mortall sinne; as being not ignorant that others who haue receaued
more fauours and graces from God Almighty then we , who were truly Saints,
and great Saints, to haue come to fall; and
this is one reason which makes the seruants of God , both liue in greater feare,
and most earnestly desire to dy . If it be
lawfull for one to wish that he had neuer
been borne, or neuer had being , on the
conditiō he had neuer sinned; how much
more reason hath one to wish to dy , seing
that sinne is a farre greater euill , then to
haue no being , and it is better neuer to
haue been, then to haue sinned ; *Bonum* Math.26
erat ei , si natus non fuisset homo ille , it 14.
had been better (saith our Sauiour , speaking of him who sold him and betrayed
him, that he had neuer been borne ; and
S. *Ambrose* explicating this of *Eccle-* Ambr.ſ.
siastes, Et laudaui , magis mortuos quàm 18.in pſ.
viuentes, & feliciorem vtroque iudicaui 118.
qui necdum natus est , saith: *Mortuus* Eccl.4.2.
præfertur viuenti, quia peccare desinit, & 3.
mortuo præfertur qui natus non est , quia

pec-

peccare nesciuit, he who is dead, is preferred to him who liueth, because he ceaseth to sinne any more, and he who was neuer borne, is preferred vnto the dead, because he neuer knew what it was to sinne, wherfore it were an excellent exercise to actuate our selues whilst we are in prayer in this deuotion: *Domine ne permittas me seperari à te*, Lord do not permit me to be seperated from thee, ô Lord, if there is no remedy but I must offend thee, take me away presently, rather then leaue me in the occasion of offending thee, for my part, I desire not life, but only to serue thee with it, and if I may not vse it to thy seruice, I care not for it; this were an exercise most pleasing vnto God, and most profitable to our selues, since herein we exercise both an act of griefe, an acte of detestation of sinne, an acte of humility, and of the loue of God, and it is a request of the most gratfull thing which we can require of Almighty God.

S. Ludo. It is recounted of *S. Lewis* King of *Frãce*,
Rex Gal. that his Mother *Blanch* would say somliæ, times vnto him, I had rather (my sonne) see the dead before mine eyes, then euer in mortall sinne, and this her wish and desire

fire

fire was so acceptable vnto God, and so
much force had this her blessing of him,
that it is reported of him; how in all his
life, he neuer committed any mortall
sinne, and who knoweth but the same
petition and desire should worke & produce the like effect in vs.

And which is yet more, we may wel wish
for death, not only to free our selues from
mortall sinnes, but also to eschew veniall,
which we so abound with in this miserable life, and that because it becometh a
seruant of Almighty God, not only to
stand resolued, rather to dy, then commit
a mortall sinne; but euen to loose his life,
rather then to tell an vntruth which is but
a veniall sinne. And whosoeuer should
giue his life for such a cause as this, should **S. Tho.**
dy a Martyr. Now it is most certaine, that **2.2 q.124**
we cānot liue without committing many **a. 5. ad 2.**
veniall sinnes, *septies enim cadet Iustus,* **Prou. 24.**
the Iust doth fall seauen times, that is to **16**
say, very often, and the longer you liue
the oftner shall you fall. Neither do the
seruants of Almighty God, desire to dy to
be deliuered only from veniall sinne, but
euen to see themselues exempt and free,
from their many faults and imperfections,

and

and so numerous tentations and calamities as they experiéce daily, wherfore that holy man said well ; O Lord what do I suffer when being in my prayer thinking on heauenly things, a wholl band of carnall things present themselues before me? Alas what a kind of life is this, where tribulations and miseries are neuer wanting; where all is set with snares, and compassed with enimies ; for when one tribulation or tentation goeth away, another cometh ; yea and during the first conflict also, many others come one after an other vnlooked for, how can a life be loued that hath so many afflictions, and is subiect to so many calamities and miseries? how is it called a life, that begetteth so many deaths and plagues ? We read of a great Saint, that she was vsed to say, that if she might haue her choice of any thing, shee should choose nothing but death ; because by means of it, her soule should be freed from feare of euer doing any thing, which might bring hinderance vnto pure loue? And in this manner, there seemes to be more perfection to desire to be out of this life, for to decline veniall sinnes, faults, and imperfections; then to shune the falling

Tho, de Kempis.

ling

ling into mortall ones, and that, becaufe
one may be moued to defire to be out
of the occafion of committing mortall
finne, more for feare of hell, and out of
felfe loue and intereft, then for the honour
of God, but to be fo inflamed with the
loue of God, as to wifh rather to dy then
commit a veniall finne or fall into faults
and imperfections, fuppofes a great purity of intention and is a point of high
perfection.

But fome one will fay, I defire to liue
vnto the end to make fatisfaction for the
faults and offences, which I haue committed; vnto which I anfwere, that if in
prolonging our life, we did go ftill cancel-
ling our paffed faults, without adding to
them new; It were a good defire, but you
do not only, not difcharge the old, but
continue ftill heaping vp new debts as
long as you remaine in life, wherby the
account which you are to make growes
euery day more heauy on your foule, and
fo your obiection hath no force at all;
S. *Bernard* fayes excellent well: *Cur ergo* Bernar.
tantopore vitam iſtam defideramus, in c.2.med.
qua quanto amplius viuimus, tanto plus
peccamus, quanto eſt vita longior, tanto
culpa

culpa numerosior. Why do we desire this life so much, in which the longer we liue, the more we sinne; & the longer our life is, the more numerous are our faults. And *S. Hierom* writeth, what is the difference do you thinke (saith he) betwixt him who dies yong and old? no more but only this, that the more aged of them, doth beare the burthen of more sinnes out of the world with him then he who dyeth yong, and hath more to answer and giue accompt to God? And so *S. Bernard* in this point doth take a better resolution and hath a saying of himselfe which in him was humility, in vs would be but truth: *Viuere erubesco, quia parum proficio, mori timeo, quia non sum paratus; malo tamen mori, & misericordiæ Dei me committere & commendare, quia benignus & misericors est, quàm de malâ meâ conuersatione alicui scandalum facere,* I am ashamed to liue (saith he) because I make so litle profit; I feare to dy, because I am not prepared, not withstanding I had rather dy, and commit and commend my selfe vnto the mercy of God, seing he is gratious and mercifull, then be the cause of scandalizing others
through

Hier. ep. ad He. liod.

Bern. de interiori domo c. 25.

through my euil conuersation; and this
is an excellent resolution . Master *Auila* M. Auila
said that whosoeuer should find himselfe
but reasonably prepared , ought more to
wish for death, then longer life, by reason
of the great danger in which we liue,
which wholly ceaseth when we come to
dy; *Quid est mors, nisi sepultura vitiorum,* Ambro.
& virtutum suscitatio ? What is death de bono
(saith *S. Ambrose*) but a sepulcher of mortis,
vices, and a resurrection of vertues. c. 4.

All these reasons and motiues to wish
for death are passing good, but that which
is the most eminent in perfection of all, is
that which *S. Paul* the Apostle had , to
see himselfe with Christ, whom he loued
so tēderly; *Desiderium habens dissolui &* Ad Phi-
esse cum Christo, ô blessed Saint what de-lip. 1.23.
sire is this of yours? why do you wish so
much to be loosed from the bōds of flesh
& blood. perhaps to auoid labour? no assuredly, but on the contrary; *Gloriamur in* Ad Rō.
tribulationibus, your glory consists ther-5.3.
in: wherfore then , to decline sinne? neither is this the cause; *Certus sum enim quia*
neque mors, neque vita poterit nos sepa- Ad Rō.
rare à charitate Dei, he was confirmed 8. 38. &
already in grace, and knew he could not 39.
loose

loose it, and therfore in that perticular he had no cause to feare ; In fine what is it that makes you so much desire to dy? that I may see my selfe with Iesus Christ, and this purely out of loue to him . *Quia amore langueo*, he languished with loue, he sighed after his beloued, and all delay seemed long ; vntill he might enioy his wished presence.

Cât. 2.5.

S. *Bonauenture* of three degrees which he makes of the loue of God placeth this the last and highest . The first is to loue God aboue all other things, and so to loue the things of the world , as not to commit any mortall sinne for them , or transgresse any of the Commandements of God,& this is that which our Sauiour said to that young man of the Ghospell: *Si vis ad vitam ingredi, serua mandata* if you desire to enter into eternall life, keepe the Commandements , and this is necessary for ail . The second degree of loue and Charity is , not only to content our selues with keeping the Commandements of God, but to adde vnto them the counsells, which is proper vnto Religious men , who procure to do not only that which is good , but also that which

Bonau. tra. 6. re- lig. c.11. 12.& 13.

Math. 19 17.

is

is better and of more perfection, conformable to this paſſage of *S. Paul* , *vt pro-*
betis quæ ſit voluntas Dei bona, & bene- **Ad R̄.**
*placens, & perfecta,*that you may proue **c. 2.**
what is the good,and acceptable,& perfect wil of God.The third degree of Charity ſaith *S. Sonauenture* is, *tanto affectu*
ad Deum æstuare: quod ſine ipſo quaſi vi-
uere non poſſis, to burne with ſuch an ardent affection and loue to God , as in a
manner not to be able to liue without him.
And hence it is , that a ſoule deſireth ſo
much to be free and looſed from the priſon of its body , to be with Ieſus Chriſt;
wiſhing its baniſhmẽt at an end,& the wal
of its body which ſeperats it from the
ſight of God , to be diſſolued and crum-
bled into duſt. Such as theſe, ſaith he,had
need of patience for to liue , life being ſo
diſtaſtfull to them , and death the obiect
of their inflamed deſire.

We read in the life of our B. F. *S. Ig-* **Lib. 5.c.**
natius , that he deſired moſt ardently to **1 vitȩ S.**
be deliuered from the Iaile and priſon of **P.Ignatij**
his body,and that his ſoule had ſo great a
longing to ſee Almighty God , as he neuer thought of death , but his eyes were
ouerflowne with teares out of pure gladnes

nes and delicious ioy ; But it was moreouer obſerued that he was not thus inflamed with the deſire of that ſoueraigne
good, for his owne ſake, that he might go
to reſt, and the ioy of that all beatifying
viſion, but much more that he might behould that moſt bleſſed glory, of the moſt
ſacred humanity of our Lord, whom he
did loue ſo deſire and tenderly. Like as
men here on earth do vſually reioyce to
ſee ſome friend whom they deerly eſteem
& loue moſt cordially, aduanced to ſome
eminent dignity: ſo did our B. Father deſire to ſee himſelfe with Ieſus Chriſt, purely for loue of him, without once thinking on his owne intereſt and felicity,
which is the higheſt and the moſt perfect
act of Charity, which we can exerciſe.

In this manner the memory of death
will not only not be bitter to vs, but
it will bring vs great content and delight;
do but ouerpaſſe it with your thought, &
conſider how within few dayes you ſhall
be in heauen, enioying that, which neither eye hath ſeene, nor eare hath heard,
nor which could euer ſinke into the
thought of man, and ſo all ſhall be conuerted into ioy and gladnes. Who would
not

not reioyce when the terme of baniſhment were out , and all his paine and labour at an end ? who would not reioyce
to arriue vnto that finall end for which he
was created ? who would not reioyce in
going to take poſſeſſion of his inheritance
and ſuch an inheritance, and to the fruition of all this happines the clew of death
doth lead vs ? *Cùm dederit dilectis ſuis*
ſomnum ecce hæreditas Domini, we can- Pſal.126.
not come to the poſſeſſion of our eternall 3.
good, but through the port of death;and
therfore the wiſeman ſays that the Iuſt
man hopes in his death ; *Sperat Iuſtus in*
*morte ſua,*it being the ſcale and ladder by Prou.14.
which he climes to heauen ; and it is alſo 32.
the comfort of our baniſhment ; *Pſallam* Pſa. 100.
& intelligam in via immaculata quando 2.
venies ad me, which words S. *Auguſtin*
doth thus explicate, my thought and my Aug.tra.
deſire ô Lord is to conſerue my ſelfe vn- 9. ſuper
blemiſhed all my life , and to make this epiſt.10.
care my ſong; of which the burthen ſhall
be, Lord when ſhall this baniſhment haue
end, when ſhall I be recalled out of this
exile into my loued Country,Lord,when
will you come to me ? when ſhall I go to
you ? *Quando veniam & apparebo ante* Pſa.41.3.
faciem

faciem Dei ? O Lord when fhall I haue
my fill of feing you ? O how that houre
lingers? Oh what ioy, what rauifhing ioy
fhall then ouerflow my heart, when they
fhall tell me, that this houre is come ; *La-*
tatus fum in his quæ dicta funt mihi , in
domum Domini ibimus : Stantes erant
pedes noftri in atrij tuis Hierufalem, I already imagine my felfe, to be ftanding a-
mong the Quiers of Angels and bleffed
foules, enioying you ô Lord for euer
more, Amen.

Pfal.121.
1. & 2.

THE XXI. CHAPTER.

Wherin that which hath been faid is cō-
firmed with fome examples.

Simon
Meta-
phraftes

S Imon *Metaphraftes* in the life of *S.*
Iohn the *Almner* Archbifhop of *Ale-*
xandria doth recount, how a certaine
rich man, had a fonne whom he loued
dearly ; who to obteine of God, for to
conferue him in life and health, befee-
ched this holy Saint to pray for him, and
withall gaue in a great fumme of gold to
beftow in Almes vpon the poore for that
intention: the Saint did as he defired, and

at the end of thirty dayes, the sonne of
the rich man dyed; hereupon the Father
afflicted himselfe aboue measure, firmely
beleeuing that the prayers of the Saint,
and the Almes which he had giuen, had
nothing auailed him. The holy Patriarch
vnderstanding of his griefe, prayed for
him, and desired of God, that he would
comfort him: God heard his prayer, and
one night sent an Angell in a humane
shape vnto the said rich man, who told
him, that he must know how Almighty
God heard the prayer which was made
for his sonnes life, and that through the
efficacy therof, his sone was now liuing &
a Saint in heauen, & that it was necessary
for his saluation to leaue the world so
timely as he did; since if he had liued, he
would haue proued a wicked man, and
haue lost all partage in the ioyes of heauen; he added moreouer, that he must
belieue, that there is nothing which happens in this life, which is not so ordained
by the particular prouidence of God, although the causes of his iudgments are
vnknowne to men, & that therfore men
were not to suffer themselues to be tranf-
ported with inordinat griefe, but receaue

P   all

all that comes, and is sent vnto them by God, with a peaceable heart, and with an equall mind: with this heauenly instruction, the Father of the diseased youth, remained much comforted, and encouraged in the seruice of God.

Hist The.
bea li. 2.
c. 10. In the *Theban* History is recorded a singular fauour which S. *Maurice* Captaine of the *Theban* band, did to a certaine Lady much deuoted to him. This Lady hauing but one sonne, vnto the end that together with his yeares, he might grow vp in good and vertuous manners, did when his childhood had scarcely resigned to youth, dedicate his riper yeares vnto the Monastery of S. *Maurice*, vnder the care and discipline of those Religious men, (as it was the custome of those holy times) the Fathers of S. *Maurus*, *Placidus* and other Romane gentlemen, in the age of S. *Benedict* hauing done the like, as also in later times *Theodora* mother of S. *Thomas of Aquin*, and the Counts of *Aquin* his brothers, disposed in like manner of him in the Monastery of *Mont Caßinus*.) This Ladies sonne was brought vp in the said Monastery, both in learnig, vertue and monasticall discipline:

In

In all which he profited wonderously;& was already well forward in musicke, in so much as he sung in the Quire with the other Religious, for sweenes of voice inferior vnto none , when a light feauer tooke him out of this life . The wofull Mother, at the first newes growne but to sadly acquainted with griefe came to the Church, and accompanied her sonnes funerall to the graue sheding infinite teares, although they all sufficed not to wash away the sorrow of his losse which shee freshly euery day renewed with lamenting ouer his Tombe, in most pittious manner, and much more was her griefe increased; when in the time of the diuine office shee heard the rest of the Religious sing, and missed her sonnes voyce among them, which vsed to be the gratefullest of them all . This Lady perseuering thus in her sad obsequies not only by day in the Church, but in her owne house by night, without admitting or taking any rest at all;once ouercome by wearines fell a sleep when the holy Captaine *S. Maurice* appeared vnto her, and said : woman why dost thou weepe so incessantly the death of thy sonne, admitting no measure in thy

teares,

teares, no côfort to thy heart. Vnto whom shee answered: all the dayes of my life will not suffice vnto my boundlesse sorrow, & therfore whilst I liue I will neuer cease to lament my only sonne, neither shall these eyes of mine, vphold from weeping till death doth close them vp, and my desolate soule doth leaue to dwell in a body so dolorous; the Saint answered her, woeman I say vnto you, do not mourne, nor deplore your departed sonne as dead, for dead he is not, but liuing, and liuing with vs in heauen, enioying eternall life; and that thou mayest know the truth of all I say, rise presently, and go to Mattins, and there thou shalt heare the voyce of thy deceased sonne, singing the diuine office among the other Religious men; neither shalt thou only enioy the content-ment of it this day at Mattins, but at all other times, when thou shalt be present there, at the Diuine office; leaue of weep-ing then, and impose an end vnto thy teares, for thou hast more cause of glad-nes then of griefe. The Lady awaking, expected with much longing the houre of Mattins to be assured of the truth of her vision, which yet but faintly she gaue

credit

credit to: the houre at laſt being come, and ſhe no ſooner entred into the Church, but ſhee plainly diſtinguiſhed the moſt ſweet voyce of her happy ſonne , whilſt the Antiphon was intoned, and therewith being rendred aſſured of his glory in heauen , ſhee baniſhed all ſorrow from her, & made no end of giuing thanks to God, for comforting her with hearing euery day his Angelicall voyce , in the harmonious muſicke, and diuine ſeruice of thoſe Religious men, and enriching her, with a fauour and grace ſo extraordinary and great.

A certaine Author writeth, how a knight once going a hunting , rouſed a wild beaſt, in the purſuit wherof, he was caſt behind with only one ſeruant with him, al the other being eager in following of the chaſe, notwithſtanding he ſpurred on a pace , and hauing loſt the cry of the hounds ſtrayed from the reſt ſo farre, as he came '(out of all way) vnto a certaine groue, where he heard the voyce of a man ſinging wōdrous ſweetly: the knight meruailing to heare any ſuch voyce in thoſe deſert places , knowing that it could be none of his followers , and no leſſe cer-

taine

taine that it was none of that Country
people. Hauing a great defire to know
whofe voyce it was, entred in farther into
the thicket, & difcouered on the fodaine,
a leporous perfon, of a horrible afpect,
whofe flefh was fo rotte, as it eafely drop-
ed of, from euery limme of him. The
knight much amazed at fuch a fpectacle,
confirmed his ftartled heart and drew
nigh, and being come vnto him, in falu-
ting him courtioufly he demanded of
him, whether it were he who had fung
fo fweetly or no, the lazer anfwered, fir
it was my felfe, and that voyce which
feemed fo fweet vnto you was mine, how
is it poffible anfwered the knight, for you
to be fo cheerfull, in fuch horrible torments, the poore men replyed, fir you
muft vnderftand that betwixt God and
me there is no other partition, then this
mud-wall of my body which you fee, and
this being once away, I fhall enioy the
cleere vifion of his diuine Maiefty. Seing
this therfore euery day falling fo faft a-
way, it maketh me reioyce and fing with
a wonderfull gladnes of heart, awaiting
ftill an entire difolution of it, vntill when
I cannot depart to enioy Almighty God,
                                                         the

the true spring and fountaine of life; from
whence flow forth those streames which
neuer dry vp nor faile.

S. *Cyprian* writes of a certaine Bishop, S Cypt.
who being in the extremity of his sicknes, lib. de
and much fearing death which he saw be- mortal.
fore his eyes, humbly beseeched our Sauiour to prolong his life, when presently
there appeared vnto him an Angell in the
shape of a beautifull young man, of comly
feature, excellent personage, a shining as-
pect, and goodly stature, who with a
vovce mixed with grauity and security
said vnto him: *pati timeris, exire non vul-
tis, quid faciam vobis?* you feare tu suffer, you are loath for to depart, what shall
I do with you? giuing him to vnderstand
that his repugnance do depart this life
was no waies gratefull vnto God; and *S.
Cyprian* adds, that the Angell spake these
words vnto him vnto the end, that he
should recount them againe, and teach
them vnto others, when he should be in
the agony of death.

Simon *Metaphrastes* relates, and *Su-* Surius
rius frō him, how the holy Abbot *Theo-* to.1.fol.
dosius, knowing how profitable the me- 237.
mory of death was vnto man, and desi-

rous through the consideration therof to
giue his disciples occasion of farther progresse in deuotion, caused a sepulcher to
be opened, and standing about it with his
disciples, he said, behould the graue open,
but who is there of you, who wil haue the
honour to be first buryed in it? and haue
his funerall celebrated by vs? One of his
disciples, named *Basilius*, a Priest, and a
very vertuous man, being well prepared
to dy, did readily offer himselfe, and falling on his knees said with great cheerfulnesse: Father giue me your benedictiō,
for I (if it may please you) will be the first
man for whom you shall sing the office of
Requiem: it was his desire, and the Saint
did grant it him. Then the holy Abbot
Theodosius commanded that they should
vse all the ceremonies which vse to be at
the funeralls of the dead, whilst he was
yet aliue, the first, the third, and ninth
dayes office, as also an other seruice for
the Quarantain, when (behould the wonder) at the end of these offices and the seruice of fourty dayes, *Basilius* being whole
and sound, without feauer, head ake, or
any other paine, as if he had falne into a
sweet and pleasant sleep, passed out of
this

this life, vnto Almighty God to receaue
of him the reward of his vertue, and that
promptitude & cheerfulnesse, with which
he had wished to see himselfe with our
Sauiour Iesus Christ. And that we might
see how gratfull vnto God, the readines
and cheerfulnes was of this religious man,
for to depart this life, this his death was
seconded by an other Miracle; For according to *Simō Metaphrastes*, for the space
of fourty dayes more after his death, the
Abbot *Theodosius* beheld him cōming vnto vespera's, & singing in the Quire with
the rest of his disciples, howbeit that none
els saw him, or heard him sing, excepting
one *Ætius*, a man of eminent vertue a-
boue the rest, who heard him sing, but
could not see him; This *Ætius* went to
Theodosius and demanded of him whither he did not heare their brother *Basilius* sing in the Quire among the rest?
yes answered the Abbot, I both heare and
see him, and if you please, will likewise
procure that you may see him too, and so
the next day being both together in the
Quire with the other Religious, during
the diuine office *Theodosius* saw *Basilius*
as he vsed to do, in the Quire singing with
the

the reſt, and he pointed him out with his
finger, to ſhew him *Ætius*, both making
their prayer together, and beſeeching of
God to open the others eyes, that he
might ſee him to, and *Ætius* hauing
perceaued him, and knowing him to be
the ſame, ranne with great feruour to imbrace him, but he could not, for the other
diſappeared, ſaying as he went, ſo as to be
heard of euery one. Farwell my deare Fathers and brothers farwell, for heare after
you ſhall ſee me (in this world) no more.
In the Chronicles of the Order of *S. Au-*
guſtin, it is related how *S. Colomban* the
Younger, Nephew and diſciple of *S. Co-*
lomban the Abbot, being afflicted with a
violent feauer, and drawing towards his
end, deſiring out of the aſſurance of his
hope to dy; There appeared vnto him, a
yong mã ſhining with glorious light, who
ſaid vnto him, vnderſtand that the prayers
and teares which thy Abbot ſheds for the
recouery of thy health, doth hinder thy
deliuery out of this mortall priſon, wher-
vpon the Saint ſweetly made his moane
and complaint vnto his Abbot ſaying in
woefull manner. Why do you conſtraine
me to liue in ſuch a miſerable life as this?
and

Chron.
ord. S.
Aug. cé.
infra 3.

and hinder me from passing to an eternall one? after which time the Abbot forbare to weape, and prayed no more for him, and so the Religious being assembled all together, the B. Saint prouided of all the requisit Sacraments, after he had tenderly embraced them all, went sweetly to our Lord.

S.*Ambrose* saith how the Inhabitants of *Thrace*, do vse to lament when Children are borne into the world, and make great feast and ioy, when as they dy; and they deplore their births and solemnize their funeralls for this reason saith S.*Ambrose* (and it is an excellent one) because their case deserueth to be pittyed & lamented, who come into this miserable world; so full of woe and camality; and on the contrary, they haue good reason to reioyce for them, when they were freed from this banishment, and deliuered from so many miseries and afflictions. Now if they who were Heathens, and were iguorant of that glory which we hope for, could do thus much; with how much more reason ought we to be glad to dy; we I say who haue the light of faith, and knowledge of those felicities, which they

Amb. de fide re-sur.

go

go to enioy who dy in our Lord? & therfore the wiseman said with farre more
reason , that the day of death , is better
then the day of our Natiuity , *Melior est*
dies mortis, die Natinitatis.

S. Hierom saith that our Sauiour when
he would depart out of this world vnto
his heauenly Father, said to his disciples,
who were sorrowfull for it; *Si diligeritis*
me , gauderetis vtique, quia vado ad pa-
trem, you know not what you do , for if
you loued me , you would certainly reioyce , because I am going to my Father,
and on the contrary, when he was about
to raise *Lazarus* from death againe , he
wept; he wept not, saith *S. Hierom,* because he was dead, seing he was presently
to be reuiued againe, but he wept, because
he was to returne againe vnto this disaste-
rous life, he wept because one whom he
so dearely loued, was to haue his part a-
gaine , of the woes of this miserable banishment.

Eccl. 7. 1.

Hier. ep.
ad Ther.

Ioan. 11.
35.

THE

THE XXII. CHAPTER.

*Of the conformity which we are to haue
with the will of God, in all afflictions
and calamities in generall which he
sends vnto vs.*

WE are not only to conforme **our**
selues with the will of God, **in**
those afflictions and particular accidents,
which do happé vnto vs, but also in those
generall calamities and desolations, which
are occasioned by famine, warre, sicknes,
death, plagues, and other the like which
God sends vnto his Church. To compre-
héd this the better, we must suppose that,
although on the one side, we resent the
miseries and afflictions, and sorrow for our
neighbours misfortunes, and harmes, **as** it
is reasonable we should: neuertheles on
the other side considering them as they
are the will of God, and so ordained **by**
his iust iudgments, to be the seeds of that
good and profit, which he knoweth resulting to his greater glory, in these I say,
we may cóforme ourselues vnto his **holy**
will, in like manner as we see a Iudge có-
　　　　　　　　　　　　　　demne

demne a malefactor vnto death, who although on the one side, he is not without feeling and sorrow, that the man must dy, out of that naturall compassion which he beareth him, or perhaps because he is acquainted with him: neuertheles he omits not to pronounce sentence of death against him, and comaunds that it be executed, because it is so necessary and conuenient for the good and welfare of the Commonwealth; and although it be true that God doth not oblige vs to conforme our selues in all these things vnto his will, in such manner as positiuely to desire and loue them, neither requireth any more of vs, then to suffer them with patience, without contradicting or resisting his diuine Iustice, or murmuring against the decrees therof; notwithstanding the diuine and holy Saints do say, that it should be a worke of farre more merit & perfection, and a resignation more entire and compleate, for a man not only to accept and endure these things patiently, but also to loue and desire them, for as much as they are effects of the good pleasure, and will of God, so ordeined by his diuine Iustice, and conferring vnto his greater glory; Imitating

S. Bona.
sent. d.
48. q. 2.
& alij.

mitating therin the blessed Saints in heauen, who conforme themselues in all accidents vnto the will of God, as *S. Thomas* and *S. Anselmus* declare by this comparison, learning vs that in heauen our will and the will of God, shall in as perfect manner agree, as the two eyes of a body, one of which cannot looke on any thing, but the other likewise fixeth its sight vpon it; whence it is, that although the eyes which see the thing, be two; notwithstanding the thing which is seene doth seem no more then one. Euen so the Saints in heauen accommodat themselues vnto the will of God in euery thing, as seing cleerly in all things the decrees of his Iustice and the end of his greater glory to which they are all directed, so also would it be a great perfection in vs, to imitate in this particular the B. Saints in heauen, by desiring that the will of God be done on earth, as it is in heauen. To will that which God Almighty wills, for the same end and reason for which he wills it, cannot choose but be precisely good.

S. Tho.
2.2.q.19.
ar.10.ad
1.
Ansel.|1.
similitu.
c. 63.

Possidonius reports of *S. Augustin* in his life, that he during the siege of the

August.

Citty

Citty of *Bonna* where he made his residence being besieged , seing so great desolation & slaughter which the *Vandals* made, comforted himselfe, with this sentence of the wiseman : *Non erit magnus magnum putans, quæd cadunt ligna & lapides, & moriuntur mortales,* he shall neuer be great, who accounts it a great wonder, to see wood and stones fall, and mortalls dy ; Now we with greater reason may comfort our selues, in considering all these things proceeding from the hand of God , and how euer the cause , why he sends these miseries and calamities be vnknowne vnto vs, yet it is not possible but they should be iust. The Iudgmēts of God are profound, and a bottomles abisse , as the Prophet saith : *iudicia tua abyssus multa* , neither are we with our shallow and scanty vnderstandings to vndertake to sound or diue into them, which would be great presumption in vs: *quis enim cognouit sensum Domini? aut quis consiliarius eius fuit?* who hath known the meaning of God, or who hath been his counsailer? It belongs only to vs , to receaue them with humility, and to belieue, that nothing either can or doth proceed, from

Psal. 3. 57

Ad Rō. 11. 34. & Isa. 40. 30.

a know-

a knowledge ſo infinit, which is not wiſe-
ly and holily deſigned, and ſo deſigned, as
to haue for its end our greater good and
profit . On this foundation we are to
ground our ſelues ſurely confiding in that
infinit goodnes and mercy of God , that
he would ſend vs nothing, neither permit
the like calamities and aduerſities , vnles
they were tending to a greater good. God
takes this way for to lead many to heauen, who otherwiſe would go aſtray and
vtterly be loſt. How many are there who
by means of theſe afflictions conuert the-
ſelues with their whole hearts to God, and
dying with true repentance for their ſinnes are ſaued , who otherwiſe had been
damned perpetually ? and ſo that which
appeares a ſcourge and puniſhmēt, is a ſingular benefit, and ineſtimable mercy.

In the ſecond booke of the *Macha-
bees* , the Author after he had recounted
that horrible and cruell perſecution , of
impious King *Antiochus*, the abundance
of blood he ſhed, which both old men
and children ; Matrons and young Virgins vaines contributed , the pillage and
profaning of the Temple , with the abo-
minations committed there by his com-

Q   mande-

mandement, concludeth in these words:

2. Mach. 32. *Obsecro autem eos qui hūc librum lecturi sunt, ne abhorrescant propter aduersos casus, sed reputent ea quæ, acciderunt non ad interitum, sed ad correptionem esse generis nostri,* but I beseech those who are to read this booke, that they abhorre not for the aduersities but that they account those things which haue happened, not to be for the destruction but for the chastising of our stocke, by the permission and disposure of Almighty God.

Greg. li. 2. mor. c. 32. S. *Gregory* saith vnto this purpose excellent well, the horseleech draweth out and sucketh the bloud of the sicke, and that which it pretends it to glut it selfe with it, and if it could, to draw the vaines of the sicke person dry ; but the intention of the Phisitian is, to haue them sucke out all the corrupted blood, and to restore the sicke vnto his health againe : the like intention hath Almighty God, in sending vs aduersities and tribulations, and as he should do indiscreetly, who would not suffer his corrupted blood, to be drawne out of him, for hauing more regard, vnto that which the Horsleech pretends, then to the intētion of the Phisitian, so in what

so

fo euer aduerfity, whether it come vnto
vs by the procurement of men, or els by
means of any other creature, we are not
fo much to haue regard to it, as vnto God
our foueraigne Phifitian, feing they all
ferue him in the nature of Horfleeches, to
draw out our corrupted blood from vs,
and to reftore vs vnto perfect health. And
confequently we are to belieue and know
that he fends them all vnto vs, for our
greater vtility and good, and although he
had no other end in them, but only as
childrë to correct vs in this life, that there
might remaine no punifhment in the o-
ther for vs to vndergoe, it were no fmall
fauour which he fhould do vs in it.

It is reported of *S. Katherine* of *Sienna*, In vita S.
Cathar.
Senen.
p. 2. c. 4.
that as fhee once was much troubled, becaufe an other had giuen falfe teftimony
againft her, in a matter which concerned
her honour, our Sauiour Chrift appeared
vnto her, houlding in his right hand a
golden crowne adorned with pretious
ftones, and in his left, a crowne of thornes
and faid: my beloued daughter, know that
thou muft be crowned with either of thefe
crownes, at feuerall times, therfore choofe
for the prefent, that which you like the
best,

beſt, either in this life to be crowned with this thorny crowne, and haue this other pretious one reſerued vntill the other life for you, which neuer ſhall haue end, or now to haue this riche and gorgious crowne, and haue the wreath of thornes kept for you till you dy? Vnto whom the holy Virgin anſwered, deere Lord I haue long time ſince forſaken mine owne will, to embrace yours, and therfore now it becomes not me to chooſe, but neuer-theles if you would haue me to reſolue I am minded as long as I ſhall remaine in life, to conforme my ſelfe vnto your ſacred paſſion, and will embrace all tribu-lations, for your deere loue and my con-ſolation, and hauing ſaid this ſhee tooke the crowne of thornes with her owne hands, out of his, and with all her might cruſhed it vpon her head, ſo forcibly, that the thornes pearced her in euery part therof, in ſuch manner, as for a long time after, the violent paine of her head, wit-neſſed the force with which they were driuen in.

THE

THE XXIII. CHAPTER.

Of a certaine means which will helpe vs much to receaue and support with great resignation, all those aduersities which our Lord shall send vs, as well in particular as in generall , which is the knowledge and feeling of our sinnes.

IT is a common doctrine of the holy Fathers, that God for the most part, doth send vs afflictions and chastisements in generall, for the sinnes which we haue committed; & it is the frequent language of the holy scripture: *Induxisti omnia hæc* **Dan.** 9. *propter peccata nostra, peccauimus enim* 28. & se- *& inique egimus, & præcepta tua non au-* quentib. *diuimus, omnia ergo quæ induxisti super nos, & vniuersa quæ fecisti nobis, in vero iudicio fecisti,* thou hast brought in all these things for our sinnes, for we haue sinned and done vniustly, and thy precepts we haue not heard; all things therfore that thou hast brought in vpon vs, and all things that thou hast done to vs, thou hast done with true Iudgment. And so we see that God punished his people

Q 3   and

and deliuered them ouer vnto the hands
of their enemies, when they had offended him & deliuered them againe, when
they did pennance and repented them of
their sinnes, returning vnto him againe
and for this cause *Achior* Captaine and
Prince of the sonnes of *Amon*, hauing
declared to *Holofernes* what a particular care God had of the children of *Israel*,
& how he sheltred them vnder the wings
of his protection, as also how he chasti-
zed them, when they departed from his
obedience, counsailed him before he en-
terprized any thing against them, to informe himselfe, whither for the present
they had offended God, seing then he
might assure himselfe of the victory, els
he had better leaue of his enterprize, for
he could not preuaile against them, nor
come of with lesse then shame and confusion, seing that God did fight for his
people, whom no man was so mighty to
withstand. And the holy Doctors do particularly gather this same, from those
words of our Sauiour in the Euāgell vnto
him who had laine eight & thirty yeares
by the *Probaticke Poole* to be cured of
his infirmity; *Ecce sanus factus es*, *iam*

noli

Iudith.
c. 5.

Ioan. 5.
14.

noli peccare, ne deterius tibi aliquid con-
tingat ; Behould (said our Sauiour after
he had cured him) thou art made whole,
herafter sinne no more, leaft some worse
thing happen vnto thee, and in conformity to this, it will be a good means, and
much helping vs in all calamities and afflictions aswell generall as particular vnto
the resigning our selues vnto the will of
God; as also to support them all with patience, to enter presently into our selues,
and consider our sinnes, and withall how
iustly we haue merited this chastisement,
because in this manner we shall receaue
in good part, and iudge it lesse then we
deserue in regard of the enormity of our
sinnes, what affliction so euer shall arriue
vnto vs.

S. *Bernard* and S. *Gregory* handle this Ber. ser.
point excellent well S. *Bernard* saith: de alti &
Culpa vero ipsa si intus sentitur perfectè, Bass.cor-
vtique exterior pana, parum aut nihil sen- dis.
titur , if the fault it selfe, be but so felt
within as it ought to be, we shall haue but
little or no feeling of the paine without; 2. Reg.
Sicut Sanctus Dauid non sensit iniuriam 16. 1.
serui conniciantis, memor fily persequen-
tis, like as the royall *Prophet Dauid,* did
Q 4   not

not feele the iniury of his seruant reuiling
him, whilst he remembred that his owne

2. Reg.
16. 1.

sonne was in Armes against him. *Ecce filius meus qui egressus est de vtero meo
quærit animam meam, quanto magis nunc
filius Iemini?* behould my sonne who
came out of my wombe seeketh my life,
how much more the sonne of Iemini?
if mine owne sonne persecute me, what
wonder is it if a straunger do the like. *S.*

Greg. li.
1. mor
c. 8
Iob.11.6

Gregory on these words of *Iob, & intel-
ligens quod multo minora exigaris ab eo
quàm mereretur iniquitas tua*, and thou
mightest vnderstand that thou art exa-
cted much lesser things of him, then thine
iniquity deserues, explicates it with an exquisit comparison, like as (saith he) the
sick man who feeles his impostume inflamed and swolne and the flesh about it to
be rotten and dead, is glad to put himselfe into the surgeans hands, and lets
him lance and cut him as he pleases, and
the more grieuous and corrupted the sore
is, the more couragiously he indures the
launcing and searing iron : so when one
hath a true feeling of the sore and sicknesse which sinne causeth in his soule, he
receaues with a good will the brand of
tribu-

tribulation, of mortification and his owne
difesteeme which God applyeth vnto this
fore to draw the filthy matter and cor-
ruption out of it, *dolor quippe flagelli tem-
peratur*, *cum culpa cognoscitur*, for the
paine of the scourge is allayed, when the
fault is acknowledged: and if you receaue
not willingly that mortification and aduersity which God presents you with, it is
a signe that you are ignorant of the sicknes of your faults, you do not feele cor-
ruption eating vpon you, and therfore
you cannot endure the lance, nor searing
yron.

The holy Saints and seruants of God
Almighty, did not only willingly receaue
these chastisements, but they desired them
with great instance and begged them ardently at the hands of God; holy *Iob* said;
Quis det vt veniat petitio mea, *& qui capit*, *ipse me conterat*, *soluat mauum suam*,
& suecidat me, *& hac mihi sit consola-
tio*, *vt affligens me dolore non parcat?* who
shall grant that my petition may come, &
that he who hath begun, should consume
me, and the same would loose his hand, &
cut me of, and this might be my comfort,
that afflicting me with sorrow he spare

not

Pfa.25.2. not, and the Prophet Dauid . *Proba me*
Pfal. 37. *Domine & tenta me*, and *quoniam ego in*
18.
Pfal.118. *flagella paratus sum*, & *bonum mihi quia*
71.   *humiliasti me*, proue me ô Lord & tempt
me, becaufe I am ready for fcourges, it is
good for me that thou haft humbled me.
The feruants of God Almighty (faith *S.*
Greg. li. *Gregory*) did fo much defire that his Di-
1.mor.c. uine Maieftie fhould chaftife them , and
7. & 8. humble them in this life,as they euen proceeded to fadnes , when on the one fide
they caft their eyes vpon their faults; and
on the other, they faw that God did not
throughly punifh them,becaufe they imagined and feared , leaft God fhould de-
ferre their punifhment vntill the other
life,where with all rigour it fhould be executed, and this is that which *Iob* adds,&
hæc mihi fit côfolatio vt affligës me dolore
non parcat,& this is my côfort, that affli-
&ting me with forrow he fpares not which
is as much as to fay , God vfeth to fpare
fome in this life,that he may punifh them
for euer in the next ; but I defire not to
be fpared in this life with them, vnto the
end that in the next he may pardon me
for euer; Let God chaftife me here like a
louing Father , that he may not punifh
                                    me

me eternally afterward, like a rigorous
Iudge, for my part I will not murmure
or complaine of the lashes of his whipp,
nec contradicam sermonibus Sancti, but Iob.6.10
it shall comfort me the more, this is also
that which *S. Augustin* saith,*hic vre hic* Augusti.
*seca, hic nihil mihi parcas,vt in æternum
parcas,* here burne me,here lance me,here
spare me in nothing,that thou maist spare
me ô Lord eternally.

It is no other then our blindnes and ig-
norance, which make corporall afflictiôs
seem so heauy to vse,and spiritual so light,
we ought not to be so sensible of aduersity as of sinne : if we did but know or
could consider the grieuousnesse of our
faults,we should esteeme all chastisements
to little.and say with holy *Iob:peccaui, &* Iob. 33.
verè deliqui, & vt eram dignus non re- 27.
cepi, words which we ought to carry im-
printed in our hearts, and often to vtter
with our mouthes, I haue sinned ô Lord
and I haue truly done amisse , offending
your diuine Maiesty & you haue not cha-
stised me according to my deserts, all
that we can possibly suffer in this life, is
nothing in comparison of that punishmêt
which one sinne deserueth. *Intelligeres* Iob:11.
                                quod

quod multò mitiora exigaris ab eo, '*quàm meretur iniquitas tua.* he who should cōsider that he hath offended the Maiestie of Almighty God, and deserued to burne eternally in the flames of hell, what paine would he refuse, what dishonour, what iniury, what contempt should he not willingly vndergoe? for recompence & satisfaction of those offences, which he hath committed against the Maiesty of Almighty God. *Si forte respiciat Dominus* *afflictionem meam, & reddat mihi Do-* *minus bonum pro maledictione hac ho-* *dierna,* said *Dauid* when Semei curst and reuiled him, hinder him not from cursing me, let him load me with reproaches, and giue me my fill of iniuries and scorne, for it may be that God will take it for sufficient payment, and exact no more punishment of me hereafter for my sinnes, but haue mercy on me, which is all I can desire, and all my happines. In the like manner are we to receaue willingly all confusion, shame and aduersities whatsoeuer, saying. On Gods name let them come, for it may be that God will be so pleased to accept of them, for payment and satisfaction for our sinnes, and so they

may

2. Reg.
16. 12.

may turne to our felicity, if we would but employ that time, which we lauish in cō-plaining and bemoaning our afflictions, in entring into our selues, we should please God more, and find more comfort and redresse.

The holy Saints made so profitable vse of this remedy in the like occasions, and were so frequent in it, that (as we read of some of them, as *S. Katherin* of *Siena* and some others) they attributed all the calamities and afflictions which God sent vnto his Church, vnto their sinnes and im-perfections, saying, this warre is hapned throug my procurement, my sinnes are the cause of this plague and affliction, which God doth send, they beeleeuing verely that their sinnes in particular did merit this and more. And we may adde in confirmation of this; that God often-times doth punish a whole nation for the sinne of one particular person; As when for the sinne of *Dauid*, he visited the whole people of *Israel* with pestilence, 2. Reg. there dying (according to the holy Scrip-24. 25., ture) seauēty thousand men in three daies space: But you will say perhaps, he was their King, and that their punishments, do

passe

passe on the people accounts with greater reason I will instance you an other for
the sinne of *Acan* who then was but a
priuat man , and tooke but only a trifle
for himself out of the anathemade goods
of *Ierico*, God punished all the people in
such sort as three thousand of the choy-
sest souldiers in the campe, not being able
to withstand their enemy, were enforced
to saue themselues by flight ; God doth
not only punish others for the offences of
the principall amongst them , but euen
the fault of any priuat man, is enough to
bring a generall plague vpon them, and in
this sense the Saints explicate that passage
which the holy Scripture doth repeat so
often that God will punish the sinnes of
the parents on their children , vnto the
third and fourth generation , the fault of
the Father (say they) passes not vnto his
children , neither hath the childrens any
reference to him. *Anima quæ peccauerit
ipsa morietur , filius non portabit iniquitatem patris , & pater non portabit iniquitatem filij*, but for as much as concerneth the punishment, God vsually chasti-
zeth the one for the others sinnes, and so
perhaps for my sinnes or yours, God may
                                   punish

*Ios.7.45.
& 11.*

*Exod.20.
5.& c.34
7. num.
14.18.*

*Ezec.18.
20.*

punish a whole house, a whole Religion.

Now let vs set before our eyes on the one side this consideration, and on the other the good pleasure of Almighty God, and in this manner we shall with ease come to conforme our selues vnto his will, in all the afflictions, which he sends to vs, and say with *Hely* the Priest: *Dominus est, quod bonum est, in oculis suis faciat,* he is Master, he is Lord, and supreme gouernour of euery thing, let all be performed and done as he shall please, and as he shall ordeine. And with the Prophet *Dauid: Obmutui & non aperui os meum quoniam tu fecisti,* ô Lord I haue not complained, of those misfortunes which you haue sent me; but haue been silent, as if I could not speake, and borne all with great patience and conformity, seing ô Lord they are proceeding from you. This ought to be our consolation in euery thing, God wills it, God doth it, God commaunds it, God sends it, in Gods name let it come, whatsoeuer it be. We should need no other reason, to perswade vs to take all things in the best part. On these words of the eight and twentith psalme. *Et dilectus quemadmodum filius vni-*

1. Reg. 3. 18.

Psal. 38. 10.

Psal. 28. 6.

vnicornium, the holy Fathers, obserue
that God cōpares himself vnto an vnicorne, becaufe the vnicorne hath his horne
belowe his eyes, & can fee to take his aime
to ftricke, wheras the Bull hath his aboue
his eyes, & goares with them at randome,
moreouer the vnicorne cures with the
fame horne, with which it did the hurt,
& fo God giues vs remedy with the fame
thing, by which he gaue the wound.

This conformity and humble fubmiffion vnder the rodd of our punifhment, is
a thing fo gratfull vnto God, that oftentimes it doth alone fuffice, to appeafe his
anger, and remit our fault without punifhment ; In the Ecclefiafticall Hiftory
we read how *Attila* King of the Hunnes,
who wafted fo many prouinces & ftiled
himfelfe *Metus orbis & flagellum Dei*,
the terror of the world and fcourge of
God, drawing nigh to the Citty of *Troyes*
in *Campania*, S. *Lupus* Bifhop of the
Citty, in his Pontificall habit accompanied with all his Clergy, went out to
meet with him, and being come into his
prefence he faid, who art thou, who rui-
neft and difquieteft all the world? *Attila*
anfwered I am the fcourge of God, then
faid

Naucler.
2.volum.

thenfaid the Bifhop , you are moft welcome to vs , and prefently commaunded
to open the holy gates, and his foldiers
entred the Toure ; but our Lord ftroke
them with fuch a blindnes, that they paffed cleane thorough without doing any
harme:for although *Attila* was a fcourge
indeed , yet God would not permit him
to be fuch to them , who receaued him as
his fcourge with fo much fubmiffion.

THE XXIV. CHAP. TER.

Of the conformity which we are to haue
with the will of God , in aridy and de-
folation in our prayer, and what is vn-
derftood by the name , of this aridity
and defolation.

WE are not only to conforme our
felues vnto the will of God , in
things exterior, humane and naturall, but
alfo in that which feemes to many euen
fanctity when we defire it with greateft earneftnes, to wit in fpirituall and fu-
pernaturall graces, fuch as are diuine confolations, vertues themfelues, and the gift
of prayer, interior quiet and tranquility of

mind,

mind, and in fine all spirituall graces and
fauours. But some one shall aske me, whither in all these things there may be so
much of our owne will, and immoderate
loue vnto our selues as may need mode-
ration euen in point of them . I answere
yes, and that from hence the malice of
selfe loue may be perceaued the better,
since euen with things so good and holy
as these, it forbeares not to mingle the
poison of its infection. Spirituall ioy and
consolation is very good, because by helpe
of them, the soule doth easely ridd it
selfe, and come to detest all feeling and
delight in worldly things, which is the
bait and nutriment of vices, and takes
heart and breath, to go on cheerfully, in
the seruice of God, according to that saying of the Prophet, *viam mandatorum*
tuorum cucurri cum dilatasti cor meum,
I haue runne in the way of thy coman-
dements then when thou hast dilated my
heart, the heart dilateth and extends it
selfe, with spirituall ioy and consolation,
and on the contrary, becomes narrow and
straight, with sadnes and desolation. The
same Prophet likewise sayes, that when
God sent him consolations, they were as
                                    wings

*Psal.118.
31.*

wings vnto him, which made him runne and fly in the wayes of vertue and the commandements of God; Spirituall consolations do moreouer helpe very much, to the breaking of our owne will, to the ouercoming our sensuall appetites, to the mortifying of the flesh, and to beare our crosse and all aduersities which may arriue with greater constancy; And therfore God vsually doth first send these spirituall ioyes and consolations vnto those, whom he intends afterwards to visit with afflictions & desolation, the better to prepare & dispose them by the one, to make their good and profit of the other.

As we see, our Sauiour would comfort his disciples with his glorious transfiguration on the mountaine, that they might afterwards be lesse troubled and deiected to see him suffer and dy vpon the crosse. We see likewise that God most commonly bestows his consolations vpon new beginners, that they may throughly forsake the delights of the world for heauenly comforts, and afterwards when he hath surely obliged them vnto him in the bonds of loue, and he seeth them well rooted and confirmed in vertue, then he

exer-

exerciseth them with aridity, that the
may the better attaine the vertues of pa
tience and humility, and merit a more a
bundant increase of grace and glory, by
seruing God purely, without the helpe o
consolation . This is the cause why some
in the begining when they are newly en
tred into Religiō, or perhaps before their
entrance, when they haue but conceiue
the desire, do feele greater consolation &
spirituall delight, then euer after, for God
then deals with them accordig to their
age, giuing them the milke of Infants, to
traine them out of the world, and bring
all temporall things into contempt and
hatred with them, but afterwards when
they are well growne and fit for harder
meats, he giues them such food as doth
become their yeares. For these and other
the like ends, God ordinarily doth send
his consolations and spirituall gusts. And
therfore the Saints commonly do counsell vs, in time of consolation, to prouide
against the comming tentations; like as in
time of peace, they vse to make the preparation for warre: for the day of conso-
tions is commonly no other, then the Euе
and vigill of tentation.

Spiri-

Spirituall comforts are therfore very good and profitable, if we know how to vſe them, as we ought to do, wherfore when ſoeuer God beſtows them on vs, we are to receaue them, with humble thankfulnes, but if any one ſhould wholly depend vpon them, and deſire them only for his owne contentment, becauſe of the guſt and delectation which the ſoule receaueth in them, it were imperfection in him, and diſordinate loue vnto himſelfe. For as in things neceſſary to ſuſtaine our life, as eating, drinking, ſleeping and the like, if a man ſhould make the pleaſure of them his end, it were a defect in him, ſo if one ſhould pretend no other end in prayer, but theſe ſenſible feelings & conſolations, it were a ſpirituall gluttony in him; Thoſe are things which are not to be accepted of, or deſired, for any proper feeling or particular delight, but only as means helping vs to arriue vnto thoſe ends which we haue mentioned. Like as one who is ſicke and can indure no meat that is good for him, is glad when he come to find ſome taſt and reliſh in it, not becauſe it is pleaſant to his pallat, but becauſe it prouokes his appetite to eate,

and

and conserues his life, so also a seruant of
God is not to seeke spirituall consolation,
as to insist vpon it, but because with the
heauenly refreshment therof, his soule is
strenghtned and encouraged to sustaine
the paine and labour of the way of vertue, and to go on with constancy. And in
this manner, comforts are not desired for
comforts sake, but only for the greater
glory of God, and so farre forth as they
redound vnto his honour and glory.

But I say yet more, that one may desire these spirituall consolations in such
manner, & for those ends which we haue
said which are good and holy, and yet for
all this there may be excesse in it, and disordinate and selfe loue may haue shuffled
in it selfe among those desires; as when
we desire them too importunatly, with too
great solicitude, and greedines, so as to
be lesse content if we obteine them not,
and lesse pliable to the will of God; but
to remaine troubled, grudging, and
in a painfull disquietnes. This is no other
then a disordinate affection, and spirituall
couetousnesse; for we are not so to depend
on these sensible feelings; and to seeke after spirituall consolations with so great aui-
dity,

dity, as to hinder our peace and quietnes
of mind, and make vs leſſe conformable
with the will of God, if he ſhould pleaſe
not to beſtow them on vs: ſeing the will
of God alone, is better and more worth
then all theſe things together, and it is
more expediēt for vs, to content our ſelues
therewith.

And that which I ſay of theſe feelings
and ſpirituall conſolations, is to be extended likewiſe to the gift of prayer, and the
feruour and facility which we deſire therin, as alſo of the internall peace and quietnes of our mind, together with all other
fauours, graces, and ſpirituall prerogatiues;
ſeing that we may be tranſported with an
affection too diſordinate, in the deſire of
euery one of theſe, as when we couet
them with ſuch impatience and anxiety,
as (if we obteine them not) to become
troubled, malecontent, and leſſe conformable to the will of God. Alſo by theſe
feelings and ſpirituall conſolations, we
vnderſtand here not only deuotion, ſenſible feelings, and ſpirituall ſweetneſſes,
but alſo the ſubſtance it ſelfe and gift of
prayer, and the facility of applying our
ſelues vnto it, and perſeuering at in it, with

R 4　　　　that

that tranquility and repose as we defire,
yea it is this of which for the prefent
we principally do treat, indeauouring
to declare how we are to conforme our
felues vnto the will of God therin,and not
to feeke it with to great anxiety and earneftnes; for concerning confolations, feelings & fenfible deuotions, there are none
who would not endure the want of thé,
fo they might haue the fubftáce of prayer,
and obteine the fruite therof: for they
know that prayer confifts not in thefe feelings,deuotions,and in tendernes of mind,
and therfore without any great vertue
they may be had, but for one to go to
prayer, and remaine there as if he were a
ftone with fo great aridity and drineffe,as
if to pray were the leaft of his bufineffe
for which he came;it feeming to him that
God hath wholly withdrawne himfelfe
from him, barring him from all acceffe
vnto him, & that that curfe is falne vpon
his head,which God long finçe did threa-
Leui. 26. ten to his people. *Dabo quoque vobis cæ-*
10. & *lnm defuper ficut ferrum , & terram æ-*
Deut.18. *neam ,* here there is need of great vertue
25.   and fortitude indeed,when euen the heauen feemes to them to be made of Iron,
                                        and

and the earth of brasse, seing that not a
dropp of water raineth downe on them,
to soften theie hearts, and produce that
fruite which should maintaine their spirituall liues, but they remaine in a perpetuall sterility and drouth : neither is it
this aridity which only tormenteth them,
but there rusheth vpon them sometimes
such variety of thoughts and wild distractions, and they perhaps so filthy & vila-
nous, as they seeme to haue come vnto
prayer vnto no other end, then to be troubled vext and assaulted with all sorts of
tentations; If you tell them , there best
way is then, to haue their thoughts on
death, or on our Sauiour crucified, which
is an excellent remedy indeed , they answere you, that they haue tryed it , but
found no fruite in it : for could they do
that ? what should they desire for more?
Sometimes one shall be so ill disposed and
dry in his prayer, that he cannot so much
as thinke vpon it, or if with much force
& difficulty he hale his thoughts vnto it,
it is in such a manner, as he is neuer moued with it, nor rendred any whit the
more recollected or attent, but they passe
it ouer without leauing any impression
in

in the foule, and this is that which we call properly fpirituall defolation, aridity or drines, and defection of mind; and herein it is neceffary that we conforme our felues vnto the will of God.

This is a point of greateft confequence it being on of the commoneft complaints, and wherwith they are moft contriftated, who giue themfelues to the exercife of prayer, for they figh and weep when they find themfelues in this manner, whilft on the one fide they heare fo much faid in the praife of prayer, and of the good ther-of, and how according as that paffes, fo the daies and liues of fpirituall men do paffe, whilft they likewife vnderftād, that it is one of the principalft meanes as we haue, as well for our owne particular pro-fit, as that of our neighbour; and on the other fide fee themfelues fo farre (in their opinion) from making any good prayer: this, this grieueth, this afflicts them much, this maks thē thinke that God hath for-faken thē, & thinks no more vpon thē, this maks thē feare they haue wholly loft his fauour, and are falne into his difpleafure and difgrace, feing it feemes to them, that he cuts them of from all refuge, all re-courfe

courfe vnto him. And this tentation is farther augmented when they fee the great
progreffe which others make in prayer,
in a few daies exercife almoft without
any paine at all; whilft they although they
labour more then their force can beare,
are nothing profitted. From whence are
begotten other tentations, yet worfe then
thefe , as to make their complaint fometimes of our Lord himfelfe , for dealing
with them in fuch a rigorous manner, and
they begin to thinke of leauing of their
exercife of prayer , imagining it a thing
vnfit for them, feing it fucceeds in no better manner with them . And all this is
made farre more and worfe, by the diuels
vexing them with that vnquiet thought,
that themfelues alone are in the caufe of
all, & that for their owne fault God deales
fo harfhly with them , and therfore fome
do liue in great difcomfort, comming out
of their praier as from fome racke or torment, fade melancholy, and both intollerable to themfelues and to all thofe with
whom they do conuerfe . Wherfore we
will now by the affiftance of the grace
of God, both anfwer and fatisfy this tentation and complaint.

THE

THE XXV. CHAPTER.

An answer vnto the complaint of those
who are troubled with aridity and
desolation in prayer.

Irst I do not say, that we are not to
reioyce when we are visited and comforted by God , for it is manifest , that
there is none so stupid, but would be glad
and delighted with the presence of his
beloued; neither do I say, that we are to
haue no recentment of his absence from
vs, when he punisheth vs with aridity and
tentations , for I see it is impossible to do
otherwise . Our Sauiour Christ had feeling himselfe to be abandoned by his heauenly Father, when hanging on the crosse
Math. 27 he vttered these mournefull words , *Deus*
46.   *meus, Deus meus, vt quid dereliquisti me?*
my God , my God , why hast thou for-
saken me? but that which is intended and
desired is, that we should know how to
make our profit of this distresse and ex-
periment , by which God commonly
doth try his elect , and with a vigour of
mind put our selues vnder the protection
                                                        of

of the will of God, in saying: *Veruntamen* Math. 26
non ficut ego volo, fed ficut tu, ô Lord be 39.
it not as I will, but as thou wilt, feing efpecially that fanctity and perfection confifts not in confolations, neither in hauing
of high and excellent manner of prayer,
and that our profit and perfection is not
meafured therby, but by a perfect loue of
God, which is not comprifed in any of
thefe things, but in a conformity and entire vnion with the diuine will as well in
bitternes, as in delicioufnes, afwell in aduerfity, as profperity, and therfore we
ought with the fame equality of mind
to receaue from the hand of God, afwell
the croffe and to be fpiritually forfaken,
as any ioy or côfolation: giuing him thâkes
for the one, and the other alike.

If you will haue me in darknes be you
bleffed, if you will haue me in light be you
alfo bleffed, if you will comfort me be you
bleffed, if you will afflict me be you likewife bleffed. And fo S. *Paul* doth coun-
fell vs: *In omnibus gratias agite, hac eft* Thomas
enim voluntas Dei in Chrifto Iefu in om- a Kêpis.
nibus vobis, rêder thanks for euery thing,
for fuch is the will of God in Chrift Ie- 1. ad
fus in all of you. If then this be the will of Thef. 5.
                                          God 17.

God what can we defire more? my life is
giuen me to no other end, then to pleafe
God with it.if then he pleafe to direct the
whole courfe of it, by thefe darke, trou-
blefome, and vneafy waies, why fhould I
feeke & wifh for paths more lightfome &
pleafant? God would haue fuch an one,
go forwards in that way which he feeth,
which he receaues guft in and loues, and
leads me through this gloomy wilder-
neffe . I will not chaunge my barrennes,
for his fertility, neither my frights, for his
fecurity, this is the language of thofe who
haue their eyes open to fee the truth, and
with this they maintaine themfelues in
côfort. Mafter *Auila* faith excellent well.

M. Auila
audi filia
c. 26.

If God would but vnuaile our eyes, we
fhould behould more cleerly thê the day,
that all things in earth and heauen, are to
little and bafe , to be defired or poffeffed
by vs, if you but feperat them from the
will of God ; and that there is nothing.
how little or bitter fo euer it be , which
would not be of great value, being once
conioyned with the will of God. It is far
better without comparifon to liue in afflictions, difcomforts, aridities, and tentations, if he fhall pleafe to haue it fo, then

ici

in all the delights, comforts and contemplations which can possibly be, if you but
take from them the will of God.

But some one shall say, if I knew that
the will of God were such, and that he
were more pleased and delighted with it,
I should soone conforme me my selfe, and remaine well contented, although it were
to passe my whole life ouer so, for I see
sufficiently my obligatiō, to desire nothing
so much, as the good pleasure of God, and
that my life is ordained vnto no other
end: but it seemes to me that God would
be farre better pleased, could I make my
prayers better, and had more attention
and internall recollection, and came with
better preparation; and moreouer that
which not a little troubleth me, is that it
is by reason of my fault and negligence,
that I cannot entertaine my selfe in prayer;
if I knew for certaine, that I had performed my duty, and that it hapned vnto me
through no fault of mine, it would not
grieue nor trouble me halfe so much. This
complaint is well set downe and there can
be nothing added more vnto it seing therin is comprised and inuolued, all the obie-
ctions of those who make the like complaints

plaints. And so if we can but well cleere
this difficulty, much of our worke is done,
since it is the ground of an ordinary and
vniuersall griefe, there being no person,
how holy and perfect so euer he be, who
hath not his share somtimes, in this aridity
and spirituall desolation . We read of *S.
Francis* and *S. Katharine of Siena*, those
great darlings and fauorites of God, that
they haue not been exempted from it, and
S. Anthony the Abbot although otherwise
he was arriued to so transcendent a degree of contemplation, that whole nights
seemed to passe away with him as a blast
of wind ; and when the morning came,
he would complaine the sunne did rise to
early this man notwithstanding (I say)
was sometimes so haunted with the importunity of wicked thoughts , as he
would cry out with a loud voice to God,
my God I would faine be good, and my
thoughts will not permit me, and *S. Bernard* hath the same complaint . *Exaruit
cor meum, coagulatum est sicut lac , factum sicut terra sine aqua , nec compungi
ad lachrymas queo, tanta est duritia cordis: non sapit psalmus , non legere libet,
non orare delectat , meditationes solitas*

non

nen inuenio. Vbi illa inebriatio Spiritus?
vbi mentis ſerenitas? & pax & gaudium
in Spiritu Sanĉto ? O Lord my heart is
dried vp, and coagulated like milke , it is
become like earth without water,& cannot be compunĉt to teares, the hardnes of
my heart is ſo great, I take no pleaſure in
ſinging, I haue no will to read , I receaue
no delight in prayer, neither do I find my
wonted meditations , where is that ine-
briation of ſoule ? where that ſerenity of
mind?& peace and ioy in the holy Ghoſt?
and therfore this doĉtrine is neceſſary for
all, and I do hope by Gods aſſiſtance likewiſe to ſatisfy euery one.

Let vs begin then from hence. I graunt
you that your faults are cauſe of your di-
ſtraĉtion, and aridity in prayer, and that
you cannot ſettle your ſelf vnto it, & therfore it is expediĉt that you know ſo much,
and ſay , it is for your paſſed ſinnes , and
preſent negligences and defeĉts for which
God Almighty doth puniſh you, with the
ſubtraĉtion of all feruours, & all feeling in
prayer, leauing you without all recolle-
ĉtion, attention, and reſt, becauſe you are
not worthy or rather wholly vnworthy
of it . Notwithſtanding it followes not

from hence, that you fhould complaine of it, but on the contrary, you ought entirely therin to conforme your felfe vnto the will of God. Shall I demonftrate this vnto you moft cleerly ? *de ore tuo te iudico?* I will condemne you, by the words of your owne mouth do you not acknowledge and alfo confeffe your felfe, that becaufe of your finnes paft, and prefent negligences and defects, you deferue to be greeuoufly chaftized by God ? I do affuredly, I haue often merited hell and therfore no punifhment can be to great for me, but all whatfoeuer befides, will be Gods mercy and my felicity, if it be compared with what I haue deferued, and I fhould efteeme it for a fingular benefit, if God would fend me fome punifhment in this life, becaufe I fhould receaue it as a pledge and affurance, that he hath pardoned my finnes, and referues me not to be punifhed in the other life, fince heere he chaftifeth me. This is enough, there is required no more, I am fatisfied, and prouided that they be not words only fpoken in the ayre, let vs come vnto the iffue and effect : behould the punifhment which God for the prefent fends you for your

finnes,

Luc. 19.
22.

sinnes, are these desolations, these distractions, and aridities, this spirituall dereli-
ction, therfore are the heauens beeome
like yron vnto you, and the earth like
brasse, therfore hath God retired and shut
vp himselfe from you, so as you can find
nothing to entertaine your selfe in prayer,
God will for the present chastise you with
this, and so remit, and expiat your sinne:
do you not thinke that your passed sinnes, and present imperfections, tepidities
and negligences do well deserue this punishment? yes vndoubtedly, and I professe
that weighed with my sinnes they are but
light, and that they are full of Iustice and
mercy, of Iustice, because I hauing so often
shut the gate of my heart against almighty
God, and giuen no eare vnto him when
he knockt without with his holy inspirations, but haue sent them conteptibly away;
wherfore I do iustly merit that he should
stop his eares, and affoard me no answere
now, whe I call vpo him, & that he should
not open, his gate of fauour to me, but shut
me out: this is a most iust punishment, but
beareth no proportio to my offences, and
thefrore is ful of mercy, because I merit infinitly more. Conforme your selfe then

S 2   with

with the will of God, in this your punishment, & receaue it with gratfull thanks,
seing he is so mercifull in chastising you,
& doth not punish you according to your
deserts. Do you not say that you haue
merited hell? How are you so audacious
then to require of God, his fauours and
consolatiõs in prayer? and to haue accesse
and familiarity with him by their addresse
enioying that peace and tranquillity of
mind which he is not accustomed to bestow on any but his children, whom he
dearly loueth and tendreth? or how dare
you complaine when you find the contrary? do you not perceaue how great this
presũption is? how intollerable this pride?
hold your selfe content that God vouch-
safeth to keepe you in his house, & suf-
fereth you in his presence; and acknowledge and esteeme it for a high fauour, &
singular benefit. If we had any humility
in our hearts, we should neuer haue complaints in our mouthes in what māner soeuer God did deale with vs, and so this tē-
tation would easely cease.

THE

THE XXVI. CHAPTER.

How we may conuert aridity and desola-
tion, into a good and profitable prayer.

WE are not ōly to suppresse in our
selues this complaint, but to endeauour to make our profit of this aridity
and desolation, and conuert it into an excellent prayer, vnto which first those
things will confer much helpe of which
we haue spoken in our treatise of prayer, Tract. 5.
to wit, to say, when we find our selues   c. 19.
in this manner, ô Lord, in so much as this
same is hapned through my fault, I am
most sorry, and heartily grieued for the
sinne and offence which I commit therin;
but in that it is your will, and a paine and
punishment which I (through my sinnes)
haue iustly merited, I accept it ô Lord, &
that with all willingnes, and not only for
the present or for a little time, but for all
the daies of my life, were they neuer so numerous I freely offer my selfe to beare this
crosse, and am ready prest to bow vnder
the weight therof, and this with all due
acknowledgment and thankfulnes; This

S 3   patience

patience and humility, this resignation
with the will of God, in this affliction, is
more acceptable to God, then my many
complaints and great anxiety that I cannot entertaine my selfe in prayer, and am
so troubled with various thoughts and
distractions whilst I am making it; If this
be not so, do but resolue me, in your opi-
niõ, whither of these two children should
please their Father more , he who is
content with euery thing his Father bestoweth vpon him, or he who is with nothing satisfied, but goeth alwaies grudging and repining, thinking nothing sufficient which he hath, alwaies crauing
more, and better things then are assigned
for him? without all doubt you will say
the first of them; and it is the like betwixt
God Almighty and vs, that patient and
quiet natured child of his, who is well cõ-
tent, and conformeth himselfe in euery
thing vnto the will of his celestiall Father,
which he shall please to send him, although it be neuer so hard and troublesome, although it were only a hard and
naked bone, doth more content & please
Almighty God, then on who is still repining, and euer complaining and moaning
with

with himself, that he hath nothing, & that nothing is beſtowed vpõ him. Moreouer I pray you reſolue me, who taketh the better way & more moueth the compaſſions of men to giue almes, and him to pitty his neceſſity , that begger who complaineth if they do not ſatisfy him preſently, and draw their purſes, at the firſt requeſt ; or he who lyeth expecting at the rich mans gate with ſilence and patience, without complaining that he waiteth to long, but hauing begged once, and implored his pitty, after he knoweth his mind is vnderſtood , waiteth there in the raine and biting cold, without crying out, or vſing importunity , there is no doubt but the rich man by this mans patience and humility, will be moued to giue him a large and liberall almes whilſt the other raſcals pride and ſturdines, ſhall ſtir him to nothing but anger and offence; & ſo it is with God Almighty and vs.

And vnto the end that you may the better perceaue the value and fruite of this kind of prayer, and how gratfull it is to God, I would faine know of you, what better prayer there is and what greater fruite expected from any prayer, then the

S 4   obtei-

obteining an inuincible patience in aduerfities, and a great conformity with the
will of God, with an excellent loue of his
diuine Maiestie? Wherfore do we pray at
all, but to arriue to these? when God
shall send you then, these aridities and tentations in your prayer, do but conforme
your selfe in this affliction, and spirituall
desolation to his holy will, and you shall
exercise an acte of patience and the loue
of God, so high and eminent, as a more
perfect cannot be imagined. It is said and
with good reason, that loue declareth it
selfe best, in suffering labour & affliction
for it beloueds sake, and that the greater the afflictions are, the more great shall
that loue declare it selfe to be; Now the
liueliest torments, and the heauiest crosse
and mortification which God Almighties
seruants can haue laid vpon them and
which goe nearest the heart of any spirituall man, are these desolations, in regard of which all corporall afflictions, in
point of riches, health, and temporall
goods, are not in way of comparison to
be accounted of. And therfore euery one
is entirely to conforme himselfe vnto the
will of God, in this barrennesse of comfort,

fort, in imitation of our Sauiour Chrift
fpiritually abandoned hanging vpon the
croffe; accepting of this fpirituall mortification for terme of his whole life, if God
fhall pleafe for to difpofe it fo, with a pure
intention, only to content Almighty God
therwith. This is an acte of great patience
and loue of God , and a moft high and
profitable prayer ; yea and fuch an on, as
there doe not want thofe who efteem
them for glorious Martyrs, who are ex-
ercifed therin.

Lud. Blo
in fpec.
fpir c.6.

Moreouer I demaund of you, wherfore you apply your felfe to prayer, vnles
by meanes of it, to obteine humility and
the knowledge of your felfe, how often
haue you defired of God , to giue you a
perfect knowledge of what you are, and
now behould God hath heard your petition, and by this meanes doth giue you to
vnderftand it. Some are of opinion that
they haue well difcharged their duty in
this point of feeking into the knowledge
of themfelues when they are ftroken with
liuely forrow for their finnes , and fpend
many teares in defaceing thē out of their
foules; but they deceaue themfelues, for it
isthe knowledge of God & not of them-
                              felues,

felues, which then they do acquire: but to remaine dry, cold, and hard as any ftone, this you haue of your felfe, and if God do not ftricke this ftone, neither hony nor water will iffue out of it, and this is that knowledge of your felfe, from whence floweth forth a thoufand benedictions vnto you, & of this you haue abundance, when your prayer in this māner fucceeds with you and if you make your: profit of it fo, your prayer will be of wonderous fruite vnto you.

THE XXVII. CHAPTER.

Of diuers other reafons which may com-
fort vs, and bring vs to conformity
with the will of God, in aridity and
defolation of prayer.

Although it is very profitable and good, to thinke for our greater cō-fufion and humility that this affliction, is procured by our owne offences, neuer-theles it is alfo neceffary for vs to know that this chaftifement, is not alwaies affli-cted vpon vs for our faults, but fometimes fo difpofed of, out of the moft profound

proui-

prouidence of our Lord, who diftribu-
teth his gifts according as he pleafeth beft,
and as it is no waies conuenient that a
whole body be compofed, only of eyes,
of feet, of hands, or heads, but that there
fhould be different mébers in his Church;
fo is it as much vnfitting, that this particular and excellent manner of prayer,
which we haue mentioned in a treatife
therofapart, fhould be communicated to
euery on, and it is as little neceffary, feing
they merit it not, or fuppofing that they
do, yet may they merit more in other
things, in the graunting of which vnto
them, God may oblige them with a greater fauour, then in beftowing vpon them
this prerogatiue. There hath been diuers
great and holy Saints, vnto whom we
do not know whither our Lord hath
in this kind been fo fauourable ; or if
this grace were added to the aboundance
of the reft; they haue faid with *S. Paul*
that they tooke no glory in it, nor had it
in any fingular efteeme, but all their glory
was to beare the croffe of Chrift: *Mihi*
autem abfit gloriari, nifi in cruce Do-
mini noftri Iefu Chrifti.

M. *Auila* treating of this hath a faying

Tract. 5:
c.4. & 5.

Ad Gala:
6. 14.]

M. Auila
to 2. epf.

ing of great consolation', God (saith he)
leaueth some in desolation for many yeares, and oftentimes for their whole liues,
and for my part I beleeue that the lot and
portion of these persons is best of all , if
they haue but so much faith, as not to
censure euill of it, and withall patience &
courage to suffer so straunge an accident
and long a banishment . If one could but
perswade himselfe that this condition is
the best for him, he would easily cõforme
his owne will to that which God desires.

The holy Saints, and Masters of spirituall
life, do bring many reasons to the declaring and prouing that this part or portion
is the better for them. Amõg the rest we
will content our selues with one of the
most important of them , confirmed by
the authorities of *S. Augustin*, *S. Hierom*,
and *S. Gregory* , as also of most of those
who haue handled this argument, which
is that all haue not sufficiẽt ability to conserue themselues in their humility, in such
a height of contemplation , seing we can
scarcely wring out a teare or two, but we
presently perswade our selues we are become spirituall men and high contempla-
tiues; whence we proceed to compare &
per-

perhaps prefer our selues to other men.
And euen the Apostle *S. Paul* himselfe
did seeme to stand in need, of some such
counterpoise, least otherwise he should
haue been swaied to vanity:*Et ne magni-*
tudo reuelationū extollat me, datus est mi-
hi stimulus carnis, angelus satanæ qui me
*colaphizet,*to the end that his being rapt
to the third heauen, and the high intel-
ligences which he had there receaued,
might not stire him vp to pride, God permitted him to be still haunted with a
tentation which might be sufficient to
humble him, and make him know his
owne infirmity. Therfore although this
way do seeme more eminent and high,
yet the other is more secure, and so God
who is most wise, and who conducts vs
vnto one end,which is himselfe,doth lead
each one that way which is most conue-
niēt for him. Perhaps if you enioyed that
great familiarity with Almighty God, in
prayer,in place of becoming humble and
making your profit of it, you would become more proud and arrogant, wheras now you are conserued in humility
and confusion, and therfore this way is
most proper for you,& most secure,how-
euer

Aug. lib.
de orā de
Deū que
est epist.
121.
Hier. su.
illud
Thrē. 3ṡ
sed & cū
clama-
uero &
rogaue;
ro exclu.
sit ora-
tionem }
meam.
Greg. li.
10. mor.
c. 21. &
24.
2. Cor.
12. 7.

Math. 20
22. euer you may be ignorant of it. *Nescitis quid petatis*, you know not what you aske.

Greg. li.
9. mor.
c. 7. S. *Gregory* to this purpose doth teach vs an excellent doctrine on this verse of Iob: *Si venerit ad me, non videbo eum;* Iob. 9. 11 *si abierit, non intelligam,* if he come vnto me, I will not see him, and if he depart from me, I will take no notice of it. Man, saith he is become so blind through sinne, that he doth not know, when he draweth nigh to God, or when he departeth from him, yea oftentimes that which he conceaus to be a great fauour of God, and wherby he imagineth himself to approch nigh vnto him, is that wherby he incurreth the offence of God, and is the occasion of his farther separation from him, and on the contrary, that which he esteemeth to be the anger of God, and wherby he gesses that God forsaketh him, and casts him vtterly into forgetfulnes, is Gods grace vnto him, and the only thing which doth withhold him from departing from him. And so, who is there that doth not thinke, when he finds himselfe plunged, in high prayer and contemplation, and on the receauing hand, of

many

many graces and fauours from Almighty
God, that he is well aduanced on the way
of a ſtraicter vnion with his diuine Maieſtie, & ſo oftentimes he cometh to waxe
proud of theſe priuacies and graces, and
too ſecure, and to confide in himſelfe too
much ; and the diuell by that way doth
bring him to ouerthrow and ruine, which
he imagined to lead directly to a greater
eminence, and to approch nigher to Almighty God. On the other ſide oftĕtimes
one ſhall find himſelfe afflicted and deſo-
late, aſſaulted with greeuous and fierce
tentatiõs, vexed with diſhoneſt thoughts,
with horrid blaſphemies and doubts of
faith, and thinke that God is mightily offended with him, and that he vtterly for-
ſaketh and leaueth him, and then he is
nigher vnto him, then euer he was before,
ſeing by this meanes, he is rendred more
humble, and more intelligent of his owne
infirmity, and ſo wholly diffiding in himſelfe, he hath recourſe to God with more
liuely vigour and reſolution, in placing
all his confidence in him, and making it
all his care that he depart not from him.
So as that is not the beſt, which ſeemeth
ſo to you, but it is conuenient you know,
that

that the way which God doth lead you, is the best and most expedient for you.

Moreouer, this very bitternes, this griefe and trouble which you resent so much, because you make not your prayers (in your owne iudgment) so well as you ought to do, may be a new cause of consolation to you, seing it is a particular grace and fauour of God, and an infallible signe of your loue to him ; for there is no griefe, where there is no loue: we cannot be sorrowfull that we serue not God enough without some will and purpose to serue him well; and therfore this paine & griefe is begotten from the loue of God and the desire of better seruing him, if you had no care how well or ill you serued him, how your prayers did go, and how your works were done, it were an euill signe, but to be sorry and afflicted because it seemeth to you, you do nothing as you ought, hath a good signification; but this feeling will be aswadged, and sorrow made sweet vnto vs, when on the one side considering them to be paine & affliction, on the other we do consider them the will of God: conforme your felfe then vnto it, and render thanks to

his

his high Maieſtie, that he hath left you,
ſo eager an appetit to do your beſt to
pleaſe him, how euer you conceaue the
worſt as may be of your actions, negligence
and languor in performing them.

Moreouer, although you ſhould do nothing
els in prayer, but only make your
perſonall appearance there, before that
diuine and ſoueraigne Maieſtie yet were
it not a little ſeruice which you ſhould do
to God, like as we ſee that it giueth a glorious
luſture, to the greatnes and Maieſtie
of an earthly Monarche, that the
Princes and Nobles giue euery day attendance
at his court, and are perſonally preſent
there at all aſſaies. *Beatus homo qui*
audit me, & qui vigilat ad fores meas Prou. 8.
quotidie, & obſeruat ad poſtes oſtij mei. It 34.
befits the glory of the diuine Maieſtie in
regard of our ſleight condition, and the
greatnes of the affaire wherof we treat,
that we ſhould be ſtil waiting at the dores
of his celeſtiall pallace, ready with thanks
when he ſhall giue vs entry, and humbling
our ſelues, when he ſhall ſhut vs
out, acknowledging our ſelues no waies
to merit it, and in this manner our prayer
will be alwaies good and profitable; With

T　　　　theſe

these helps and other the like we are to
serue our selues, in conforming vs vnto
the will of God in this desolation, and
spiritual defection, receauing it with gratfull thanks and saying: *Salue amaritudo*
amarissima omnis plena gratiæ: haile most
bitter bitternes, full of all grace & good.

F Barth.
de Matt.
Archiep.
Bracha-
rensis in
suo cō-
pē, c. 26.

THE XXVIII. CHAPTER.

That it is a great deceite and grieuous
tentation, to leaue of our prayer, be-
cause we find our selues in the said
manner in it.

IT followeth from that which we haue
said, that it is a great deceit and grieuous tentation, for one when he feeleth
himselfe so dry, and desolate in prayer, to
giue it ouer, or not to perseuere in it, as
thinking that he getteth no profit by it,
but only for his paines hath losse of time.
This is a tentation, wherwith the maligne
spirit, hath made not only diuers seculars,
but also many Religious, leaue of the exercise of prayer, or (failing of so much) at
least to go more rarely to it, and not to
employ in it, so much time as otherwise
they

they could conueniently. Diuers begin to apply themselues to prayer, and as long as they find sensible comfort and deuotion in it, do prosecute it with great care and feruour, but when they chaunce to fall into distraction and aridity they presently imagine, that it is no prayer which they make, but rather a new sinne, to be there in the presece of God with so much distraction, and so little reuerence. And so by little and little they come to neglect their praier, in presuming that they should do God better seruice, in employing themselues in some other exercise and occupation, then in such manner to remaine in prayer. And as soone as the diuell hath any inkling of this their faint heartednes, he presently taketh hold of the occasion, and is so diligent, to helpe them with these distractions in their prayer, and to see they haue no want of tentations to second them: he casts into their thoughts, that all the time they spend in prayer is as good as lost, and so by degrees bringeth them to leaue it of, with losse of their vertue, and oftentimes with yet a worse effect. This we know hath been the begining of the ruines of many; *Est*

T 2   *amicus*

Ecclef. 6.
19.

*amicus focius menfa, & non permanebit
in die neceffitatis*, faith the wifeman, to
be delighted with God, there is none but
hath defire, but to indure and fuffer for
him, is an infalible figne of a true loue
to him, when you find comfort and de-
uotiõ in prayer, it is no wonder if you per-
feuere in it, & entertaine your felfe with
it for diuers howers, for you may be moued to it, only by the guft and contentment which you find in it, as it is a figne
you are, when you continue it no longer
then whilft you haue fuch a baite as this
to intice you on. When God doth vifit
one, with defolation diftraction & aridity, then cometh the tryall of true frends
indeed, and thofe faithfull feruants of his
then manifeft themfelues, and fhew that
they feeke, no intereft of their owne, but
purely the good will and pleafure of Almighty God; and therfore particularly in
fuch occafions we are to perfeuer with all
patience and humility the wholl time

B Ignat.
lib. exer.
fpirit.
anot. 13.

allotted for our prayer, and rather longer;
as our B. Father counselleth vs, the better
to ouercome the tentation, and fhew our
force and valour againft the enemy.

Palad. in

Palladius recounteth of himfelfe, how

that

that ōce being shut into his cell, to bestow
himselfe with more quietnes on the consideration of celestiall things, he was grie-
uously assaulted with the tentation of
aridity, and wondroufly disquieted in his
thoughts, in so much as he begā to thinke
of leauing of his exercise begun, as a thing
for which he was wholly then vnfit, herupon he had recourse to *S. Macharius*
of *Alexandria*, and declaring to him his
whole tentation, he desired of him counsell and remedy. The Saint answered him,
whē those thoughts are suggested to you
againe, that you should be gone, & actuat
your selfe in those pious considerations no
more; *Dic ipsis cogitationibus tuis, propter*
Christum parietes cellæ istius custodio,
say to those thoughts of yours, for Chrifts
fake I keepe the walles of this cell of mine,
as much as to fay vnto him, that he should
perseuer, & content himselfe to performe
that holy action purely for the loue of
Chrift, although for his owne part, this
were all the fruite which he should reape
from it; and this is an excellent answere,
to put of such tentations as these, for as
much as the principall end, which we are
to pretend in his holy exercise, and the

T 3   inten-

intention with which we ought to apply
our selues vnto it, and to be exercised in
it, is not to haue our owne particular taſt
& cōfort in it; but to perfoume a good and
holy action, which may be pleaſing and
gratefull vnto God, & withall to ſatisfy &
defray according to our ſmall ability, the
intereſt, of that great and principall debt,
which we owe him for his being what he
is, and for thoſe innumerable benefits
which we haue receaued from his omnipotent hand. And in fine ſeing that he willeth and pleaſeth that I ſhould be for the
preſent ſo emploied, although it ſeem to
me that I do nothing at all, yet I ought
to be moſt content therwith. We read of
S. *Katharin* of *Sienna*, that ſhe was for the
ſpace of many daies, deſtitute of all ſpirituall conſolation, and had no feeling left
of the feruour of her wonted deuotion,
being moreouer vexed with moſt wicked
and filthy thoughts, from which by no
meanes ſhee could deliuer herſelfe, and
yet notwithſtanding ſhee neuer omitted
her prayer, but perſeuered in it, as well as
ſhee could, and with as much circumſpe-
ction and care as was poſſible, ſpeaking
vnto her ſelfe in this manner. O thou moſt
vile

Bloſ.c.4.
monil.
ſpirit.

vile and wreched sinner, thou dost deserue no consolation; for what? ought it
not to suffice thee although thou wert to
suffer these afflictions & spirituall nights,
thy whole life long if finally thou mightest not be damned as thou deseruest: assuredly thou madest choice to serue God,
on no such condition as to receaue consolations from him here, but that thou
might enioy him in heauen for all eternity. Arise therfore, and prosecute thy
wonted exercises, and continue faithfull
to so good a Lord.

Let vs then imitate these examples, &
conforme our comfort vnto this saying Tho. de
of that holy man. O my Lord I esteeme Kempis.
this my consolation, to be well content
to want all humáne comfort, and if comfort from thee do fraile me, thy will and
righteous probation of me, shall serue me
for the best of all contentments. If we be
but once arriued to this height of perfection to esteeme the good will and pleasure of God, to be all our ioy and delight,
so as euen to take pleasure to be depriued of all comfort, in considering it to
be his blessed will and pleasure, then we
shall be in possession of true content in-

T 4   deed,

deed , and such as nothing in the world can bereaue vs of,

THE XXIX. CHAPTER.

Wherin that which hath been said is con-
firmed by some examples.

B.Fracif. **I**T is recounted in the Chronicles of
de Ca-   the Order of *S. Dominicke* , how on
ftillo. 1.
p. lib. 1. of the Principall Religious of that Order,
c.6. hift. liued many yeares in that holy Order a
Ord.Pre- singular patterne of exemplar life, and of
an excellent purity of mind, without euer
enioying any consolation, or finding any
taft or delight , in the performance of his
Religious exercises , neither in medita-
ting prayer, or spirituall reading. This Religious man, hearing on the otherside frequent mention made , of those great fauours high graces and spirituall feelings
which God did vsually communicate to
others, became halfe desperate , and one
night in a deepe discontent he burst out
in his prayer before a Crucifix into these
much vnaduifed words which were accompanied with many a bitter teare . O
Lord, I heare it commonly reported of
you,

you, that in goodnes and sweetnes you
surpasse all your creatures:behold me here
who haue serued you many yeares, and
suffered for your sake, much tribulation,
hauing made a willing sacrifice of my
selfe, to your only seruice ; had I serued
any Tyrāt but a quarter of this time,with-
out doubt he would haue long since some
waies declared,himselfe well pleased with
me, either by a good word had I desired
so much, or a gratefull looke , or some
pleasant smile or other , but you ô God,
you haue not done me the least good, or
fauour, or shewed me any of those graces
which you do to others,but you,you who
are sweetnes it selfe , haue handled me
more cruelly then a hundred tyrants, oh
God what is the meaning of this ? miserable as I am, why do you ordeine it so?
he had no sooner vttred these fearfull
words, but he heard so mighty and horrible a cracke, as if the whole Church had
been shattering downe, and on the roufe
was such a hideous noise,as if a thousand
rauenous hounds had been tearing vp the
planchers with their teeth , wherupon
being astonished & all trembling through
feare, he cast vp his head for to serch out
the

the cause ; he perceaued ouer his shoul-
diers standing the most horrible and
vglie sight as euer man had seen, a diuell
weldeing a huge barre of yrō, with which
he gaue him so mighty a blow vpon the
body as he strokc him flat to ground,
without being able to lift vp himselfe a-
gaine; neuertheles he inforced himselfe
so much as to crawle to the protection
of an Altar not farre from him, where he
found himselfe so pittifully bruzed , that
he could not stire a limbe, all his body remaining as if it had been broken and dis-
ioynted with the force of blowes; In the
morning when the Religious came into
the Church to Prime, they found him all
streched at length, lying vpon the ground
without any motion , as if he had been
dead, and without being able to gesse the
cause of such a sodaine and dolefull accident they caried him into the infirmary,
where he remained for three weeks together iu most miserable torment, brea-
thing from him a stench so filthy & horrible , that the Religious could not approch vnto him, to bring him any remedy or reliefe, without first stopping their
noses, and preparing themselues before
with

with certaine preseruatiues at the end of this time he began a little to recouer strength, and as soone as he perceaued himselfe able to go vpon his legges, he (to cure his foolish presumption & pride, and seeke remedy at that place where through his fault he had receaued his wound) went into the Church, and with a profound humility seasoned in many teares, he made a prayer far different from the former, confessing his fault, and acknowledging himselfe vnworthy of any spirituall fauour, but on the contrary, meriting the greatest punishments. Wherupon our Lord did comfort him with a voice from heauen, saying vnto him, if thou desirest to enioy spirituall gust and consolation; thou must be humble, and acknowledge thine owne basenes and vility, knowing thy selfe to be more contemptible then durt, and of lesse value then the very wormes, which thou dost crush to earth vnder thy feet: & herwith he toke so faire a warning that therupon he became a perfect Religious man.

We read an other example far different from this of our B. F. *S. Ignatius,* who (as it is recorded in his life) reflecting vpon

Lib. 5. & 1.vitæ S. P. Ignat.

vpon his faults, and deeply forrowing for them , was wont to say , that he defired in punifhment of them that our Lord would fometimes depriue him of the de-liciousneffe of his confolations , vnto the ēd that feeling the curbe therof; he might be put in mind ; to carry himfelfe with more care and circumfpection , in God Almighties feruice . But the mercy of our good God was fo great towards him, and the multitude of his fweetnes, and fuauity of his grace fo aboundātly great that the oftener he fell, and the more earneftly he defired to feele the punifhment in fome such rigourous manner, the more gra-tious our Lord did fhew himfelf vnto him, and in the greater aboundance did he fhower downe vpon him the treafures of his infinit liberality. And fo he vfed to fay, that he did verely beleeue , there was not a man in the world , in whom was to be found , two things fo paffing oppofit as was in him , firft to fall fo often into im-perfections, and continue fo ingratfull to Almighty God ; and on the other fide to receaue fo great and continuall fauours from his Almighty hand.

Blof. c.   *Blofius* writeth of a certaine great fer-

uant

uant of God Almighty, vpon whom our
blessed Lord had bestowed many graces
& fauours, giuing him great illustrations,
and communicating to him in praier high
& admirable things, this holy soule out of
his profound humility, did begge of God,
if so it might stand with his better will and
pleasure, to take from him that his aboũ-
dant grace, and our Lord at his petition,
for fiue yeares together left him without
all consolation, in greeuous tentations, in
great anxieties and afflictions, and when
once, whilst he bitterly wept, two Angells presented themselues to cõfort him,
he told them, that he requested no consolation of them, but he should be aboundantly satisfied, if the most acceptable
will of God might be effected in him.

The same *Blosius* relateth how our Sauiour once said vnto *S. Brigit* why my
deare daughter are thou so troubled and
solicitous; vnto whom shee answered, because I am afflicted with diuers vaine and
euill cogitations, of which I can by no
meanes rid my selfe, and the feare of thy
Iudgment doth much disturbe my soule:
this is exact iustice answered our blessed
Lord, that as thou hast been formerly delighted

lighted on the vanities of the world a-
gainst my will , so now against thy will
thou shouldest be troubled with as many
various and wicked thoughts therof: Neuertheles feare my iudgment with mode-
ration and discretion, firmely euer confiding in me who am thy God, for thou art
to hold it for most certaine true; that such
euill cogitations, which the mind striueth
against and doth abhorre , both purify
and crowne the afflicted soule : if thou
canst not auoid them, beare them patiēt-
ly and keepe thy will, resoluedly bent a-
gainst them. And although thou dost not
consent vnto them, notwithstanding feare
least thou become proud therof, and so
come to fall, for whosoeuer stands, is sup-
ported with the only force of God.

Tauler'   *Taulerus* saith and *Blesius* recoūteth it
in his *Cōsolation of the Pusilanimous* that
there are diuers who whē they are vexed
with any tribulation do vse to say vnto
me, Father I am much afflicted, all goeth
very ill with me, for I am greatly peltered
and perturbed with many afflictions and
much griefe and sorrow; and I tell them
that it goeth well with them: then they
will reply, ô Sir but my fault is only the
                                        cause

caufe of it, to whō I anfwere againe whither your fault be caufe of it, or no, beleeue neuertheles that it is a croffe of affliction impofed by God vpon you & rendring thanks vnto him, fuffer it patiently, and refigne your felfe vnto him. Then will they tell me, oh but I euen internally pine away, with that great aridity, and fpirituall obfcurity in which I liue; vnto whom I finally reply, beare it patiently my deare child, and it will be more for your foules good, then if you were in neuer fo much and great fenfible feeling of deuotion.

We read of a great feruant of God Almighty who faid, it is fourty yeares fince firft I ferued our Lord, and haue been conuerfant in prayer, and yet I haue neuer knowne what fenfible feeling or confolation was, but only this I haue found; that daie when I haue duely made my prayer, I am much ftrégthned, & enabled to go thorough with the exercifes of vertue, wheras if I euer omit it or performe it tepidly, I am fo infeebled, that I cannot raife my felfe on wing to do any thing which is good and vertuous.

THE

THE XXX. CHAPTER.

*Of the conformity which we are to haue
with the will of God, for as much as
concerneth the diſtribution of others,
vertues, and ſupernaturall gifts.*

L Ike as we conforme our ſelues vnto
the will of God, in what manner ſo
euer he ſhall diſpoſe of vs in prayer, ſo alſo
are we to do, in all other vertues & gifts
of God, and in all ſpirituall fauours and
prerogatiues, it is good to haue all vertues
in deſire, to aſpire vnto them, and indeauour to attaine them; but we are in ſuch
manner to deſire to become better, and to
go forwards and increaſe in vertue, as not
to be diſquieted if we obteine not that
which we deſire, and to conforme our
ſelues vnto the will of God, and place our
whole contentment and delight therin.
If God be not pleaſed to beſtow vpon you
an Angelicall purity, but would haue you
ſuffer in that kind violent tentations, it is
farre better for you to haue patience in it,
and to accommodate your ſelfe vnto the
will of God, in this tentation and extre-
tremity,

mity , then to difquiet and trouble your
felfe , with bootleffe lamenting of your
cafe that you cannot attaine vnto that
purity and candour of the bleffed foules,
in heauen. If God be not pleafed to beftow
vpon you fo profound a humility as *S.*
Francis had, neither a mildnes, anfwerable to that of *Moyfes* or of *Dauid*, nor in
fine fo great a patience as that of holy
Iob , but letteth you experience the contrary motions & appetits, your beft courfe
were to humble your felfe and to embrace the fhame , which may giue you occafion of hauing your felfe in a more vile
efteeme ; which will not be effected if
you remaine troubled with it, and fpend
your felfe in filly complaints and lamen-
tations , becaufe God hath not indowed
you , with an equall patience vnto holy
Iob, or fuch a humility as *S. Francis* had.
We muft conforme our felues vnto the
will of God euen in fuch things as thefe,
or els we fhall neuer enioy true quietnes.
M. Auila faith excellent well : I do not
belicue (faith he) that there hath euer
been Saint in the world, who defired not
to become better then he was , but that
notwithftanding did not hinder quiet of

Auila c.
23. Audi
filia.

V　　mind

mind since they desired it, not out of any cupidity of their owne (for that is insatiable & neuer cryeth enough) but only for God, with whose distribution they should haue been content, although he had giuen them lesser then they had, esteeming it the part of on who loueth loially and truly indeed, to content himselfe with that which is giuen him, rather then to desire more, how euer selfe loue may preted that it is to be able to serue Almighty God the better.

But some will say, that our speech seemeth to tend to this, that we should not be very forwards and feruent in desiring to be more perfect and vertuous then we are, but that we ought to remit our selues wholly vnto God as well in matter of soule, as of our body, and from thence they may imagine that we may giue occasion to some, of becoming more tepide and negligent, and neuer to striue to become perfect, or make progresse in vertue. This point is well to be heeded, seing it is not of little importance; this obiection and reply, is so forcible that there is nothing more in this treatise to be feared. There is no doctrine, how sound or good ſo euer it be, which may not be abuſed by thoſe who know not how to apply it as they ought , & of this number are as well thoſe things which appertaine to prayer, as thoſe which concerne all other vertues, and ſpirituall gifts, and therfore it is need-full that this be well declared and vnder-ſtood. I do not ſay that we are not to de-ſire euery day to be better & holyer then other , and to be alwaies imitating thoſe who are more perfect , with the greateſt diligence and feruour as we can , for we are come into Religion , only vnto this end, and if we do not this we are no good Religious men: but that which I ſay is, that we are to carry our ſelues in this point, as we do in exteriour things , where a man muſt be diligent to procure them, but not anxious, nor too couetous, as the holy Do-ctors ſay , and our Sauiour prohibiteth it in the Euangell ; *Dico vobis ne ſoliciti* Math. 6. *ſitis animæ veſtra, quid manducetis , nec* 25. *corpori veſtro quod induamini,* where that which he reprehends is a care and anxiety too inordinate, and an appetit of thoſe things too immoderate: but he for-bideth not a moderat care, and requiſit di-ligence, but rather comaundsit, and hath

V 2   by

Gen.3.
19.

by way of pennance imposed it on vs: *In sudore vultus tui vesceris pane tuo* . It is requisit that men should vse labour & diligence to liue, or els it were a tempting of Almighty God. In this manner we are to behaue our selues in spirituall things, and in the obteining of vertues and the gifts of God; wherin we haue need to be very diligent and vigilant, yet so, as not to bereaue our selues of our minds peace, and conformity with the will of God . You are to do all which poshbly you can, and if with all you do, you cannot arriue vnto that high perfectiō to which you do pretend, you are not to be transported with impatience, for that were worse then the faults which hinder you , yea although it should seeme to you, that it were occasioned through your owne lukewarmnes (which is a thing that vsually afflicteth many) you are to procure to vse all diligence you can to the compassing of it; when if you find your selfe defectiue, & falne into in any faults you are not to be dismaied, or to loose courage, for it is a common case with vs all. You are a man and not an Angell , Infirme and not yet sanctified; Neither is God ignorant of our
misery

misery and infirmity , *quoniam ipse cog-* Psal. 102.
nouit figmentum nostrum, and would not 14.
haue vs discouraged therfore, but that we
should repent and humble our selues, and 2. p. tra.
presently rise againe & beg new forces of 6. a. 3.
him , indeauouring both in the interiour
and exteriour , to liue more contentedly:
for it is farre better that you should presently with cheerfulnes enterprise a new
(which would redouble your courage) to
serue God better for the time to come,
then to torment your selfe for your
offences; which whilst you thinke to do
for the loue of God , you displease the
same God in your ill seruing him with a
tepid heart, and a deiected mind, and o-
ther the like branches of imperfection ,
which vse to sprout from such a corrupted root. There is nothing els to be feared
here then the daunger wherof we haue
formerly spoken, which is least our tepi-
dity do increase, and we omit of our parts
to do what lieth in vs vnder the pretext
of saying it is God who is to bestow this
on me, all is to proceed from his hand, for
my part I can do nothing more : and we
are likewise to take the same heed in
that which we haue said in matter of
　　　　　prayer,

c. 26 &
seq..
& prayer, & least slouth also deceaue vs there
under the same pretense. Hauing then
stopt and made good this breach, and
done truly on our parts that which we
ought to do. God will be more pleased
with our patience and humility in these
weaknesses of ours, and spirituall wants,
then with the melancholly and excessiue
discontent of those, who thinke their progresse in vertue and perfection no waies
answerable to their desire, & their prayer
not to succeed so well, as otherwise it
might if they were not in fault. For this
arte of prayer, and perfecting our selues,
is not required, by being sad or lesse
satisfied with our selues, or by violence or force of armes, but it is God who
doth instruct vs in it, and doth bestow
it vpon whom he pleases, and also when
he pleases; and it is most certaine that
euen among those who are to be blessed
in heauen, there is inequality of glory,
and therfore we are not to be discouraged
if we are not of the best, yea perhaps not
of the middle sort, but we are in euery
thing to conforme our selues vnto the will
of God, and render infinit thanks vnto
our gratious Lord that he hath giuen vs
hope

hope by his great mercy to be saued at
last, and if so be that we cannot hold
our selues from falling into faults in this
mortall life of ours; let vs thanke God at
least for this, that he hath giuen vs the
knowledge of those faults of ours. And if
we cannot obteine heauen; by the subli-
mity of our vertues as some others do, let
vs be content, to make our selues a way
thither, by the knowledge and sorrow of
our sinnes, as do the greater part. *S. Hie-* Hier. in prolog galeat.
rom saith that others offer in the Temple
of God according to their ability, one
gold, an other siluer, and pretious stones,
others silke, purple, scarlat and cloth of
gold, for me it suffices to make my offering in his holy Temple with goats haire
and the skines of beasts: and so, let others
present their vertues to God, their excellent and heroicke actions, their high and
eleuated contemplations; it is enough for
me to sute my offering to my base condition, and to acknowledge and confesse
my selfe before the face of God a sinner
& imperfect, & present my selfe before his
omnipotent Maiestie as a poore & needy
wretch. And euen in this I am to reioyce,
and to thanke and praise Almighty God
that

that he hath not depriued vs of those gift,
whatsoeuer they be which he hath bestowed vpon vs, considering our offences
and vile ingratitude.

S. Bonauenture, Gerfan & diuers others
do add vnto this an other point, by which
that which we haue said is better confirmed, which is, that diuers perfons do ferue
God better without this great vertue and
recollection, (fo that on their parts their
desire and induftry be not wanting) then
if it were graunted them; feing that by
this meanes they are preferued in humility, and they proceed with care and dili-
genee, procuring withall earneftnes their
farther progreffe in fpirit, hauing for that
end frequent recourfe to God : whereas
if they fhould once become familiar with
vertue, perhaps they would be proud and
negligent, and goe flowly forwards in the
feruice of God, imagining that they had
already attained that heigth of perfection
which was neceffary for them, & would
neuer put thefelues to the paines of endeauouring to become more perfect thē they
were. All this which we haue said ought
to be an incitement vnto vs to do on our
parts precifely all we can, and to proceed
                                          al waies

Bonau.
opufc.de
profectu
Relig. li.
1. c. 33.
Gert. tra:
de mōte
contēpl
F. Barth.
de mart.
Archiep
Brachar.
in fuo
cōpend.
p. 2. c. 15.

alwaies with all care and diligence to the
purchasing of vertue and perfection, and
then to hould our selues content with
what soeuer our Lord shall please to bestow vpon vs, and not to be deiected nor
disquieted for that, vnto which we cannot attaine, and which is aboue our reach;
for this (as *M. Auila* very well obserueth) Auila to.
were no other then to afflict our selues 2. epist.
because we haue not wings to fly in the fol. 32.
ayre.

THE XXXI. CHAPTER.

Of the conformity which we are to haue
with the will of God, in that which con-
cerneth felicity and glory.

WE are not to conforme our selues
ōly vnto the will of God, in those
things which concerne grace, but also in
point of heauenly glory; in which a true
seruant of Almighty God ought to be so
farre estranged from all interest of his
owne, as he is no farther to reioyce in it
then that he seeth the holy will of God
accomplished, and not for any commodity of his owne. It is a high perfection
(saith

(faith deuout *Thomas a Kempis*) not to
feeke our owne ends neither in little nor
much, neither in things temporall nor
eternall, and giueth the reafon of it, in
thefe words becaufe your will ô Lord and
the loue of your honour ought to be transcendent vnto all, and it becomes vs to be
more content and comforted therewith,
then with all the benefits which either
we haue or may poffibly receaue.

Tract. 3.
c. 14.

This is the content and ioy of the Bleffed in heauen, where the Saints efteeme
their happines greater in the accomplifh-
ment of the will of God, then in the ex-
ceffiueneffe of their owne glory, they
being fo ftraictly vnited to his will, that
they defire not fo much the glory which
they poffeffe, neither the beatitude which
they enioy, for any profit refulting to thé
from thence, neither for the content
which they receaue therin, but only becaufe God is well pleafed therwith, and it
is his will for to beftow it on them. And
hence it proceedeth that euery one is foe
well content wirh that degree of beatitude which he hath, as he affecteth no
other, neither is difpleafed that any one
es aduanced aboue himfelfe; becaufe whofoeuer

foeuer enioyeth the vision of Almighty
God, becomes so transformed into him,
that he wholly leaueth of all proper will,
and beginneth expresly to haue the same
will with God, & he taketh all his cōtēt-
ment and delight therin, in considering
that it is the will & pleasure of God that
it should be so. And we see how illustrous
this vertue hath been in diuers great
Saints, as in *Moyses* and *S. Paul* who for
the saluation of soules, and the greater
glory of God, seemed so wholly to haue
forgot themselues, as they were not so
much as mindfull of their owne glory.
Aut demitte eis hanc noxam, aut si non
facis, dele me de libro tuo quem scrip-
sisti, either ō Lord forgiue these people
(said *Moyses*) this fault of theirs, or if
thou wilt not blott my name out of thy
booke of life, and *S. Paul, obtabam ego*
ipse anathema esse à Christo pro frari-
bus meis, I my seife wished to be excom-
municated from *Christ* for my brothers
sakes. And *S. Martin* who together with
many other Saints, did follow the doctrine of so excellent Masters, said in the
article of dying: *Si adhuc sum necessarius*
populo tuo, non recuso laborem. O my
God

Exod. 32
32.

Ad R6.
9. 3.

God if yet it be needfull for thy people
that I liue, I do not refuse the labour.
They neglected willingly their owne repose, and vnfainedly renounced all right
which they had to glory, when they were
euen vpon the point of enioying it, offering themselues afresh to more paine and
labour for Gods greater seruice. This is
truly to do the will of God in earth, as it
is in heauen, to cast wholly into forgetfulnes our owne commodity, and repose
all our content in the accomplishing of
the will of God, esteeming the contentment of his diuine Maiestie more, then
all our owne profit, or the possession both
of heauen and earth.

And from hence may be clearly perceaued how great perfection is requisit
to the exercise of our conformity to the
will of God : for if we must haue no regard of any interest of our owne, of any
spirituall good, no not eternall, nor what
is more, of blessednes it selfe, to keepe
our sight more obseruant of Gods good
will and pleasure; how much lesse are we
to care for humane, respects and all these
temporall things ? Whence also we may
perceaue how far short they come of this
per-

perfection who find repugnance to conforme themselues vnto the will of God,
in such things as we haue treated of in the
beginning; as in residing here or there, in
liuing in this Colledge or in that, in being
employed in one or the other office, in
enioying perfect health or being infirme,
in being much or little esteemed by o-
thers: for as we now affirme, we are more
to esteeme the good pleasure and will
of God then all the prerogatiues which
may redound vnto vs, either from our spirituall or eternall good, wheras you are
still insisting on these things which in cō-
parison of the other are but drosse and
basenes itselfe. He who had but such an
ardent desire to pleafe God, and to ac-
complish his holy will, as to disdaine willingly his owne glory, & to be contented
with the meanest place, not out of any
lesse desire, of doing heroicall acts to cō-
mend his seruices & labours to the highest place, but only because he hath in
chiefest esteemation the pleasure of Almighty God; he, I say, shall find no difficulty in any other thing, seing he hath renounced for the loue of God the highest
degree of excellency to which he could
arriue

arriue, and this is the chiefest thing which
we can depart with, and leaue for to conforme our selues vnto the will of God. If
it be Gods pleasure that I should die instãt-
ly, an which haue lesse glory, I had rather do so,
then liue twenty or thirty yeares more,
although I were to merit a higher degree
of glory. and on the contrary, although
I were assured of the glory of heauen, if
I died at this present, yet if God should
please to retaine me yet longer for diuers
yeares, in this prison and banishment of
mine in suffering many labours and miseries, I should rather do it then go presently to heauen, seing the good pleasure
of God, and the fulfilling of his holy will,
is my only content and glory, *tu es gloria*
mea, & exaltans caput meum.

There is recounted of our B. F. S. *Ig-*
natius, a rare and remarkable example in
this kind, he being on day with *F. Laynes*
and others, vpon the occasi n of a discourse they had, said to *F. Laynes:* what
would you do, in case our Lord should
propose to your choice in this manner. If you will dy presently, I will re-
lease you from the prison of your body,
and bestow vpon you my eternall glory,
but

Psal. 3.4.

Lib 3.c.
2.vitæ S.
P. Ignat.

but if you will liue longer, I giue you no
certainty of what may happen to you,
but vpon your perill be it , so as if you liue
and perseuer in vertue I will reward you
for it eternally : If you cease to be good , I
will Iudge you according to your works.
If,I say,our Sauiour should say thus vnto
you, and you in remaining longer in life,
could do some great and notable seruice
to his diuine Maiestie what do you thinke
should you choose, what would you answer him ? vnto whom F. *Laynes* replyed. I confesse ingeniously to your Reuerence , that I should choose to go in-
stantly to enioy Almighty God , and put
my saluation in security , leauing nothing
to daunger in a thing of so high conse-
quēce. Then said our B. Father to him,for
my part I do assure you I should not do so,
but if I imagined that with longer liuing
I could do God any particular seruice, I
should humbly beseech him , to giue me
life so long vntill I had discharged it and
should haue no regard vnto my selfe,but
all to him,without careing either for mine
owne daunger or security . And in this
doing he was not of opiniō that he should
put his saluation in ieopardy or daunger,
but

but rather that he should the more secure
it, seing that out of confidence in God,
he had chosen for his greater seruice, to
remaine here exposed still to daungers.
For what King, or Prince is there in the
world, said he, who after he had offered
his seruant some extraordinary recompence for his seruice, and the seruant had
respited the acceptance of it, the better
to do some important thing for him,
who would not hold himselfe in a manner obliged, not only to reserue it for
him, but to giue it him afterwards with
addition, seing that he had depriued himselfe of the present possession of it only
out of loue to him, and his affection to
do him greater seruice. Now if men who
are so forgetfull of benefits and ingratfull,
will do so much, how much more are we
to hope for, from such a Lord, who with
his grace hath so preuented vs, and obliged vs with so many speciall fauours? how
can we feare that he will abandon vs and
let vs fall, when we haue differd our beatitude, and forborne the fruition of it, for
his sake alone? We cannot beleeue nor
feare so much, of such a Lord as he.

THE

THE XXXII. CHAPTER.

Of conformity, vnion, and perfect loue
of God, and how we are to apply this
exercise to practise.

THat we may the better perceaue the perfection and excellency which is comprized in this exercise , as also how farre we may arriue by means of it , we will (for end and conclusion to this trea-tise) speake somewhat of that sublime ex-ercise of the loue of God , as it is tought by the Saints and Masters of spirituall life ; and it seemeth to come fitly for our purpose , seing that one of the principall effects of loue (according to *S. Denis* the *Areopagit*) is to make the will of the be-loued its owne , so as to will and not will the same in euery thing: whence the more one hath of conformity with God Al-mighties will , the more he hath of the loue of God; and the more loue he hath, the more straitly is he vnited and confor-med vnto his will. To declare this the bet-ter it is necessary that we ascend into hea-uen with our consideration , and behold in what manner the blessed there are louing and conforming themselues vnto

S. Dion.
cap. 4. de
diuin.
nomin.

the likeing & the will of God, in hauing
one will with him, since the nigher we
shall cóforme our selues to that, the more
perfect shall be our exercise. The glorious Apostle and Euangelist *S. Iohn* saith
that the vision of God, doth beget in the
blessed a similitude vnto him; *Quoniam*
cum apparuerit, similes ei erimus, quo-
niam videbimus eum sicuti est, and that

Ioan.3.2. because in seing God they are in such ma-
ner vnited with him, and transformed
into him, that they haue in common but
one will and liking; Now let vs see what
is this will, liking, and loue of God, that
we may withall arriue to know what
the desire and will of the blessed is, and
gather from thence what our will & perfect loue ought to be. The will of God
and his most soueraigne and perfect
loue, is his owne glory, and his being
so supremly perfect and glorious as he is;
and this is the same loue which possesseth
the blessed in heauen; so that the loue of
the Saints and blessed is, a loue and desire.
by which with all their forces they loue
and desire that God should be what he
is, and of himselfe so good. so glorious, so
worthy of all honour, and so mighty as he
is,

is , and seing they behold in God all
which they do desire ; therfore is it that
they reioyce in full fruition of that fruite
of the holy Ghost , of which the Apostle
speaketh , *fructus antem spiritus est gau-* AdGala.
dium, to wit, an vnspeakeable ioy to be- 5, 22.
hold him whom they so dearly loue , so
rich in himselfe with euery better thing.
Frō that which we see ordinarily to happen in this world we may giue an imperfect gesse at the Diuine Ioy which the
blessed in heauen receaue in this particular. Do but marke how great the ioy and
contentment is of a child here on earth, to
see his Father whom he tenderly respe-
cteth, beloued , honoured , and gratfull
vnto all ; or wise , rich , mighty and gratious with his King? assuredly there are
children of so toward nature, and choyce
education , as will not sticke to say , that
there is no ioy in the world to be compared, to that which they receaue frō seeing
their Fathers in so prosperous state . Now
if this ioy here can be so great, where loue
is so cold, and the things which occasion
their ioy so slight and poore , what may
the contentment of the blessed be , to see
their rightfull Lord , and Creator ; and

their

their celestiall Father, into whom they are so transform'd through loue, so good, so holy, so excellently faire; so infinitly powerfull and great; how all created things haue their being and beauty from his will alone, without which not a single leafe can shake vpon a tree: which saith the Apostle *S. Paul* is a ioy so great, as neither eye hath seene, nor eare hath heard, nor any heart hath comprehended it. This is that deepe and mighty riuer which *S. Iohn* saw in his reuelations, flowing forth from the Throne of God and from the Lambe, reioycing the Citty of Almighty God, of whose waters the blessed in heauen do drinke, and being inebriat with this holy loue, chaunt out perpetually that *Alleluia* of which *S. Iohn* doth speake, together blessing and glorifying God. *Alleluia, quoniam regnauit Dominus Deus noster omnipotens, gaudeamus & exultemus & demus gloriam ei*, there they reioyce and are delighted with the greatnes of God Almighties glory, congratulating with him, and rendring him a thousand benedictions for the same with an incredible ioy and iubilation. *Benedictio, & claritas, & sapien-*

tia,

1.Cor.2. 9.

Apoc.22. 1. & Psal. 45. 5.

Apo. 19. 6. & 7.

Apoc. 7. 12.

tia, & gratiarum actio, honor & virtus
& fortitudo Deo nostro in sacula saculo-
rum, Amen.

This is the loue which the Saints do
beare to Almighty God in heauen, this
is their vnity & conformity with his blef-
sed will, speaking in proportion to our
meane capacity, and this is that which according to our small ability, we are to indeauour to imitate on earth, that the will
of God may be done on earth, as it is in
heauen. *Inspice & fac secundum exem-* Exod.25.
plar, quod tibi in monte monstratum est, 40.
marke well, and do according to that patterne which hath been shewed you in the
mount, said our Lord vnto *Moyses*, when
he commaunded him to erect him a Ta- M. Auila
bernacle: and so ought we to do all things to. 1.ep.
here, conformable to that modell and P. Fran.
sampler which is proposed vnto vs to Arias p.
worke after, on that high mountaine of 2.profect
glory, and so are we to loue and desire 5.c. 3.&
that which the blessed in heauen loue & 4.
desire, as also that which God himselfe P. Lud.
both willeth and liketh, which is his de Puct.
glory, and his being soueraignly perfect 2.to. me.
and glorious. dit. p. 6.

Now vnto the end that each one may

the better bestow himselfe vpon this holy
exercise, we will in briefe declare the practise of it. When you are in prayer, consider with your vnderstanding the infinit
being of God, his eternity, his omnipo-
tence, his infinit wisdome, beauty, glory,
and blessednes; and then exercise the affections of ioy and pleasure with your will,
making it your only delight and comfort
that God is what he is, that he is God, that
he hath his being and endles goodnes
only depēdant on himselfe, without standing in need of any one; wheras all besides do stand in need of him, in that he
is omnipotent, supreamly good exceeding
glorious, and all within himselfe. In the
like manner are we to consider, all the
other perfections and infinit good which
is in Almighty God. This as S. Thomas
saieth and with him the diuins in generall,
is the greatest and perfectest acte of the
loue of God, and so likewise is it the most
supreme and excellent exercise of conformity with the will of God, seing there is
no greater nor perfecter loue of God, thē
that which God doth beare vnto himselfe, which is the loue of his owne glory
and being, towit souerainly perfect and
glo-

S. Tho.
31. q. 28.
art. 5. ad
3. & ar. 1

glorious, neither can any one haue a better
will then this. Therfore the more excellent and perfect your loue shall be, the
greater resemblance it shall haue vnto the
loue which God doth beare himselfe, and
the more great and perfect likewise shall
be our vnion and conformity with his
omnipotent will. Moreouer the Philosophers do teach, that *amare est velle* Aristot.
alicui bonum eius causa, & *non sui ip-* Rhet. li.
sius, to loue is to wish good vnto an other, 2. c. 4.
not for his owne sake, but his only whom
he loueth, whence it followeth that the
more good we wish an other, the more
loue we beare him. Now the greatest
good which we can wish Almighty God,
is that which he hath already, as his infinit being, his goodnes, wisdome, omni-
potence, and endles glory. When we
beare affection to any creature, we are
not only delighted with the good which
he is owner of, but haue also scope to
wish him some good, beyond that which
he hath already, seing the goodnes of all
creatures may receaue addition: but we
cannot wish any good to God which already he is not possessed of, seing he is
euery way infinit, and so can haue no

X 4   more

more power, no more glory, no more
wisedome, nor more goodnes then
he hath. And for this cause the greatest
good which we can wish to him, and
consequently the greatest loue which
we can beare him, is to be glad and reioyce, and to take all our pleasure & contentment that God hath so much good
as he hath, that he is so good as he is, so
rich, so powerfull, so infinit and glorious.

Hence it is that, as the Saints which are
in heauen, and the most sacred humanity
of *Chrift* our Sauiour, together with his
glorious virgin Mother & all the Quires
of Angels, do reioyce to see God so beau-
tiful & superabounding with euery good:
which ioy and delight of theirs cannot
conteine it selfe from bursting forth into
loud praises of such an excellent Lord;
neither can they be satisfied with blessing
and praising of him without end. And as
the holy Prophet singeth. *Beati qui ha-*
bitant in domo tua Domine, in sacula sæ-
culorum laudabunt te, euen so ought we
to vnite our hearts, and raise our voyces
to that high pitch of theirs, as we are
taught by our holy Mother the Church,
cum quibus, & noftras voces, vt admitti
iubeas

Pſal. 83.
5.

iubeas deprecamur supplici côfessione dicentes, Sanctus, Sanctus, Sanctus Dominus Deus Sabaoth, pleni sunt cæli & terra gloria tua. We ought perpetually (or with the greatest frequency as we can) to praise and glorify God, in reioycing and delighting our selues with that glory and soueranity which he hath; blessing him, and congratulating with him for the same: wherby we shall resemble in our imperfect manner the blessed in heauen, and Almighty God himselfe; exercising tho highest act of loue, and the most perfect conformity with the will of God, as can possibly be imagined.

THE XXXIII. CHAPTER.

How much this exercise is commended vnto vs and inculcated in holy scripture.

WE may yet better comprehend the value and excellency of this exercise and conceiue how acceptable it is to God, in that it is so much recommended and often iterated in the holy scripture; whence also we may lay hold
on

on the occasion to exercise it more, and
insist vpon it longer. The Royall Prophet Dauid in his Psalmes doth almost
in euery verse inuite vs to this holy exercise. *Lætamini in Domino & exultate
iusti, & gloriamini omnes recti corde.
Exultate iusti in Domino. Delectare in
Domino & dabit tibi petitiones cordis
tui.* Reioyce in our Lord, and exult ô yea
iust, and glory all you of a right heart.
Yea righteous exult in our Lord. Reioyce in him (and in his infinit goodnes)
and he will graunt you the petitions of
your owne heart, or rather, all which you
shall desire and stand in necessity of. For
this is a prayer, by which without setting
your selfe to pray, you pray, and God
heareth the desires of your heart, to
shew how much he is delighted with this
prayer of yours. And the Apostle *S. Paul*
writing to the *Philippians* saieth, reioyce
alwaies in our Lord: *Gaudete in Domino
semper*, and thinking it not sufficient to
haue said it once, he adds, *iterum dico gaudete*, I say againe to you, reioyce. And this
was the ioy which informed the sacred
Virgins purest heart, when in her Canticle shee said; *Et exultauit spiritus meus in*
　　　　　　　　　　　　　　　　　　Deo

Psal. 31.
11.
Psal. 32.
2.
Psal. 36.
4.

Ad Phil.
4. 4.

Luc. 1.
47.

Deo salutari meo, and my soule hath exulted in God my saluation. And with this
ioy likewise was our B. Sauiour *Christ*
replenished when (as the sacred Euangell
testifieth of him) *exultauit Spiritu Sanc-* Luc. 10.
sto: he reioyced in the holy Ghost. And 21.
the royall Prophet said, that the ioy and
contentment was so passing great which
his soule receaued , from the consideration of the great felicity & glory of God,
and so becoming it was for euery one,
to reioyce in that infinit goodnes which
is in him, as euen the soules ioy out of its
aboundance had influence into his body,
and set his flesh on fier with the same
loue of God; *Cor meum & caro mea ex-* Psal. 83.
ultauerunt in Deum viuum, my heart & 3.
flesh haue exulted in the liuing God, and
in an other place : *Anima mea exultabit* Psal. 34
in Domino,& delectabitur super salutari 9.
tuo; omnia ossa mea dicent, Domine quis
similis tibi? my soule shall reioyce in God,
and be delighted with the Author of it
saluation , and all my bones shall say, ô
my Lord who is like to thee ? And because this loue is a thing so celestiall and
diuine, our Mother the Church directed by the Holy Ghost , in the beginning

ginning of her Canonicall howers, inuiteth vs by this *Inuitatorium*, to soue our Lord in this manner, to reioyce, to triumph in his endles perfection and it is the beginning of the 94. Psalme: *Venite exultemus Domino, iubilemus Deo salutari nostro, praeoccupemus faciem eius in confessione, & in Psalmis iubilemus ei,* come all and reioyce in our Lord, and sing canticles of iubilation to his eternall praise, who is our saluation, seing he is God and a mighty Lord and King aboue all Gods seing the sea is his and he made it, and his hands haue founded the dry Land: *Quoniam Deus magnus Dominus & Rex magnus super omnes Deos &c. Quoniam ipsius est mare, & ipse fecit illud & aridam fundauerunt manus eius,* for this reason and the same end the holy Church concludeth all it Psalmes with this versicle. *Gloria Patri, & filio, & Spiritui Sancto. Sicut erat in principio & nunc & semper, & in sacula saculorum, Amen,* & this is that entrance into the ioy of our Lord which our Sauiour spoke of in the Ghospell. *Intra in gaudium Domini tui,* where we are made partakers of the infinit ioy of God, by reioycing & delighting

our

Psal. 94. 1. & 2.

Mat. 25. 21.

our selues with him for his glory, beauty, and riches, all infinit.

Now to the end that we may take pleasure in this exercise, and endeauour to proceed alwaies therin with this cheerfulnes and ioy, it will much helpe vs to consider how good God is, how faire, how glorious: in all which he is so passing infinit, that his only vision doth render those who do enioy it blessed; in so much as should but the damned in hell, once haue a glimps of him, all their paine and torments would be turned to ioy, & Hell would be changed to a Paradyse; *Hæc est autem vita æterna, vt cognoscant te solum Deum verum,* saith our Sauiour *Christ* in the Euangell of *Saint Iohn.* Ioan. 17. 3. This is eternall life, that they know thee the only true God; this is that which maketh them blessed, and that not only for a day, or yeare, but for eternity, in such manner as neuer to be satiat with seing God, but the delight therof shall be alwaies new vnto them, according to that of the Apocalyps. *Et cantabunt quasi canticum nouum,* they shall alwaies sing, as if their song were new. This seemeth to me sufficiëtly to declare the infinit goodnes Apo. 14.
3.

nes beauty and perfection of God, but notwithstanding there is alwaies some-what to adde, yea infinitly more. God is so faire, so glorious; that euen in seing himselfe he is made happy: so as the glory and felicity of God, is to see & loue himselfe. Imagin therfore, what reason we haue to be glad and to reioyce, in a goodnes, beauty and glory, so infinitly great, as to fill with delicious content the whole Citty of God, rendring all the Citsens blessed who inhabit it, & euen God himselfe happy in knowing and louing of himselfe.

8. Th. 1. p. q. 26. ar. 2.

THE XXXIV. CHAPTER.

How we may yet farther extend this holy exercise.

WE may yet farther dilate and en-large our selues vpon this subiect, in descending to the consideration of the most sacred humanity of *Christ* our Lord, from the contemplation of his di-uinity; obseruing the great dignity and perfection therof, and from thence re-ceauing particular pleasure and delight in

that

that the sacred humanity of *Christ* is so
highly exalted , and straitly vnited to his
diuinity, that it is enriched with all aboū-
dance of grace and glory, that it is the instrumēt of the diuinity , to exploit those
highest mysteries of the sanctification and
glorification of all the elect, and impart
those supernaturall gifts and graces which
God distributeth and bestoweth on men.
And finally we are to reioyce & receaue
exceediog pleasure from euery particular
of the perfection and glory of the most
blessed soule, and sacred body of our Re-
deemer Iesus Christ ; insisting therupon
with a truly viscerall loue & delectation;
In such manner as the Saints do contem-
plate him , and the sacred virgin beheld
him on the day of his glorious resurrection , rising from death so bright and
triumphantly; in fine with such affection
as the holy Patriarch *Iacob* did declare, Gen. 45.
when(as the scripture saieth) hearing that 38.
his soone was yet liuing, and Lord of all
Egypt, he was surprized with so excessiue
ioy that his decayed spirits being reuiued,
therby, he said , it is sufficient if my sonne
Ioseph liueth, I desire no more, then only
to go and see him, and then I shall be content to dy.   And

And we may extend this exercise vnto
the glory of the immaculate virgin, and
all the other Saints, and it would be a
good and laudable deuotion, vpon their
particular feasts, to spend some part of
our prayer in this exercise, seing it is the
most especiall seruice and honour which
we can exhibit to them, as declaring the
greatest loue that we can beare them,
which is, to wish them all the good which
they can possibly haue, and reioyce and
congratulat their great & excellent glory.
Which exercise the holy Church propo-
seth to our deuotions on the feast of the
euer glorious Virgin: *Hodie Maria virgo
cælos ascendit, gaudete, quia cum Christo
regnat in æternu*, to day the virgin *Mary*
ascendeth vp to heauen, reioyce therfore
because shee raigneth eternally with God.
And the office of the holy Masse, both in
this solemnity and diuers others, doth inuite vs to this holy exercise, and incite vs
by the example of Angells in this office
imployed. *Gaudeamus omnes in Domino
diem festum celebrantes, sub honore beatæ
Mariæ Virginis, de cuius Assumptione
gaudent Angeli, & collaudas filium Dei*,
let vs euery on reioyce in our Lord, in ce-
lebra-

lebrating this feast day, in honour of the
B. Virgin *Mary* , for whose Assumption
the Angells reioyce , and praise the sonne
of God. There is moreouer an other great
good and profit resulting from this deuotion vnto the Saints, and particularly vnto
the sacred humanity of *Christ* our Lord;
which is, that from hence we come by
little and little to raise our selues, vnto a
higher light of the diuinity, seing as *Christ* Ioan.10.
our Sauiour saieth this is the way, & gate 7. & Ioa.
which leadeth vs vnto the eternall Fa- 14. 6.
ther,

This exercise of considering God so
far forth as he is God , hath likewise its
degrees ; and we may render it more familiar vnto vs by descending vnto the
consideration of worldly things; for although it is most certaine , that God in
himselfe can receaue no increase, seing he
is euery waies infinit , and therfore there
is no good falling within the compasse of
our wish which he hath not already: neuertheles he may accidentally in his creatures become greater and increase, when
he is better knowne, more loued & serued
by them ; and therfore there is place for
vs to employ our selues in this act of loue,

Y   in

in wishing to God the addition of this exteriour good. And so the deuout soule by considering in prayer, how most worthy God Almighty is, to be loued, honoured and serued of his creatures, is to wish and earnestly desire that all the soules which are, or euer shall be, may know him, loue him, praise him, and glorify him in euery thing (and out of the depth of its deare affection say) ô Lord who shall conuert all the Infidells and sinners of the world, so as there may not be left any to offend you more, but that all may be obedient to you, and employ themselues wholly vnto your seruice, both now, and for euer more: *Sanctificetur nomen tuum. Omnis terra adoret te & psallat tibi, psalmum dicat nomini tuo.* And here we may insist and imagine with our selues a thousand waies wherby creatures may come to serue Almighty God, and wish them all particularly put in practise.

Marc. 6.
9.
Psal. 65.
4.

From hence is each on to descend vnto a desire of performing the will of God, & procuring his greater glory in euery thing which belongeth to them to do; euer endeauouring to do whatsoeuer we may know to be the will of God & redounding

ing

ing to his greater glory. Conformable
to that which our Sauiour saieth of himselfe in the Euangell, *quia ego quæ placita* Ioan. 8.
sunt ei, facio semper, I do alwaies that 29.
which is pleasing to my Father. For as *S.*
Iohn the Euangelist saieth, *qui dicit se* Ioan. 2.
nosse Deum & mandata eius non custo- 4.
dit, mendax est, & in hoc veritas non est,
he who affirmeth that he knoweth God,
and doth not keepe his cõmaundements,
is a lyer, and there is no truth in him; *Qui*
autem seruat verbum eius verè in hoc
charitas Dei perfecta est, but he who
obserueth his word hath the charity of
God perfectly indeed within him.

So that to loue God, and to haue an
entire conformity with his will, it is not
sufficient that a man conceaueth a great
ioy and delectation, for the felicity which
God enioyeth, or desireth that all creatures may loue and glorify him, but it is
requisit that he resigne himselfe wholly
to the accomplishmēt of the will of God:
for how can one say with any colour of
truth that he desireth the greater glory of
God, when euen in those things which
lie in him to do, he procureth it not? And
this is that loue which a soule actuateth,

when

when in prayer it conceiueth good purposes and true desires of performing the will of God, in this or that, or any particular thing which may present its selfe; with which exercise we commonly entertaine our selues in prayer.

Thus haue we laid open a large field, to exercise our selues for long time together in prayer, and declared the great profit, and rare perfection which is comprehended in this exercise: wherfore there only remaineth that we set our hand to worke, and begin be times on earth to take essay, of that which we are euer after to practise in so excellent a manner in heauen. *Cuius ignis est in Sion, & caminus eius, in Hierusalem*, here we are to enkindle in our selues that fier of loue, but the flame therof must shine and spread it selfe, and its height and sublime perfection appeare in the celestiall Hierusalem, which is our lasting glory.

Isai. 31. 9.

THE

THE TABLE OF THE
CHAPTERS.

THE I. CHAPTER.

Chap.

The Table

FINIS.